William Boyd Carpenter

The permanent elements of religion

Eight lectures

William Boyd Carpenter

The permanent elements of religion
Eight lectures

ISBN/EAN: 9783337259877

Printed in Europe, USA, Canada, Australia, Japan

Cover: Foto ©Lupo / pixelio.de

More available books at **www.hansebooks.com**

THE PERMANENT ELEMENTS
OF RELIGION

EIGHT LECTURES

PREACHED BEFORE THE UNIVERSITY OF OXFORD

IN THE YEAR 1887

ON THE FOUNDATION OF THE LATE REV. JOHN BAMPTON, M.A.,

CANON OF SALISBURY

BY

W. BOYD CARPENTER, D.D., D.C.L.,

BISHOP OF RIPON,

HONORARY FELLOW OF ST. CATHARINE'S COLLEGE, CAMBRIDGE

London

MACMILLAN AND CO.

AND NEW YORK

1889

[*All Rights Reserved*]

To My Mother

I OWE MY EARLIEST THOUGHTS

OF RELIGION:

To My Mother

I DEDICATE MY LATEST.

EXTRACT

FROM THE LAST WILL AND TESTAMENT

OF THE LATE

REV. JOHN BAMPTON,

CANON OF SALISBURY.

——"I give and bequeath my Lands and Estates to
" the Chancellor, Masters, and Scholars of the Univer-
" sity of Oxford for ever, to have and to hold all and
" singular the said Lands or Estates upon trust, and
" to the intents and purposes hereinafter mentioned;
" that is to say, I will and appoint that the Vice-
" Chancellor of the University of Oxford for the time
" being shall take and receive all the rents, issues, and
" profits thereof, and (after all taxes, reparations, and
" necessary deductions made) that he pay all the re-
" mainder to the endowment of eight Divinity Lecture
" Sermons, to be established for ever in the said Univer-
" sity, and to be performed in the manner following:

"I direct and appoint, that, upon the first Tuesday
" in Easter Term, a Lecturer be yearly chosen by the
" Heads of Colleges only, and by no others, in the room
" adjoining to the Printing-House, between the hours of
" ten in the morning and two in the afternoon, to
" preach eight Divinity Lecture Sermons, the year
" following, at St. Mary's in Oxford, between the com-

Extract from Canon Bampton's Will.

"mencement of the last month in Lent Term, and the
"end of the third week in Act Term.

"Also I direct and appoint, that the eight Divinity
"Lecture Sermons shall be preached upon either of
"the following Subjects—to confirm and establish the
"Christian Faith, and to confute all heretics and
"schismatics—upon the divine authority of the holy
"Scriptures—upon the authority of the writings of the
"primitive Fathers, as to the faith and practice of the
"primitive Church—upon the Divinity of our Lord and
"Saviour Jesus Christ—upon the Divinity of the Holy
"Ghost—upon the articles of the Christian Faith, as
"comprehended in the Apostles' and Nicene Creeds.

"Also I direct, that thirty copies of the eight Divinity
"Lecture Sermons shall be always printed, within two
"months after they are preached; and one copy shall
"be given to the Chancellor of the University, and one
"copy to the Head of every College, and one copy to
"the Mayor of the city of Oxford, and one copy to be
"put into the Bodleian Library; and the expenses of
"printing them shall be paid out of the revenue of the
"Land or Estates given for establishing the Divinity
"Lecture Sermons; and the preacher shall not be paid,
"nor be entitled to the revenue, before they are printed.

"Also I direct and appoint, that no person shall be
"qualified to preach the Divinity Lecture Sermons
"unless he hath taken the degree of Master of Arts
"at least, in one of the two Universities of Oxford or
"Cambridge; and that the same person shall never
"preach the Divinity Lecture Sermons twice."

PREFACE.

THE publication of these Lectures has been delayed much longer than I hoped or intended. Constant occupation and incessant interruptions must bear the blame of this delay. More than once the proof sheets have been left for months untouched. Various reasons have also rendered the task of preparation for the press unusually difficult. The Lectures, I should explain, are little better than corrected short-hand writer's reports. As such I trust that they will be read. Had leisure been at my disposal, I should have re-cast and re-written the whole. The delay, which I otherwise regret, has, however, enabled me to gather some illustrations from works published within the last two years. In addition to those whose works I have used, I desire to thank the Dean of Windsor, the Archdeacon of Durham, Canon MacColl, Canon Waugh, and Mr. Brownlow Maitland, who, in various ways, have given me much personal help. To these I must add the name of Professor Max Müller, who, besides other kind help, allowed me the privilege of seeing the advance sheets of his Gifford Lectures. No acknowledgment would be complete which did not speak of the uniform kindness and helpfulness of the authorities at the British Museum, and here my thanks are specially due to Mr. Fortescue and Mr. Bendall.

I must not make the kindness of these kind friends in any way responsible for the many mistakes and defects which my want of time or of wit may have left in the pages which follow. I am aware of my own feebleness; but I am more and more convinced that in the path along which I have been stumbling, lies the solution of many of our present-day difficulties.

W. B. RIPON.

Ripon,
   Aug., 1889.

CONTENTS.

INTRODUCTION.

LECTURE I.

PROBABLE PERMANENCE OF RELIGION . . . 3

An age of transition makes men ask, Will religion survive?

I.—There are reasons for believing that religion will survive.

These reasons are derived from
1. The experience of the past, which shows that religion lives, though religions die.
2. The nature of man—which is (a) permanent, and (b) religious.

II.—Further, it is not impossible to indicate some of the conditions of religion in the future, and to which any religion which aspires to be enduring must conform; for the permanence of man's nature means the permanence of certain spiritual conditions or principles, which, for the sake of convenience, we may call laws. There are seemingly four:
1. The Law of Environment.
2. The Law of Organism.
3. The Law of Sacrifice.
4. The Law of Indirectness.

The existence of these gives us a guarantee of the survival of religion and the conditions on which any religion can hope to survive among men.

Thus the survival of religion is likely, and the religion of the future must conform to certain conditions.

LECTURE II.

SOME ESSENTIAL ELEMENTS OF RELIGION . . . 47

One guarantee of the permanence of religion is the permanence of man's nature, and that permanence is expressed in certain spiritual laws.

It may be asked whether we cannot predict any of the elements which will be found in the religion of the future.

I.—It is likely that we can: for a large field of investigation is being opened up to us in the comparative study of religions. The history of religions may suggest to us the elements which the nature of man has demanded in religion.

II.—The elements which man's nature asks are three:
Dependence.
Fellowship.
Progress.
 1. Two of these are indicated by Definitions of Religion.
 2. All three are suggested by general considerations, but the evidence that they are, as a fact, demanded by mankind must be sought in the history of religions.

III.—The evidence on this point will be given by
Non-universal or minor religions.
Universal religions.
 1. Hints of these elements meet us on the threshold.
 2. The witness to them in some non-universal religions.
  (a) The religion of Mexico.
  (b) The religion of Israel.
  (c) The religion of Greece.
The need of these three elements for man.

LECTURE III.

ESSENTIAL ELEMENTS OF RELIGION WITNESSED IN THE HISTORY OF THREE UNIVERSAL RELIGIONS   77

The permanence of religion and the permanence of man's nature are correlated. There are certain essential elements demanded by man in religion. The main evidence on this point must be sought in the history of the three universal religions:

I.—Islamism in its history illustrates this demand. The original element in Islamism is Dependence The Sufite movement is the demand for Fellowship. The Mo'tazilite movement is the effort after Progress.

II.—Buddhism in its original form attempted to meet the demand for Fellowship. Later developments show the demand for Dependence. The worship of the Buddha. The multiplication of Deities. The practice of Prayer. The element of Progress is recognized in the hope of a Future.

III.—Christianity in its history shows the reiteration in various ways of the demand of human nature for these three elements:
  (i.) The teaching of Christ.
  (ii.) The witness of history and controversy—
    1. To Dependence.
    2. To the need of Fellowship.
      (a) Montanism. (b) The struggles of Athanasius. (c) Asceticism. (d) Saint Worship. (e) Mysticism.
    3. To the need of Progress—
      (a) The Schoolmen. (b) The School of nature.
  (iii.) The existence of parties as a witness to the need of Dependence, Fellowship, Progress.
Thus mankind in all periods has shown the need of three great elements in religion.

LECTURE IV.

THE RELATION OF THE THREE UNIVERSAL RELIGIONS TO THE ESSENTIAL ELEMENTS OF RELIGION ... 127

The question now assumes another form. Hitherto we have been asking what elements man demands in a religion. We have now to ask how far any religion has the native power to meet this demand.

With the view of answering this question, it is needful to examine:—

I.—Islamism.
  1. The element of Dependence is natural and indigenous.
  2. The element of Fellowship is found to be an artificial growth.
  3. The element of Progress has no natural home.

II.—Buddhism.
  1. Fellowship akin with its earliest features.
  2. Dependence demanded in later developments: North India, China.
  3. Progress recognized: Maitreya Buddha.

III.—Christianity.
　The three elements originally present:
　　1. In the teaching of Jesus Christ:
　　2. In its theological drift.
　　3. In the teaching of Apostles.
　Thus Christianity alone of the three universal religions possesses originally and indigenously the three elements of religion which the History of Religions shows that man's nature demands.

LECTURE V.

RELIGION AND MORALITY 171

　It being admitted that Religion is natural, two questions may be raised: whether Religion is (1) necessary, (2) ethically helpful to mankind.
　Taking the latter first, this Lecture is occupied with the relation of Religion and Morality.
　Ethical efficiency may be taken as a test of Religion.
　I.—The question considered as one of Fact.
　　(i.) The Fact is that the influences of Religions on morals have been not wholly evil or good, but mixed.
　　(ii.) The interpretation of this Fact.
　　　1. The results of Religion due to more than one factor. Man a factor, no less than Religion.
　　　2. Examination of this factor. Religion never sown in virgin or passive soil.
　　　3. Evil may result from man or from religion
　II.—The question considered as one of Principle.
　　(i.) The statement that religious principles are immoral.
　　　1. The statement is ambiguous.
　　　2. The statement confuses Religion with its shadow—Religionism.
　　(ii.) The principles of Christianity in relation to morals.
　　　1. Christianity in principle hostile to Religionism.

2. The consideration of three charges of demoralising influence.
   (a) Orthodoxy preferred to morals.
   (b) Sentiment preferred to conduct.
   (c) Energy diverted from the world-life.
(iii.) Conclusion with regard to Christianity.
   Its principles embrace all life.
   Its orthodoxy is the highest morality.
Conclusion.—Religion gives a sort of Eternalism to Righteousness.

LECTURE VI.

THE NECESSITY OF RELIGION 250

Religion being natural to a man, and having capacity as a moralizing factor, the question meets us—Is religion necessary? Is there, in other words, any adequate substitute for religion?

I.—Morality must be preserved.
   (i.) The indispensable elements of real morality.
   (ii.) The connexion of these elements with
      1. The laws of man's spiritual nature.
      2. The needed elements of religion.
   (iii.) Danger of moralism; the shadow of morality.
II.—Proposed substitutes for religion:
   (i.) Three considered as substitutes.
      1. Knowledge.
      2. Altruism.
      3. Drift of the world, or evolution of morals.
   (ii.) The defectiveness of scientific moralism in relation to
      1. The dark side of life.
      2. The unfit and the unfortunate.
      3. The deeper side of man's nature.
   (iii.) The indebtedness of social sentiment to religion.
      1. As a fact in history—Influence of religion.

B

2. Ethically—the ideal set up.
3. Sociologically.
Conclusion.—Religion seems necessary to men.

LECTURE VII.

RELIGION AND PERSONALITY 243

No adequate substitute for religion being found, religion is a necessity in the future. In a perfect religion, religion and morals should be inseparable. The need, therefore, of a principle or basis on which religion and morals unite.

This is to be found in the recognition of personality, *i.e.*, in the recognition that religion and morals are meaningless except they express relationships between beings who have wills and affections.

I.—The recognition of Personality not an empty phrase. The power at work which aims at the education of man as a personal being.

(i.) History shows the danger of forgetting that man is man.

(ii.) Nature educates man to—
 (*a*) The consciousness of self.
 (*b*) The sacrifice of self.
 (*c*) A certain completeness of character.

(iii.) Recent knowledge shows us stages of evolution in the same direction—(*a*) Physical, (*b*) Psychical, (*c*) Social.

II.—The recognition of Personality affords a basis of reconciliation between religion and morals.

(i.) The reconciliation afforded by the idea of personal beings—
 (*a*) The word Personality as applied to God.
 (*b*) Anthropomorphism inevitable to man.

(ii.) This recognition applies to (*a*) the source as well as to (*b*) the subject of religion.

(iii.) To the varying standards of morals.

III.—The religion of the future must be based on a Person, not on Creed, or Code.

(i.) No necessary loss to Definiteness and to Conduct.
(ii.) But an enormous gain to religion in Creed
and Worship.

Conclusion—Creed so based contrasted with the creed of
science.

LECTURE VIII.

THE RELIGION OF THE FUTURE 287

The survival of Religion being probable, the question
arises whether any existing Faith can fulfil the conditions needful for survival.

I.—The conditions needful.

(i.) Religion must—
1. Satisfy men's wish for unity.
2. Give guarantee of Permanence.

(ii.) Religion must supply the three elements—
Dependence, Fellowship, Progress.

(iii.) Religion must possess a Power of Inspiration.

II.—The application of these conditions to existing
Religions.

(i.) How far existing Faiths possess needful con
ceptions.

1. Non-Christian Systems—
Islâm, Buddhism, Positivism.

2. Christianity.
(a) The three elements—Dependence, Fellowship and Progress. (b) The test of unity
and permanence. (c) Some further features.

(ii.) The power of Inspiration.
1. This both in subject and object of Religion.
2. The relation of this inspiring power to—
(a) Law of Environment. (b) Law of Organism. (c) Law of Sacrifice. (d) Law
of Indirectness.
3. This power pervades Christianity.

Conclusion.—Changes of form may be expected, but
Christianity in its essential elements abides.

INTRODUCTION.

Necessity of the Study of Religion.

THE unsettled meaning of the word "Religion" has caused inconvenience and misunderstanding. The question, for example, whether there were any races or tribes wholly destitute of religion would have been simpler if there had been agreement about the meaning of the word religion. But the discussion became confused when, with some, religion meant any tokens in rite, custom, or belief, which indicated the possession of a religious sentiment, however crude—while, with others, it meant religion in vertebrate form, or religion "worthy of the name."

It might be said, then, that the inconvenience would end with the definition of religion. But this is not so simple a matter. The historical school will tell us that we can only define after we have collected the material facts upon which alone a definition can be based. Before we can say what are the indispensable features of religion, we must study the religions of different races and times all the world over. To define a word by the exercise of the easy dogmatism of our study chair is not a scientific proceeding. The only definition worthy of the name is that which results from a large induction of facts. If we are to learn what religion is, let us leave our own preconceived ideas on one side, and let us interrogate mankind. From the study of man, and his needs and requirements, we shall receive, if not a clearer answer, yet one which will be founded on fact.

We have therefore to study religions before we can define religion.

Advantage of the Study.

There is a further advantage which may possibly arise from the study of the religious history of man. A change has come over our mode of presenting arguments for faith. Certain lines of argument, once popular, are not felt to be appropriate to the mind of our age. It is not my task to deal with the reasons of this change. Whether it is due to a mere change of taste, or to our having drifted away from the standpoint from which the force of such arguments can be estimated—whether we are, as some imagine, more clever, or, as others believe, more dull than our ancestors, the fact remains that arguments which were freely advanced a hundred or even forty or thirty years ago, fail to produce much impression on the men of to-day. We do not now find apologists employing arguments from

Introduction. xxiii

miracles or from prophecy as their predecessors did. It would be unwise to say that those arguments have for ever lost their value. It is true to say that they are like mines no longer worked, because there is no longer the same demand for their produce. The demand diminishing, it has happened in theology as in commerce, that energy and enterprise have betaken themselves to mines which are being developed in other regions: the workers leave the shafts deserted and ply their toil elsewhere in the produce of more marketable commodities. Is it want of faith to believe that there is a protective function in nature; that when the sources of wealth fail in one quarter they may be discovered in another; and that arguments derived from physical nature may, with advantage, for the time be replaced by those which result from the study of the realms of man's psychical and moral nature? In one of his essays, brilliant with dexterous argument, and bewildering with startling paradox, the late Professor Clifford concluded that, out of the clouds which gathered round our path, the face of our forefather man looked down upon us, and that in the future, not the kingdom of God, but the kingdom of man was at hand. There is a sense in which we may accept the idea. Led away from the evidence of cosmical contrivance, and driven to undertake the study of the growth and origin of religion, the witness to the abiding strength and permanence of religion may be found in humanity. In the hour of the world's despair, amid decaying creeds, she may find that the key of deliverance lies concealed in her own bosom. The investigation of the laws and conditions of the kingdom of man may yield fresh and reliable testimony to the eternal kingdom of God.

In what field is this discovery more likely than in the history of man's efforts to find God, or, which is the same thing more fitly expressed, in the history of God's methods of leading man to Himself?

Natural Limitation of the Study.

Such a study deals with religion mainly from its subjective side. It is the history and study of the religious sentiment in man. It cannot deal with the objective truth of any religion. But, notwithstanding this, the study may bear indirect, and none the less convincing, witness to the truth of religion. It may afford a test of fitness which may create a strong presumption in favour of or against the permanent value of one religion or another. We may at least ascertain those elements which man imperatively demands in a religion, and which, therefore, must be supplied by any religion which rightly aspires to permanence. These elements we may call permanent elements of religion.

Range of the Study.

For the purpose of ascertaining what these elements are, we must treat as religious whatever is religious to any race or people. But we must distinguish the varying value of the materials at our command. In other words, we must classify. In doing so, we may be misled by some unconscious bias; but the risk of this may be minimised by observing the results of different modes of classification.

Classification.—One Class Excluded.

One class may be excluded—the class of modern manufactured religions. That which is made wilfully, and of malice aforethought, so to speak, can never be accepted as religion. It lacks the element of faith or simplicity, which is essential to everything religious. They be no gods that are made with hands, and they be no religions that are wilfully invented. We may call things by any name we like, but to devise a system and call it a religion will not make it such. We may analyse, and by doing so we may ascertain those elements which are essential to a religion; but when we put them together they do not make a religion; they want the divine element, the breath of God from the unseen and infinite beyond to give them life. Build up the image as carefully as we may, we know that it is an image. No man can worship the work of his own hands, knowing it to be such. If he can persuade himself that a Divine hand has touched it—that it is He or It, the great Spirit, and not he himself, who has made it—if by magic, rite or consecration he can bring himself to believe that the great unseen Power has transmuted its nature, then he may bow his head and worship. But when religion is reduced to the level of an analysis, and from its elements every touch and flavour of aught surpassing man's knowledge has been deliberately rejected—of the residue that is left, man cannot make himself a religion. The grouping of those elements which are essential to religion can no more make a religion than can colour and canvas make a picture, or linen and sawdust make a doll. The moment a creed becomes scientifically measurable, the religious power of it evaporates. Men may dislike or distrust the dogmatism of the Athanasian Creed, but there is more religion in the grand roll of its declaration of faith in the Father incomprehensible, the Son incomprehensible, and the Holy Ghost incomprehensible, than in a self-styled

religion whose position and proportions can be
laid down upon a diagram and measured upon a
plane. If we may so speak, the trajectory of
religion must rush away towards the infinite
beyond, if it is to keep its place as a religion
towards men. The scientific creeds must extend
towards the Unknown and Infinite before they
can become religions in any true sense. Man
must cast his anchor into depths into which he
has never descended, if he is to ride sure amid the
storms and waves of life. To cut off, as Positivism
does, all that is unknown, is to cut religion adrift
from its most needed anchorage.

Ought Buddhism to be Excluded?

Do the same arguments or similar ones exclude
Buddhism? I think not. In the first instance
the element of simplicity is present in the dawn
of Buddhism. There was no deliberate invention
of a religion. It was not built up; it grew.

But Buddhism has been described as a religion
without God. Is not such a description a contradiction in terms? Here, again, we must not
be misled by an ambiguous word. Buddhism is a
complex term. It is true that in some of its
aspects it presents the paradox of a religion
without God. But in its later and in its far larger
and wider developments, it accepts gods as objects

of worship. Further, even in its earlier aspects it never cuts itself away from some sort of touch with the Infinite and Unknown which is above or beyond us. It is an Agnosticism more than a Positivism. It is nearer to Mr. Herbert Spencer than to Mr. F. Harrison. Indeed, in some of its aspects I have been tempted to call Buddhism an unconscious Theism. Its ultimate is the wish to reach that which is above the change of phenomenal life, outside the reach of time or passion, which is beyond consciousness and unconsciousness. It has here a link with that which is above thought or time-life. We must, therefore, include Buddhism in our study. But we must exclude those manufactured systems which, though styling themselves religions, lack the religious ἦθος. With this exception we must treat all that as religion, which is religious to any race or people. From the study of these we may ascertain what man needs in his religion.

But though we cannot ascertain the essential elements of religion except in the study of religions, we may yet gain some glimpses of the nature of these elements by considering (1) the various modes of classifying religions, and (2) the definition of religions adopted by those who have given special thought to the subject.

Introduction. xxix

Modes of Classification.

We may group religions, as Professor Max Müller does, into book-religions and religions without sacred books. We may arrange religions according to the races which have produced them, and consider separately the religions of the Aryan, Semitic, Mongolian, Nigritian, and other families. We may divide them into "race-religions" and "individual religions," *i.e.*, into those which have grown up, so to speak, unconsciously with the growth of a race or people, and those which owe, or seem at least to owe their origin to some distinct individual founder. Again, we may divide them according to their special characteristics, arranging them as Professor Réville does, as "Legalistic" and "Redemptive;" or again, as "national" and "universal."

In each of these methods there is something to be gained, since each method gives prominence to some special feature. If our aim be to discover what man says of himself and his own religious needs, every classification will be useful, in so far as it yields up some principle of man's need or man's nature.

We may illustrate this by considering severally some of the proposed classifications.

1. No special principle of man's nature is

perhaps to be found in the distinction between "book religions" and "non-book religions," but this classification nevertheless furnishes a valuable caution.

Those religions which possess sacred books may be studied with the consciousness that we have dependable material upon which to base our study. Difficulties arise respecting dates, no doubt, and it is important to study the various books with scrupulous regard to their place in the chronology of their religion.

But when we come to study the non-book religions, and especially when we meet with those religions which belong to races destitute of all literature, our difficulties increase in proportion to the doubtfulness of the material at our command. In studying, for example, the old Pelasgic religions we may put ourselves under the guidance of some expert, such as M. Alfred de Maury, feeling that we can to a degree correct his conclusions by reference to the pages of classical literature. But when our studies are of races without literature, and our only materials consist of the reports of travellers and their mutually discordant accounts of the same race, then the difficulty is very greatly increased, and a feeling of doubt haunts every conclusion.

2. The classification of religions into "national"

and "universal" may be objected to, but it cannot be denied that it has served to emphasize the great difference which exists between religions which seem to be limited in their range, and those which are capable of over-passing the land of their birth ; between those which are for one people and those which are for all. It is true that in a sense no religion can be called universal till it has vindicated its right to the title by over-spreading the whole world ; but the existence of a religion which has spread its influence over divers nationalities and races, and has shown itself capable of breaking the fetters of class and family, making little of race distinctions and much of universal needs, witnesses to the possibility of a religion which may claim to be universal in a larger and truer sense.

3. The classification of religions, according to race, for instance, into Aryan, Semitic, Nigritian, etc., calls attention to what may be called characteristic differences.

As a fact it is admitted that the religions of the Aryan races possess characteristics which distinguish them from those of the Semitic races, while these again differ in religious thought from the Nigritian and Mongolian races.

These characteristic differences do not imply that there are no resemblances. They rather refer to the degree of emphasis with which certain features of religion prevail among one people as compared with another. The idea of sacrifice, for instance, finds place in almost all religions; but one religion might give it such special prominence that it would be fair to say that sacrificialism was one of its characteristics. The features which tend to appear everywhere are universal features. The features to which special prominence are given in any religion may be called its characteristic features.

For instance, the Aryan religions are theanthropic, while the Semitic are theocratic. In the latter the emphasis is laid upon the sovereignty of God: in the former it is laid on the kinship or friendship of God. It is not meant that the Aryan could not recognise the gods as rulers, or that the Semite could not recognise God as friend, but still the characteristic difference remains true. To the Semite, God was the Sovereign, the Mighty One, the Lord. Man was the subject under the protection of the Sovereign Lord. In the strongest and most uncompromising form (for instance in Islam) the creed is essentially that of faith in the Absolute Sovereign. Allah is Emperor, submission is the first virtue. In this way the Semitic race gave special witness to Dependence as an element of religion.

The Aryan religion, on the other hand, seized

hold of the relationship between the human and divine. The Godhead is Father, Brother, Friend. In the extreme forms the gods are so like men that they share the weaknesses and vices of human beings. The Aryan races were alive to the element of Fellowship in religion. This element was not, indeed, outside the range of the Semitic mind. Abraham was the friend of God. "The Lord God walked with Adam in the cool of the day." But the greatness of God impressed the Semite; the kinship of God attracted the Aryan. These great races gave, therefore, their emphatic witness to two great elements of religion—Dependence and Fellowship.

4. The classification of religions as legalistic and redemptive, deals with some of the deepest human needs. The redemptive religions (Buddhism and Christianity) bear witness to the need of emancipation from inward discord, from the tyranny of lust and desire, from the thraldom of moral evil. They are alive to the cry, "O wretched man that I am, who shall deliver me?" Buddhism and Christianity arising in the world pronounce sentence upon mere legalistic religions. They touch the heart of human need in their realization of the need of redemption.

Their differences are instructive. In Buddhism redemption comes from below; in Christianity it is from above: in Buddhism it comes from man; in Christianity it comes from God. This is not surprising. The race characteristics of which we have spoken might have prepared us for this. Buddhism is Aryan, Christianity is Semitic, in origin. Yet the wonder will remain how Christianity escaped the limitations of its Semitic surroundings.

5. Take the classification of religions as national and individual. This classification has been criticized. Religions which have had no apparent personal founder, have yet grown up through the influence of distinguished individuals. Religions which seem to owe so much of their life and origin to individual founders have derived much of the material which the individual prophet vitalised, from the slow, unconscious accumulation of national thought. There is truth no doubt in this statement. But the classification into national and individual religions still remains valuable. Nothing can alter the tremendous fact that the three religions to which alone the title "universal" is accorded are associated with the story of individual lives, and are popularly described by names which have practically become proper names of their prophets. Mohammedanism, Buddhism, and Christianity are the pre-eminent individual as well as universal

religions. They seem to bear witness to the principle that a purely philosophical religion must fail, and that it is only when a religion is vitalised by personality that it has power to live and move and have its being.

These various classifications call our attention, therefore, to certain features or elements of religion. The naturalness of religion, the possibility of a universal religion, the importance of the elements of Dependence and Fellowship, the need of redemption, and the power of personality, are among these features.

It will be seen that we reach here the suggestion of some possibly permanent elements of religion. Every classification is of service, as we are only seeking to know what man has asked for in his search after religion.

Definitions of Religion.

There is great variety in the definitions of religion; but this variety has its value, as it serves to show what elements are deemed essential to the idea of religion by various writers and thinkers. Some of these give special prominence to Dependence. Schleiermacher, for instance, says, religion consists in our consciousness of absolute dependence on something which, though it determines us, we cannot determine in turn.[1] This is

[1] Given by Prof. Max Müller, " Hibbert Lectures," p. 19.

a very strong statement of Dependence. Hegel criticises it, saying that, if this be so, a dog would possess more religion than a man. But the view of Schleiermacher becomes less limited when we notice that he recognizes an inward appropriation of the power on which we depend. "Religion is neither knowing nor doing, but an inclination and determination of our sentiments, which manifests itself in an absolute feeling of dependence on God."[1] "Religion is the immediate consciousness of all that is finite within the infinite, of all that is temporal within the eternal."[2] The sense of dependence is thus accompanied by a realization of the infinite significance of life, and by a sentiment of our union with Him on whom we depend.

Hegel is the advocate of the element of freedom. "Religion is, or ought to be, perfect freedom." This freedom, however, involves dependence of a very marked character. "Religion is the knowledge acquired by the finite spirit of its essence as absolute spirit."[3] This would seem to be the declaration of the emancipation of the finite spirit from its limitations. But the freedom becomes veritable dependence when religion is said

[1] "Christliche Glaubenslehre," § 3.
[2] Quoted by Prof. Max Müller, "Gifford Lectures," p. 68.
[3] See "Gifford Lectures," Prof Max Müller, p. 69.

Introduction. xxxvii

to be "the Divine Spirit becoming conscious of Himself through the finite spirit."[1]

We have thus the elements of dependence and freedom contending for expression in religion. It can hardly be otherwise when religion is conceived of as a relationship between the finite and infinite.

This thought is expressed in the definition adopted by Pfleiderer in his earlier work, and mentioned with approval by Tiele, according to which religion is the synthesis of dependence and freedom.[2] The finite is to become free, capable of the fullest exercise of its powers, by its voluntary and conscious recognition of its dependence upon the infinite. In a sense it enters then into fellowship with the infinite. The freedom it finds is the power to express that which otherwise it would have failed to express. Freedom is found in service. We rule by obeying. This is the liberty of the children of God. This is that service of God which is perfect freedom.

Professor Caird has admirably combined these elements in his definition of religion : " Religion is the surrender of the finite will to the infinite, the abnegation of all desire, inclination, volition that pertains to me as this private individual, the

---

[1] See " The Origin of Religion," Prof. Max Müller, p. 20.

[2] See Art. on "Religion," in " Encyclopædia Britannica," 9th Ed.

giving up of every aim or activity that points only to my exclusive pleasure and interest, the absolute identification of my will with the will of God."[1] If religion be thus the surrender of our will to the will of God, the element of Dependence is included in the definition, but inasmuch as the surrender is a voluntary identification of our will with the will of God, the communion or fellowship of the Divine and the human will has taken place. The finite finds itself in the infinite, and the infinite finds expression in the finite. The element of Fellowship is here.

Schelling's definition presents parallels, but touches on an aspect of religion which the definitions so far have not brought into explicit prominence. "Religion is consciousness, the highest unity between what we know and what we do."[2] Religion, so defined, might seem to be little more than consistency. But we must not narrow down the range of *know*, or limit it to mere scientific knowledge. It rather, I imagine, corresponds to the range of the Ideal which transcends the real as rendered by us. The infinite significance of life, when perceived, puts to shame the insignificance of life as we make it. Religion seeks to realize the ideal, and to bring

[1] " Philosophy of Religion," p. 296.
[2] "Werke," vol. i., p. 55.

about the lofty consistency which lifts the low actual into view of the ideal.

We are here within reach of the question of conduct or morality as related to religion. Kant considered religion (as subjective) to consist "in the recognition of all our duties as if they were divine commandments."[1] It is duty with the consciousness of the infinite significance of duty. It is duty seen with a kind of majestic self-enforcing power.

Beside this we may place Fichte's definition: "Religion is conscious morality, a morality which, in virtue of that consciousness, is mindful of its origin from God." Or again, "Religion is the living power of morality, a power which has become conscious of its origin, and which manifests itself ceaselessly in moral achievement."[2] Here we may recognise the infinite significance of duty. Its voice bears witness to more than the passing act of duty. It has behind it the emphasis of the Infinite and Eternal. It never dies in one achievement. It is a living force which works ceaselessly. In such a view we can see the element of Dependence. There is a majestic kinship between duty on earth and

[1] "Religion innerhalb der Grenzen der blossen Vernunft," ch. iv. 1.

[2] "Ethik," vol. i., p. 23.

the power behind duty. But the eye of duty goes not only backward to its source, but forward to the unconquered realms and contemplates ceaseless moral achievement. The element of Progress finds place here.

Spinoza seems to include this power of moral activity when he defines religion as "the love of God, founded on a knowledge of His divine perfections."[1] The element of Fellowship is present here. The soul is bound by love to God; but that love has been called forth by the recognition of what God really is. Dependence is implied, and moral or spiritual activity will follow. This definition includes the Power or Force which can evoke an admiring and grateful love. It assumes that there is a real object of love or admiration before the soul of the worshipper. Whether false or true in its view, religion is not in this definition considered as a series of subjective feelings viewed apart from the Infinite Cause or Object which calls them forth. The same is true of all the definitions which either implicitly or explicitly postulate the infinite or the unknown greater than self. Religion may, like a dream, produce emotions in the mind of the dreamer by a series of unreal images, but the moment the dreamer knows that they are unreal, the dream ends; the emotions depend

[1] Given by Prof. Max Müller, "Gifford Lectures," p. 66.

for their existence on the assumed reality of the images. The sentiments or emotions produced in men by the sense of the infinite or unknown Power of the universe cannot be called religious except in so far as they arise from the reality or supposed reality of that Power. In other words, the existence of that vast Reality, other than ourselves, the existence of God, or some equivalent of God, is an element of these definitions.

If these definitions are correct, there must be some defect in definitions or descriptions of religion which leave this element out of sight. When, for example, religion is said to be the faculty of "habitual and permanent admiration,"[1] we feel that, compared with some other definitions, it errs by defect. Religion postulates the idea of the great Beyond and Unknown, the Infinite, with which relationship is somehow possible, the Great Power or Force behind nature, which evokes our feelings of awe or reverence.

It is true, however, that religion ought to awaken our feelings towards all life. The sentiment of awe called forth by the sense of the Infinite would not be sufficient. According to Goethe, "a threefold reverence has to be called forth in man by religion: a reverence for what is above,

[1] "Natural Religion," 1882, ch. iv., p. 74.

for what is around, and for what is beneath us."[1]

Similarly Darwin says : "The feeling of religious devotion is a highly complex one, consisting of love, complete submission to an exalted and mysterious superior, a strong sense of dependence, fear, reverence, gratitude, hope for the future, and perhaps other elements."[1] We have here the recognition of Dependence, Fellowship (love), and Progress (hope for the future), allied with the recognition of the Power beyond and greater than ourselves.

The necessity for the recognition of the Infinite or Unknown finds its fit prominence in the definition of Religion given by Prof. Max Müller :— " Religion consists in the perception of the infinite under such manifestations as are able to influence the moral character of man."[1] Two elements seem to me to be implied : (1) that of dependence ; and (2) that of progress as far as regards moral character.

The definition given by Teichmüller, and quoted by Prof. Max Müller, is given in shorter and longer forms. Religion is the "disposition which, being joined to God-consciousness, symbolizes

---

[1] Quoted by Prof. Max Müller, in his recently published work "Natural Religion" ("Gifford Lectures," 1888), p. 65; note on p. 69; p. 188.

itself in the common function of knowledge, feeling, and action;"[1] or again: "Religion consists

"(1) Of personal feelings of *fear*, of complete dependence on unknown powers, which form a motive leading man to seek comfort in a view of the world not supported by experience.

"(2) It consists of *æsthetic* feelings, which surrender themselves in admiration to the Beautiful, and lead to the erection of an ideal world.

"(3) It consists of *moral* feelings, which lead to an attempt to construct such a system of the universe as should in turn make them (our moral feelings) intelligible."[1]

The longer definition, it will be seen, deals with disposition or feelings. It is occupied with the subjective side of religion. The "view of the world," the "ideal world erected," "the system of the universe constructed," may be untrue and unreal, but unless these were true and real to the worshippers, they would not be religious. It seems to me, therefore, that the definition errs by not sufficiently recognising the necessity of the *reality* of the objective in the mind of the worshipper. This defect is remedied in the shorter definition by the introduction of the word "God-consciousness." The consciousness of the

[1] *Ibid.*, note on p. 63, p. 64.

Unknown or other than self is an indispensable element of religion. The first clause of the longer definition gives a place to the feeling of dependence. The second clause, in setting forth an ideal world, awakens the instinct of progress; the third clause gives expression to the necessity of pure synthesis between things as they are and as they ought to be. This is the religious feeling which asks reconciliation or fellowship.

Réville, in his definition, gives a prominent place to this element of fellowship. "Religion," he says, "is the determination of human life by the sentiment of a bond uniting the human mind to that mysterious Mind whose domination of the world and of itself it recognises, and to whom it delights in feeling itself united."[1] The idea of union or fellowship pervades the whole of this definition. Religion is the sentiment of a bond which unites: the human mind delights in the consciousness of this bond. But near and glad as this union is, it is the link which unites man to that which is greater than man—the sense of dependence is never absent. The acquiescence which the spirit feels in the ruling mind carries with it a readiness of co-operation—we accept the domination of the mysterious mind—we delight in identifying ourselves with it inwardly and out-

[1] "Prolegomena of the History of Religions," p. 25.

Introduction. xlv

wardly in thought and in action. This implies the element which I call Progress.

Pfleiderer gives almost equal prominence to the element of Fellowship. "Religion is the relation of our life to the world-controlling Power, which is to become a community of life with it."[1] Here there is community of life. There is the idea of dependence in the recognition of the world-controlling power. There is the idea of soul-progress implied when we speak of the future and of that which is to become richer and fuller than it is at present.

Martineau defines religion as "belief in an Ever-living God, that is, of a Divine Mind and Will ruling the Universe and holding Moral relations with mankind."[2] Dependence is recognised here. Fellowship or spiritual union is possible wherever moral relations exist. Belief in the Everlasting One, who rules the universe, carries with it confidence with regard to the future and that progressive order of life which can never fail or become capricious, when all things are ruled by an Ever-living God.

Definitions might be multiplied. The above are to a degree typical, and probably sufficient for our purpose. It will be seen that they vary in

[1] "Die Religionsphilosophie." vol. ii., p. 29.
[2] "The Study of Religion:" Introduction, p. 1.

completeness and exhaustiveness; but on the whole, it appears to me that there is a general consensus of opinion that a sense of dependence is indispensable to religious feeling in man; but this sense of dependence is sooner or later accompanied by a desire of union or self-identification with the object of worship, or that on which man depends. Further, that there is always a hint of a glance forward to the future, in the recognition of an ideal to be aimed at, or of a Golden Age to be reached. The quenchless desire of progress asks a place in man's religious thoughts. These feelings yield the three elements which I call dependence, fellowship, and progress. But none of these can be satisfied except on the supposition of the truth and reality of the object of worship. To resolve this into a mere ideal is to destroy the basis of religion. Unless man feels that he yields allegiance or submission to some Real Power greater than self, he has no religion in the true sense.[1]

It follows that definitions, which deal only with subjective feelings, or which seek to make religion consist of only these, are defective.

Feuerbach, for instance, regards religion as selfishness.[2] This is simply exaggeration. To

---

[1] *Cf.* Renouf, "Hibbert Lectures," p. 253.
[2] "Wesen der Religion," p. 100.

say that there is a recognition of the needs and desires of self in religion is true enough—for man is the subject; but to make religion consist wholly in this is to forget that there is an Other-than-self element in religion. Religion is a relationship of some sort between self and some Other-than-self. To define it in such a way, that only one factor in the relationship is reckoned with, is to miss the mark.

The same objection lies against the definitions given by Wundt and Gruppe. Wundt says: "All precepts and sentiments become religious as soon as they have reference to some ideal existence which can supply the wishes and requirements of the human heart."[1]

Gruppe declares that " religion exists because it satisfies certain selfish instincts."[2] In his view, it has no other *raison d'être*. It is no doubt true that religion can be given a selfish form by selfish people. Selfishness is sufficiently strong in human nature to allow of this. But all human wishes and requirements are not selfish, and religion as often as not appeals to man, awaking generous passions to make war against selfish desires. Religion in many of its phases insists on a self-surrender. One is inclined to ask whether the writer has not

[1] Quoted in "Natural Religion," Prof. Max Müller, p. 73.
[2] "Die Griechischen Culte und Mythen." 1887. p. 216.

mistaken the remedy for the disease. How can religion, which is selfishness, get rid of selfishness, unless Satan can cast out Satan?

Professor Max Müller has devoted some pages in recently published " Gifford Lectures " to Gruppe's position. It is enough, perhaps, to say here, that in all these hostile definitions of religion there appear to be radical defects. The writers forget the sense of the infinite reality which enters so largely into man's religious thoughts or sentiments. They further confound men's legitimate Egoism with selfishness; all self-affirmation, self-preservation, self-possession, self-mastery, all effort to make the best of self is not selfishness. It is not a sin to seek joy, or to find gladness in union with Him who is higher than ourselves. Self is a sacred thing; and the religion which seeks to set it aside, rather than to lift it to true self-possession, has set the seal of doom upon itself. You cannot define religion in terms which do violence to human nature.

Religion, according to Mr. Herbert Spencer, will change, but not die.[1] Whatever components of the religious sentiment disappear, those which are due to the consciousness of unfathomable mystery and an Omnipresent Power will abide. Our capacity for wonder will grow while the one

[1] "Religion, a Retrospect and a Prospect," and "Last Words about Agnosticism." ("Nineteenth Century," July and November, 1884.)

absolute certainty will remain, that we are in the presence of an Infinite and Eternal Energy from which all things proceed. It seems to me that there is a flavour of Semitic faith in this conception. It deepens our sense of Dependence. Agnosticism has kinship with Semitic Naturism.

Positivism, on the other hand, cuts off the whole sphere of the Unknown. In its view the incomprehensible can have no kinship with us. We must create our philosophy of life and religion without the Infinite or the Beyond. We can find sympathy in woman. We can have kinship with the *Grand Être*. An active religion can derive its impulse from the recognition of duty, based on a kinship with all Humanity. The point which is emphasized here is kinship. We may worship Humanity, which is akin to us: we cannot worship the Infinite. Thus, while Agnosticism dwells on the infinite, and therefore unknown, Positivism dwells on the finite, because known. These two modes of thought give prominence respectively to the elements of veneration and kinship, to dependence and fellowship. Like the Aryan and Semitic races they attest in their place some of the special elements which man needs in his religion. Each mode of thought witnesses to a truth, neither is complete without the other.

So-called Non-Religious Peoples.

But how are we to deal with the cases of those peoples and races who are said to have no religious sentiment whatever? There are no books to guide us, and the reports, however honest, may even mislead us. As M. Renouf says, " The habits of savages without a history are not in themselves evidence which can in any way be depended on."[1]

In the first place we may estimate the position of the argument on the supposition of the facts telling on one side or the other. Suppose, for example, that the facts go to show that there are no races destitute of religious sentiment, then it must be allowed that religion is natural to man. Suppose that there are races destitute of all religious sentiment, then it would seem that we have discovered peoples who are in the condition of children in whom certain feelings and instincts are wanting. The discovery of these would not necessarily forbid our saying that religion is natural to man. If there are infantile races in whom religious consciousness is dormant or dead, we need not be greatly surprised. We do not measure man by his infantile, but by his adolescent or adult powers. In all adult races religion exists, and is as natural

[1] " Hibbert Lectures," p. 125.

to man as his hair, even though hairless men are to be found.

In the next place, what are the facts? The evidence of the existence of non-religious races is doubtful. It is doubtful, because frequently the cases cited have been proved to be mistaken. The case of Darwin and the natives of Terra del Fuego, the view of Sparrman about the Hottentots, and of Liechtenstein about the Kaffirs, may serve as illustrations. Other examples are given in the Lectures. It is doubtful, because the study of the native races has been undertaken with an unconscious bias. It is easy to see how the missionary, with strong views of the superiority of the faith he has to teach, may be blind to the value or significance of the tokens of religious sentiment among native races. It is easy to see how the anthropologist, in his desire to find evidence of the low levels from which present-day humanity has been evolved, may be blind to the same tokens. Added to this is the secretiveness of the barbarous races. Secrecy is the strength of oppressed peoples as "deceit is the fist of the weak."[1] Lastly, there is the difficulty of language, which prevents travellers from understanding what these races really do believe.

Against this doubtfulness which hangs over the

[1] Goldwin Smith, "Cowper," p. 9.

evidence on one side, we may put the weight of authority on the other side. The same facts which led Sir John Lubbock to declare that there were non-religious races led Professors Roskoff and De Quatrefages to declare the opposite. "As a matter of fact, the tribes are not found,"[1] says Professor Tylor. On the whole, therefore, we may conclude we are not at the end of the discoveries; we must wait for further light. But meanwhile the weight of evidence is on the side of those who affirm that wherever there is man there is also some religious sentiment. "A religious system," writes Mr. Herbert Spencer, "is a normal and essential factor in every evolving society."[2] On the whole we are justified in speaking of religion as natural to man.

The Religions to be Studied.

The true field of evidence on the subject of man's religious needs is the history of religions. Here we can observe what directions man's efforts have taken; and what elements he has incorporated into his faith and worship. At times some one element has been given undue prominence; but sooner or later nemesis has followed its exaggeration, and the neglected elements have in turn risen into importance. In the Lectures I have endeavoured to show what may be learned from

[1] "Prim. Culture," vol. i., p. 418.
[2] "The Study of Sociology," p. 313.

Introduction. liii

the record of the three religions called universal. I am not concerned to justify or condemn the use of the word universal as applied to these religions. Strictly speaking, no religion is universal till it has spread over the whole world, and gathered all races and peoples under its sway. No religion has as yet completely accomplished this triumph. Christianity has made the largest advances in this direction. She has embraced the greatest variety of race and people under her wing. Islâm has made little way among Aryan peoples. Buddhism has found small favour among races of Semitic blood. Christianity, rising among the Semites, has made its home among people of every tongue and of every blood. In the history of each, three elements, which I call Dependence, Fellowship, Progress, have been demanded by man. The witness of Islâm, Buddhism, and Christianity is the witness of three-fourths of the human family.

The history of other religions seems likely to yield the same results, and to show that sooner or later man asks that religion shall meet this threefold demand of his nature. The religion of Mexico has been touched on in the Second Lecture. Had time and space permitted, I should have followed this out more fully, and treated also of the witness given by the religions of the Jew and of the Greek.

The religion of ancient Egypt, as unfolded to us in the delightful pages of M. Le Page Renouf's "Hibbert Lectures," indicates the same instinctive demand.

The element of dependence is clearly marked. The word Nutar, which is translated God, means Power. It corresponds to the Hebrew El.[1] It was applied indifferently to any powers believed to be active in the universe; but "a Power without a name or any mythological characteristic is constantly referred to in singular number, and can only be regarded as the object of that 'sensus numinis,' or immediate perception of the Infinite."[2] This Power, or God, is spoken of as forbidding and commanding. He gives the fields to till. Treasure grows through His gift. He knows and smites the wicked. He will protect His servant in his affairs. He is in the light above the firmament. Sentences like these clearly state the dependence of man on the Power greater than man. "A sense of the Eternal and Infinite, Holy and Good, governing the world, and upon which we are dependent, of Right and Wrong, of Holiness and Virtue, of Immortality and Retribution—such are the elements of the Egyptian religion."[3] It will be seen

---

[1] "Hibbert Lectures," 1879, p. 98.
[2] Ibid., p. 100. [3] Ibid., p. 251.

that we have here not the mere naked element of Dependence. It is dependence with an ethical factor added. But whenever we get this recognition of a moral or righteous order, we are on our way to the element of Fellowship. Since the righteous order demands conformity to itself, man must recognise in his religion more than the idea that the gods can be persuaded to help him to his wishes: he must realize that he himself must be in harmony with the righteous rule. The realization of this righteous order is strong in Egyptian religious thought. "The recognition of law and order as existing throughout the universe, underlies the whole system of Egyptian religion. The Egyptian *maāt*, derived, like the Sanskrit *rita*, from merely sensuous impressions, became the name for moral order and righteousness."[1] We can thus see the elements of Dependence and Fellowship, joined with the recognition of a Power infinite and beyond man's comprehension. The element of Progress has a place in these passages, in which gifts and talents are recognised as divine. "It is He (God) who granteth genius with endless aptitudes."[2] We may compare, on this point what M. Le Page Renouf says of the significance of the Egyptian word *Ka*.

[1] "Hibbert Lectures," p. 250.
[2] "The Maxims of Ani," ibid., p. 102.

"The genius was a sort of spiritual double of each individual. . . . The Egyptian word corresponding to the Latin *genius* is *ka*. Its original signification is 'image.'" It acquired later the meaning of a divine gift.[1]

The Three Elements of Religion.

The words which I have used to describe these three elements are Dependence, Fellowship, and Progress. I do not claim that they are the best words, nor am I tied to their use. They seemed to me to express popularly and most nearly what I wanted to express. Their meaning will be made clearer in the Lectures. But here I may say in explanation, that the order of religious life in the world seems to move through three stages of consciousness, and at each stage to gain something which tends to complete the religious idea.

1. The first stage I call Nature or God-consciousness. Those who accept the theory of a primitive revelation will admit this at once. For those who do not, I grant that it might be more exact to spell the word God with a small *g*—for the stage I speak of is consistent with very low notions of the Supreme Being. It is the stage in which the powers of nature are felt. Man has no real consciousness of himself as greater than

[1] "Hibbert Lectures," pp. 147—152.

the animals, or even the trees around him. But he has a keen sense that there are powers, or that there is a power greater than himself, and that he is dependent on it or them for his safety and comfort. It may only be the sense of the good which the sun brings to him, warming his body and delivering his eye from the terror of the night; but it is the recognition of the greater than self, and it enforces on his mind the idea of dependence. The history of religion shows the elevation of the idea of the power greater than self. The conception of God reached higher and yet higher ranges; but the first step out of mere animalism is the consciousness of Dependence on other than self. It is certainly anterior to any polytheistic or henotheistic stage. It is the stage of naturism if you will; but it is the stage in which man conceived of the powers about him as powers which were alive. It is recognition of a life and power other than his own. It is what I call Nature or God-consciousness.

2. The second stage is self-consciousness.

This stage is the dawn of the ethical idea. For man to become conscious of himself is to realize what we call his personality, and to be aware of his power of self-direction. He begins to determine his actions; his will is in play. He perceives that there is an order of life about him; misfortune when it comes is realized as involving some mistake or fault on his own part. Nature has prohibitions. Nature avenges the violation of her prohibitions. The gods have a way or order of their own: he must conform his practice to their will or wish. He has learned to blame himself. Related to this stage is the propitiatory sacrifice. If we may, without committing ourselves to the interpretation, draw an illustration from the early chapters of Genesis, we might regard the sacrifice of Abel as typical of the dawn of the self-conscious stage. Cain is the type of man in the mere Nature or God-conscious stage. Abel has reached the stage in which to God-consciousness is added self-consciousness. This stage is at first crude; it is often allied with gross superstition: human sacrifices darken its movements. But crude or dark, the element which it reveals and nourishes in man is the recognition that he must somehow unite himself with the power above him. The relationship must not be that of mere dependence. It must be one of communion or fellowship. In its highest stages the feeling of dissatisfaction with self becomes full of keen and poignant anguish : the righteous order presses upon the self-consciousness of man, alive to his failures and waywardness. Its language is the cry of despair from the lips of one who perceives the

Introduction. lix

strife between the life as prescribed by the ideal of righteousness and the life as self-will has made it. Then we hear the wail, " O wretched man that I am!" The recognition of the idea of sin belongs to this stage. The idea of sin is the witness to the element of Fellowship. The idea of sin (not the sense of sin in individuals) loses its power whenever the union between the Divine and the human can be established as complete and uninterrupted. The propitiatory sacrifice is no longer offered, being no longer needed. The world has seen one vivid example of this. Wherever the story of Christ has been accepted as a way of life, there all propitiatory sacrifice has ceased. In one sense, sacrifice is the heart of the Christian system. In another, sacrifice, except in the ethical and eucharistic senses, is no part of it. The stage of self-consciousness is followed by another stage.

3. The last stage is world-consciousness.

It is only comparatively late in the world's history that the claims of the world and of the race have been recognised among men. The claims of the family or of the clan were recognised as the recognition of community of interest grew. But the view that every human being all the world over had claims on his brother man seems to me to stand on a different footing. Altruism, to whatever source we trace it, is a nobler thing than clanship or the claims of *goel*. It is not the consciousness of a mere extended self-interest; it is a world-consciousness, and implies not merely an enlarged range of view, but a clarified vision. It seems to stand upon the recognition of the fellowship between God and man, which makes man conscious that he has a place in working out the great aim of God. He was once dependent; like the animals, he sought his meat from God. He is still dependent, but not in the old sense, for he has recognised the moral order, and he has seen that in righteousness lies life; but becoming one with God, he views the world with the eyes of God. The Father cares for the children—the eyes with which the Son of God beholds the world are the eyes of Love. Like St. Paul, such an one feels that he is a debtor to all—Jew, Greek, Barbarian, Scythian, bond or free—what matters the name? He owes his life-energy to all. Out of this spirit grew the recognition of the claims of humanity. There is a goal towards which humanity can travel. Progress is recognised here. It becomes a necessary element when out of God-consciousness and self-consciousness has grown world-consciousness. Sinai is the expression of the righteous order, but it would have no meaning except to those who had reached the stage of self-consciousness. But the code of Sinai is before the Sermon on the Mount. This latter deepens the sense of self-consciousness, but it also opens the stage of world-consciousness. "Do good, and lend, hoping for nothing again; and ye shall be the children of the Highest; for He is kind unto the unthankful and to the evil."[1] Can world-consciousness find nobler expression than this, or Progress find a truer inspiration?

It is worth noting the connexion of these three elements with those conceptions of God which have been current from time to time in the world.

Deism proclaims the transcendence of God. It leads to absolutism in religion. It is allied with fatalism in life: it cuts man off from the sense of kinship.

Pantheism, when viewed as a reaction from Deism seems to bring God nearer, but it does so at too great a sacrifice. It touches all the movements of existence and the Universe with a passing brilliancy: all motion, all advance, are the pulsations of the life of God in the Universe. Progress is a divine thing. God is near to Nature and to man; He is in Nature and in man; nay, He is Nature—nearer than this he cannot be; but this is not nearness, it is annihilation. In no

[1] St. Luke vi. 35.

true sense can the desire of kinship, which makes man reject Deism, be satisfied by this doctrine of God's nature. He may be immanent in Nature, but how can man have fellowship with Him if He be all Nature, and if man be Nature too? In this confusion of substance, to borrow a phrase, there is no scope for Fellowship. Pantheism destroys the possibility of the kinship which at first it seemed to promise.

God must be near and akin to man. He must be working in the great order of the Universe. He must be near us, and yet above us. The realization of the three elements—dependence, fellowship, progress—protects us against erroneous, inadequate, and unsatisfying conceptions of the Divine Nature.

Similarly, the true conception of the Divine Nature meets man's needs, and proves adequate and satisfying to man's nature.

These three elements are witnesses of man's needs. He is conscious alike of his feebleness and of his greatness. He must find the Strong and Eternal One on whom to depend ; he must become one with the order of the world in which he is placed ; and he must express himself in achievement. His sense of dependence, his desire for kinship, and his ambition of progress, claim to be heard. These three things are as

Introduction. lxiii

laws of the kingdom of man, and they discover to us man's nature. The needs of man witness to the nature of man :· they meet with response in the nature of God. The impression on the coin corresponds to that on the die. The conceptions formed by man of the nature of God have often been grotesque : they must always be imperfect ; but they may be true, though inadequate. To be real to man they must be correlated to man. This correlation we meet in Christianity. If man's nature asks satisfaction in dependence, kinship, progress, the conception of the nature of God given in Christianity corresponds. On the Eternal Father, man may depend; in the Eternal Son, man finds fellowship and true harmony with the order of life ; in the Eternal Spirit, there is the guarantee of all true progress.

If our position is true, these elements enter into the foundation of the religious nature of man, and they are also of the eternal order of the Universe. They have been demanded by man : they have been steadily maintained amid changes and controversies. Interpret them as we may, they refuse to be discarded. An unseen Power has presided over the history of man as his religious conceptions have developed into greater clearness. The presence, but not the nature of this power, has been almost universally recognized. It is the faith of some of us that the world has never been left without the guidance of the Maker of all, and that it has lived and does live in the grace of our Lord Jesus Christ, the Love of God, and the Communion of the Holy Spirit.

LECTURE I.

PROBABLE PERMANENCE OF RELIGION.

An age of transition makes men ask, Will religion survive?

I. —There are reasons for believing that religion will survive.

These reasons are derived from
1. The experience of the past, which shows that religion lives, though religions die.
2. The nature of man—which is (*a*) permanent, and (*b*) religious.

II.—Further, it is not impossible to indicate some of the conditions of religion in the future, and to which any religion which aspires to be enduring must conform; for the permanence of man's nature means the permanence of certain spiritual conditions or principles, which, for the sake of convenience, we may call laws. There are seemingly four:
1. The Law of Environment.
2. The Law of Organism.
3. The Law of Sacrifice.
4. The Law of Indirectness.

The existence of these gives us a guarantee of the survival of religion and the conditions on which any religion can hope to survive among men.

Thus the survival of religion is likely, and the religion of the future must conform to certain conditions.

LECTURE I.

PROBABLE PERMANENCE OF RELIGION.

"Hereafter ye shall see heaven open."—*St. John* i. 51.

TIMES of transition are times of question and of doubt. Our age is such; and it is said that the age has lost its faith. The saying is uttered by some who fear that it is true; it is echoed by others who wish it to be true. But it is not true because prejudice and fear say so.

An age which has its face towards the future, and in which men are full of plans for the welfare of the world, is not an age which has lost its faith. Its temper of mind is constructive; it is eager for new institutions, keen for new ideas, and has already a half belief in a future in which all things will be new.[1] The republic of the future, the Church of the future, the religion of the future, are phrases which betray hopes for the future on the part of those who use them; and hope is never unbelieving.

[1] Mat. Arnold, " Lit. and Dogma," ch. xi. and xii., Pop. Ed.

If the age has not lost faith, has it lost faith in religion? and is Christianity slowly taking its place among extinct things, like the flora and fauna of earlier times, doomed because lacking power to adapt itself to changed conditions? To these questions I shall try to give answers. I shall try to give reasons for believing that the age has not lost its faith in religion; to shew, too, that the days of Christianity are not numbered, that her eye is not yet dim, nor her natural strength abated—that she holds within her bosom elements which are indestructible, that she has the power of survival in her capacity of adjusting herself to the shifting conditions of the world, and that thereby she gives promise of carrying on her beneficent ministry among succeeding generations. She has been misunderstood by the world; she has been misrepresented by her followers; but she has, if I mistake not, powers, the force of which has hardly yet been realized; she is much greater than any of us know—when rightly understood her morrow shall be as to-day, and much more abundant. This is my belief; but belief is not argument.

For the present I wish to leave aside the question of the survival of Christianity, and to attempt a consideration of the earlier question. For it will easily be understood that we cannot expect the survival of Christianity if all religion is doomed.

I.—There are reasons for believing that religion will survive.

1. Experience affords no ground for thinking that religion will die. It is perfectly true that we say in melancholy fashion—"All things die": and then we ask why should religion be exempt from the common lot? But the history of religion is a tale of transfiguration rather than of death. Certain forms of religion have died. "The Greco-Roman, Germanic and Scandinavian mythologies—the Semitic polytheisms of Nineveh, Babylon, Biblos, Tyre and Carthage—the rich pantheon of ancient Egypt—the solar worship of the Incas—all these are dead, gone for ever. And we could add to this funeral list."[1] But though these have passed away, religion lives on. Religions die: religion lives. The forms of religion may be said to die: the spirit and power of religion endure. Of religion it may be said, that though the outward man perishes, yet the inward man is renewed epoch by epoch. Threatened with death, she passes into the cloud, is transfigured in the cloud, and comes forth invigorated.

[1] Réville, "Prolegomena of the History of Religions," Eng. Ed., 1884, p. 2.

We are not now dealing with the truth of this religion or that. We are only noting facts in the history of religions. Brahmanism was threatened by Buddhism. To men then alive, the time must have seemed one in which religion was about to perish. The event, however, showed not destruction, but transfiguration. Judaism was threatened by Christianity, men feared that faith would die. But religion, transfigured, gathered fresh energy, and started on a new and victorious course.[1] In those days, as now, there were not wanting men who cried out, some with despair, others with eager triumph: Religion is doomed. If we have been frightened by these cries, it is perhaps well to call to mind the shrewd saying of Archbishop Whately: "A man does not die because his coffin is made." It is so easy to say, because certain institutions, customs, faiths have passed away, therefore all will perish. A calm spirit will discriminate, will reflect that there are certain principles, elements, laws— call them what you will—which survive change, and smile in the face of every death. Nothing can rob us of that which is eternally true. The minor aspects of truth may alter; the rubbish

---

[1] *Cf.* Matheson, "Can the old faith live with the new?" pp. 5-7.

which has gathered for years round the temple may be cleared away; the tables of the moneychangers may be overthrown; false, defective, unworthy statements of truth may disappear. The history of the past teaches this, but it also teaches us that there are things which cannot be shaken. Religion has passed through many a crisis, and yet she survives. Like force, though she changes her form, she never dies. Now seen as light in pure and luminous thought; now bursting forth as heat in burning enthusiasm, she always remains a force, wielding her sceptre amongst men. Thus experience shows that religion survives: it is the form alone that alters: the living force abides.

2. And the nature of the case might lead us to expect religion to survive.

We say that this is a world of change; and as we speak we think of the rapid and startling changes which we have experienced, but we forget that there are elements which do not change. Our sentiment and our sadness lead us to fix our thoughts on the things perishable; and we forget the things which endure. We are as one who meets his friend after long years of absence, and whose first thought is: How changed he is! his hair has blanched, his eye is dim, his head no longer erect, his step no longer firm, how changed he is! It is true, but these things are on the surface. The friend has not changed, his hand is outstretched as freely and as warmly as of old; the light of recognition which kindles in his eye glows with the light of a love which has not died, and which knows no change. No! the friend has not changed. And we, like him, are all liable to be deceived by the outside of things; we take the outside as if it were the whole; we are sorry materialists and sad literalists, and we cannot believe in the unchanging heart of things.

Apply this thought. Religions die, we say; and we expect therefore to see all religion pass away. But here again we are misled by the outside of things; we note the things which undergo change, as the modes of thought, the special doctrines or conceptions of an age or a nation—even the popular phraseology of a creed or of an epoch. We see these pass away, but we forget that there are elements which do not alter. Man may change his language, his customs, his dress, but man's nature is permanent; the roots of his character and disposition scarcely alter from age to age; he may be better or worse; more learned or less learned; but he is man still, whether the sky over him be northern or southern, whether he draws his breath under the rule of the Pharaohs, or is born under the flag of the American Republic.

(a) The permanence of man's nature is as a key which unlocks the door of the past; it creates that freemasonry which enables the characters of widely differing times and places to understand one another. Were it not for this, the past would be a sealed book to us, and the most glorious creations of ancient literary genius undecipherable hieroglyphics; but because man is man, whether in Athens or in London, we can enjoy the works of Æschylus and of Shakespeare, of Molière and of Goethe, and find in them characters who appeal to our nature as beings who thought and struggled, sinned and sorrowed, failed and succeeded as we have done. Prometheus and Macbeth, Tartuffe and Faust belong not to one country only: they are the possession of every land and of all time. It is this fact which makes variety possible to the modern novelist. We read for instance the works of Mr. Marion Crawford. He sets his scenery in the far East, and we listen to the speech of Buddhists in Northern India; he transports us to Italy, and we are made intimate with the palaces and aristocratic pride of Italian nobles; he puts before us the scenes of to-day, and we hear the language of enterprising Germans and versatile Americans; he carries us to the distant past, and we live in the age of Zoroaster. But in all these books, dealing with whatever place or time, man is still man. We read in all of ambitions and jealousies. Man is the same creature of misunderstandings, hopes, fears, of love lost and found, of resolutions made and broken. The tragedy of life, and the comedy of life, move together through all ages; the draperies change, the scenery shifts; but the characters bear a family likeness; the nature of man is unchanged. When calculating, therefore, the chances of the survival of religion, it is not wise to dwell merely on the accidental features of life which are subject to alteration, or on the intellectual forms of man's faith which naturally vary with enlarging knowledge. It is necessary to remember that there are things which do not change. Man's nature is so far constant that we can recognise in him the same being of hopes and fears, of convictions and doubts, of chivalry and selfishness; a being timid, confident, loving, passionate, capable of high aspirations and profound regrets; a being who, in spite of all the weaknesses which provoke our contempt, is yet the one being whose story in all ages attracts us, and whose destiny fills us with the deepest curiosity and interest. He is seen in every age asserting himself in the midst of tremendous and

Probable Permanence of Religion.

baffling difficulties as one who has rights, and is greater than the circumstances which seem to crush him; slowly winning his way to the mastery of the forces around him, he reveals in his history, if not a continuity of purpose, still a constancy of nature.

(b) And one feature of that nature stands fixed by the witness of history and investigation. This being, whose nature is constant in all ages, shows himself to be incorrigibly religious.[1] Exceptions have been taken to this statement; but, as far as we can ascertain, these exceptions tend to disappear. It has been stated over and over again that there are tribes and races amongst which no religion has been found. Travellers have affirmed that they have sought in vain for any traces of religious system or belief. But negative testimony is not conclusive on this question, as the three following considerations will show. The difficulty of language has more than once led to misapprehension. Long residence among native tribes is needful before the religious significance of their phraseology is perceived. Again, the very lowness of the type of religion existing among some races leads to its being overlooked. There have been travellers who have declared that certain savages have no re-

[1] See Appendix, Note 1.

ligion, because the religious system is so low that it is not worthy of being called a religion at all. This is clearly not a very logical method of carrying on important enquiries. To ignore phenomena because they seem insignificant is to miss the opportunity of advancing the growth of scientific knowledge. This is true always; it is especially so when we are investigating the doctrine of tendencies; the lowest and crudest fetishism is, in one sense, as significant of human tendencies as the most elaborate worship. Lastly, the very human nature which is being studied puts a further difficulty in the way of the investigator. The love of secrecy, strong in many natures, is perhaps strongest of all among those whose intelligence and civilization are low. Ignorance and timidity are almost always secretive. The fear lest the betrayal of what they know may be used against them, and the pride of knowing something which those who are felt to be their superiors do not know, are forces which promote secretiveness. An Englishman lived for twenty years among the natives of Australia. He became so friendly with one of the tribes that in token of their confidence and esteem they made him a chief. He had closely observed them during those twenty years with opportunities more favourable than any which an ordinary traveller could possess;

yet during the whole time he had not been able to discover so much as a trace of any religious belief higher than fetishism. But at last he made the discovery that the tribe had been in the habit of meeting to worship a God to whom they gave the name, Father. The secret, entrusted only to the men, had been jealously guarded, and kept from the knowledge of the white man, even though he had been deemed worthy of chieftainship.[1]

The difficulties of language, the low type of the religion, the secretiveness of the natives conspire, therefore, to place difficulties in the way of the investigator, and sufficiently explain the fact that tribes, which at one time were thought to possess no religion, are now recognised as having one. "Little by little," writes De Quatrefages, "the light has appeared, and the result has been that Australians, Melanesians, Bosjesmans, Hottentots, Kaffirs, and Bechuanas, have, in their turn, been withdrawn from the list of atheist nations and recognised as *religious*."[2]

But even if the case were not so strong, the

---

[1] This incident was related to me by one whose work in the Colonies is well known. Similar evidence is given by a Benedictine missionary.—See Prof. Max Müller, "Origin of Religion," pp. 16, 17, 97, 98. See Note 1 in Appendix.

[2] "The Human Species," p. 475. *Cf.* Introd. xlviii.

fact would remain that man is religious. The existence of some exceptions would not make it untrue to say that man is religious. We say that man is sociable, though there are numbers whom we call unsociable; we say man is a calculating, musical, laughing animal, though there are thousands who will never understand mathematics, thousands more who never really relish music, and probably thousands who never laugh. The statement that man is religious can be fairly made, even were the exceptions spoken of conceded. On this point the controversy recently revived concerning the existence of what is called a Primitive Revelation may help us. I do not now deal with the question whether there was or was not a primitive revelation. It is enough for my purpose to say that there either was or was not such a Revelation. If there was, then man had a religion from the very earliest times. If there was not, then man must have been naturally religious, seeing that, without external aid, his religious conceptions and customs grew as from a soil whose seed was in itself. "As soon almost as we know anything of the thoughts and feelings of man, we find him in possession of religion, or rather possessed by religion. The oldest literary documents are almost everywhere religious. 'Our earth,' as Herder says, 'owes all the seeds of all higher culture to a religious tradition, whether literary or oral.' "[1] "Religion," writes Professor Réville, "such as we define it, is inherent in the human mind and *natural*. We are justified in applying these terms to that which throughout history and over the whole surface of the habitable globe shows itself inseparable from human nature. The ancients, when they began to look beyond their own country, were greatly struck by this *consensus gentium*, the result of which was that in spite of all diversities, they found everywhere a religion. The more acquaintance with the world has been extended, the more this observation has been confirmed. Ancient Asia, America, Africa, Malaisia, Polynesia, Australia, the Polar regions, have successively furnished their testimony. Religion is a human fact in the strictest sense of the word, and here we are in accord with Benjamin Constant, who .... has enunciated this principle, constantly verified ever since, that religion is an indefectible and perfectible attribute of our species."[2]

We are now in a position to answer, so far, the question: Will religion survive? The answer must, we think, on any ground, be

[1] Max Müller, "Hibbert Lectures," p. 4.
[2] "Proleg." pp. 32, 33.

"Yes." The destructive elements in the world, at any given time, cannot really destroy; they can only transform—but transformation implies the permanence of some essential principle or elements. The nature of man remains the same, and the more widely our knowledge of man's nature is extended, the more clearly do we perceive that he is religious. I have said that he is incorrigibly religious. The epithet can be justified. As the needle to the pole, "through all its aberrations, the human mind always turns towards the Divinity. Efforts have been made from time to time to impress upon it a contrary tendency. It has always resisted, and taken again as soon as possible its constant direction. It also might say to us, This is my nature!"[1]

We may calculate, therefore, upon the survival of religion.

II.—But can we calculate upon any of the features of the religion which will survive? Can we mark any of those elements which are likely to endure after the shaking and sifting of all things? There are two ways in which we may approach this question. We may take our stand upon the convictions of our faith, and say, "Those things which we have from God are certain to endure; those

[1] Réville, "Proleg." p. 63. See Appendix, Note 1.

truths on which we have lived are among the things which cannot be shaken." It is obvious that though this position may be perfectly sound, it is not a position which can be accepted by all. We turn to another method of approaching the question. The ladder between heaven and earth has a foot which rests on earth as well as a summit which reaches to heaven. We may reach the human from the Divine; but we may also approach the Divine through the human. We may ask what the nature of man has to say on this question. If human nature is the same always, and in all ages, and
"Every human heart is human,"[1]

then we may be sure that whatever the nature of man imperatively demands will be supplied by religion. This statement may be open to misinterpretation. It will be said that, of course, whatever man wants in the form of his religion, he will be ready enough to invent—that nobody ever doubted the religious inventiveness of human nature. This criticism, however, does not invalidate the position here adopted. The question is: Can we forecast any of the features of the religion which will survive? The answer is: If man is a

[1] Longfellow, Introduction to "Hiawatha."

religious being, we may discover what are the constant elements in his religious nature; and we may be sure that the only religion which has a chance of survival is that which meets the essential religious demands of his being. Further, we are not now considering whether the religion which will survive is true or false, provable or disprovable. We are only dealing with the question of facts in human nature—such as the fact that man's nature is religious—and we are asking whether we can lay our finger upon any principles which seem so essentially bound up with man's nature as to demand a place in the religion of the future? Negatively, we may say that no religion will survive which violates any essential law or principle of man's nature. Positively, we may say that the religion which is likeliest to survive is that which shows itself most capable of meeting the wants of man's nature. To ascertain, therefore, what features may be expected to survive in the religion of the future, we must betake ourselves, for the purposes of this argument, to the study of man's nature; we must try and ascertain what are its spiritual laws; we must trace these, not only in man studied alone, but as displayed in the history of religions; we must examine religions with the view of ascertaining how far they meet these spiritual requirements of man; and from this study we may infer the probability or improbability of their permanence. The survey of the religious history of mankind will show us the universality of certain principles. Meanwhile, it will be convenient, if, before going into the region of history, we point out certain spiritual laws of man's nature. We shall thus bring ourselves closer, as it were, to the heart of the question, and clear our path somewhat before advancing.

Those conditions which, with all diffidence, I call laws of our spiritual nature may be stated, for convenience hereafter, as three; but for the purposes of clearness, I propose to divide them now into four. The last two, in reality, are but branches of one law, simple in itself, but needing subdivision in consequence of the weakness of man, and of the theological questions which have gathered round it. The remainder of this Lecture will be occupied with the consideration of these laws, stated in fourfold form, laws which cannot, I believe, be safely ignored or set aside by any religion pretending to be universal or hoping to be eternal.

Can we fix on any elements, laws, or conditions marked out for permanence?

It may be well to notice that all spheres of life

show us that there are laws or elements which abide in the midst of change. The man who is rich and increased in goods may pull down his barns and build greater; he may reconstruct all the farm buildings, so that the whole external aspect of his estate may be altered; the yield of his land may continue to increase; but the laws by which the corn, and wine, and oil are supplied remain the same. He may change buildings and crops, but the laws of growth remain unchanged. Similarly, man may increase in knowledge and experience, his treasury of faith may be enriched, his learning may grow; he may pull down the old systems, theories, and assumptions, and in doing so he may extend the borders of the domain of knowledge, and add new wealth to his store of science; but the laws of thought remain unchanged. And man, too, may reconstruct his religion; he may alter its outer framework; he may enlarge his intellectual conceptions; he may destroy his ancient creeds and put new ones in their place; he may find his notions of sacrifice obsolete, his theories of expiation defective in moral significance, his doctrine of inspiration purely mechanical, his conception of revelation dry and barren: but while thus he pulls down his barns, and seeks (perhaps vainly) to build greater, the elements of his spiritual

I.] *Probable Permanence of Religion.* 21

nature, the laws by which his spiritual nature grows, remain unchanged. And these are not, as we think, destined to change; they are likely to be as strong, as imperious, and as exacting in the future as in the past.

I wish to speak of some of these elements. There are four, which may be called laws of man's spiritual nature, destined, I think, to be such as long as man remains man, and allied with principles the possession of which is needful to any religion which aspires to permanence. These laws, closely knit together with man's moral and spiritual growth, will be found to suggest ground of reconcilement between many things now at variance.

1. The first of these laws may be stated thus: *As we think, we are.* This, inasmuch as our thoughts are as a constant environment round our hearts and spirits, I venture, though conscious of its inadequacy, to call a Law of Environment. I place this first, not because it is first in importance, but because it is somewhat overlooked, and, if not overlooked, viewed with suspicion, as favouring too much the standpoint of the dogmatist. I am perfectly prepared to admit the vices of the dogmatist; he is an intellectual pedant, prone to exaggerate the importance of those few opinions which he is in

the habit of calling momentous truths. But exaggeration does not warrant rejection. It is cheap and easy to say, "Let us abolish creeds, and get rid of doctrines;" and every wise man will be ready to discard doctrines which have proved themselves untrue: but it is not sufficiently considered that, as it is impossible to get rid of the exercise of private judgment, so it is impossible to get rid of doctrine or creed. There is no system in the world without them. Even those who most mightily decry them are possessed of them. Emerson said: "As men's prayers are a disease of the will, so are their creeds a disease of the intellect."[1] There may be truth in this; doubtless our weak and blind prayers are often the expression of our passionate and petulant will; doubtless our cherished beliefs are often only the expression of our intellectual weakness rather than of our moral strength. But if Emerson meant to disparage all doctrine, we can but reply that it would not be difficult to exhibit a system of doctrine underlying Emerson's teaching; nor is it with the slightest want of appreciation of his great powers that we say Emerson was, notwithstanding his apparently undogmatic method, as truly a dogmatist as John Calvin. The truth is, the effort to get rid of dogma is vain and illusory. A ladder

[1] Emerson, Essay on "Self-Reliance."

must have its foot on the earth, and truth must be capable of intellectual statement; and intellectual statement is dogma whether we like it or not. Dogmas are everywhere; Comte needs them no less than John Knox, physical science no less than theology. The doctrinaire may be a nuisance,[1] but he is not essentially a fool. He has a real work to do. He embodies a protest on behalf of the important place held in the world by our intellectual conceptions; he calls our attention to the sovereignty of ideas; he exists to remind us that as we think, so we are.

It is not difficult, perhaps it is scarcely needful, to show the importance or the truth of this law. Failing to remember it, we often lose the significance of history; and what is perhaps most curious is the fact that the strongest assaults made upon religion are based upon the assumption of the truth of this law. "Look at the horrible things," it is said, "done at the bidding of religion, and learn its injurious effects." But what is this if it be not saying in other words, "When men's notions of religion are debased, their conduct will be debased?" Religious notions count for something in the forming of conduct. When the Indian widow was burned on the funeral pyre of her husband; when the multitudes prostrated

[1] See Appendix, Note 2.

themselves and sought death beneath the bloodstained wheels of Juggernaut's car; when the Mexican crowned the victim with flowers; when the devout and sorrowing friends put corn in the hand of the corpse—they were acting in obedience to religious notions. We ask, naturally enough, what was the idea in their minds when they did this or that? The idea, whatever it was, represented the doctrine which they received, and which inspired their conduct.

It is noteworthy that Mr. Buckle seems to have overlooked this simple law. I say, seems to have overlooked it, for I would not speak with certainty. But, as far as I can judge, he has not reckoned with it. He twits moral laws with their inability to effect improvement in regard to the great evil of religious persecution;[1] but it is well to remember that religious persecution arises largely from false ideas—"Whosoever killeth you will think that he doeth God service." (St. John xvi. 2.) The conduct in this case is the result of a religious idea; there is a theory or doctrine behind the action—a false theory, no doubt, but that is immaterial; it serves just as well to establish the law that conduct follows ideas. It is argued, indeed, that ideas wait on sentiment, and that only as our moral senti-

[1] "History of Civilization," vol. i., pp. 164, 188 *et seq.*, and 208.

ments vary do our theological notions change; *i.e.*, that our theological notions are the result of our moral feelings. There is a truth in this; it is the case, as we shall see shortly, that our perceptions are coloured alike by our sentiments and by our character; but to admit this does not get rid of the fact which is also true, that our characters grow under the influence of our ideas.

The truth is, that, among the various sovereignties of the world, the sovereignty of ideas holds high place. Homer writes a poem; but his poem becomes more than an epic; it fills the minds of people with ideas; and on these ideas a great people is nourished; the ideas are appropriated; and the characters of the people take form under their influence. Homer's "poems became the Book of the Law for the Hellenic peoples, so that he became for them what Moses was to the Hebrews. Never again shall we see a society regulated on the plan of an epic .... Greek society, in fact, tended by a constant approximation to form itself on the ideal of the Iliad and the Odyssey .... Greece was not untrue to the image that had thus been revealed to her; on the contrary, she has made of the poem a truth, of fiction a reality, of presentiment a history."[1] In the same spirit the same writer said that

[1] Quinet, "Génie des Religions," chap. vi., sec. 2.

the institution of polygamy was regarded as sacred when the principle of pantheism was applied to the family. "A new earth is always the result of a new heaven," is his doctrine in a work, the leading object of which is to show "how entirely each of the civilisations was the offspring of a religious dogma."[1]

In the same spirit Ruskin speaks of the beauty of Greece as dependent upon the laws of Lycurgus, the beauty of Rome on those of Numa, and our own beauty on the law of Christ.[2] Ideas and thoughts thus count for something; yes, for much in the formation of character. "If you wish to alter the destiny of a people," said a great French preacher, "you have only to alter its ideas; doctrines are sown in the soil of the mind; they are ripened by the sun of the centuries; they spring up in action."[3] The age of revolution has almost always been preceded by a doctrinaire age; the teachers to-day, the actors to-morrow; Christ and his Apostles to-day, a Christianised Empire to-morrow; Luther and Erasmus to-day, the Reformation to-morrow; Diderot, Helvetius, and Raynal to-day, the revolution to-morrow. We need not wonder at the law. We, who live in a time

---

[1] See "Edgar Quinet," by R. Heath, pp. 265, 294.
[2] Ruskin, "Art in England," pp. 105, 106
[3] "Père Felix."

when the influence of the environment on the organism is spoken of as a real factor, need hardly be surprised to find, that man's character takes colour from the thoughts and ideas which he habitually cherishes. The lad who feeds on the criminal column in the newspapers, and makes the police news his study, is certain to find his character sink to the level of the thoughts on which he nourishes it. "Give me a great thought that I may feed upon it," has been the cry of more than one great man. Character rises with great thoughts. "Nature is subdued to what it works in, like the dyer's hand."[1] Our characters grow or shrink with our thoughts. If

> "Love, like an insect frequent in the woods,
> Will take the colour of the tree it feeds on,"[2]

the same is true of character. "The key to every man is his thought,"[3] says Emerson; and the quality and tone of a man's thought are ennobled or debased according to the ideas and truths amongst which he dwells. As we think, we are. It is the Law of Environment.[4]

Hence the religion of the future cannot afford

[1] Shakespeare, Sonnet cxi.
[2] Sir H. Taylor, "Philip Van Artevelde." *Cf.* Schopenhauer, "The World as Will and Idea," p. 304.
[3] Emerson, "Essay on Circles."
[4] Further illustrations of this law will be found in the Appendix, Note 3.

to ignore ideas and thoughts. She must ally herself with the sovereignty which thought wields in the world. Laws, as we call them, are little more than the compact statement of truths derived from facts. The laws of nature are the formulated account of an observation of facts. These become, in their turn, vehicles of knowledge; but they become more, they become rulers in the realm of progress. Every system which has grown into influence has made use of them. Without them, our knowledge would be chaotic, and we should be the victims of eternal flabbiness. Life would be like a game of tennis, played against a feather bed, instead of against a firm responding wall. The religion of the future cannot ignore this principle—she must have a message to the region of thought. If she can supply no thoughts, reveal or teach no lofty ideas, if she be void of doctrine, she can hold no place in the confidence of man. If she have no link with man's thoughts, man will learn to think without her, and so learn to live without her. She will fail if she ignore this law: *As we think, we are.*

2. The second law may be stated thus: "*As we are, we see.*" If the first law may be called the law of environment, this may be called the Law of Organism. It is correlated with the first law, and is its complement. Our conduct is largely the result

of the thoughts, views, and opinions which we have inherited. The principles, which we have been taught, tend to form our characters; our characters reflect them, as a mirror reflects the object presented to it, but the reflection is not wholly due to the object; the condition of the mirror exercises a modifying power, and can make or mar the image. The creature grows by influence of its environment; but it is not wholly the victim of its environment; it exercises some force, and moulds the environment to its need. The same conditions may bring life or death; the things which one man receives and on which he grows great, come to another man and degrade him. We do not see with our eyes only, nor perceive with our minds only; we see and perceive also with our hearts: "As a man's heart is, so is he."[1] Our thoughts take colour from our wishes and from our character. We are not pure, impartial mirrors. Something of the colour or texture of ourselves mingles with the reflected image; the image of the object and the object itself are not identical in every respect. The truth of this law is not hard to see. Proof of it may be found in the realm of nature. The river primrose is but a yellow primrose to some; it is a beauty and a revelation to others.

[1] Prov. xxiii. 7.

The jaded sensualist looks upon the Thames below Richmond and sees in it only a volume of flowing water, which streams by with irritating and exasperating monotony. The man whose eyes are opened sees in the same river entrancing sights. "Not in nature, but in man," says Emerson, laying down the very law we speak of, "not in nature, but in man is all the beauty and the worth he sees." In the same strain, Mrs. Barrett Browning sings :

"Earth's crammed with heaven,
And every common bush afire with God."

The heart, full of its own thoughts, cannot escape from them, but imparts their hue to every vision. Shakespeare, in his play of Julius Cæsar, gives us an illustration of this principle. It is to be found in a minor scene, which stirs us strongly. Like the scene in Macbeth, when the sound of the knocking at the door is heard, its power over us is unquestionable. The reason is clear. The scene reveals the intensity and variety of feeling in the minds of the actors. "Here lies the East," says Decius. "No," answers Casca, with his heart full of the conspiracy. Cinna interposes, agreeing with Decius:

"O, pardon, sir, it doth; and yon gray lines
That fret the clouds are messengers of day."

I.] *Probable Permanence of Religion.* 31

Then Casca rejoins :

> "You shall confess that you are both deceived.
> Here, as I point my sword, the sun arises,
> Which is a great way growing on the south."

The calm thoughts of Cinna can contemplate with simple natural pleasure the lines of luminous gray, which are the pathways of the morning; but Casca's heart is full of other things; he sees a new day for the republic, which will dawn through the lines drawn by a sword; and that day is nearer than his companions dream.[1]

In Art the same law shows itself. The artist's nature shines through the artist's work. For better or for worse, there it is. Ruskin has preached this many times to the men of this generation. "To Rossetti the Old and New Testaments were only the greatest poems he knew; and he painted scenes from them with no more actual belief in their relation to the present life and business of men than he gave also to the Morte d'Arthur and Vita Nuova. But to Holman Hunt, the story of the New Testament, when once his mind entirely fastened on it, became what it was to an old Puritan or an old Catholic of true blood,—not merely a Reality,

[1] "Julius Cæsar," Act ii., Scene 1.

not merely the greatest of Realities, but the only Reality." [1]

In poetry—in all the realms of great thoughts—the same is true. Great thoughts grow greatest in those who are great of soul. Gray thoughts reflect the spirit within,

"Doubtless I am old, and think gray thoughts, for I am gray."

No man is degraded in his powers, who is not first degraded in his tastes.[2] The same principle lies in the lesson which our own Laureate has taught us in his matchless music. The Holy Grail—the glorious vision of the true meaning and power of the life which is both divine and human—is seen in various measures by various men. "Ye have seen what ye have seen," is King Arthur's language to the Knights. The vision is to them as they are to it. Some see it in its unveiled glory: some see it as a casual gleam: some see, but only think they see it, and what they see is veiled: and how could it be otherwise? A Galahad, whose "strength is as the strength of ten, because his heart is pure," can see the vision of God given only to the pure in heart. Sir Percival may see, but not so fully and so clearly. Sir Lancelot will look up from his

---
[1] Ruskin, "The Art in England," pp. 7, 8.
[2] Dr. Johnson, "Essay on Dryden."

land of sand and thorns, and see what is only a great doubt proving a great certainty.

To this law Réville refers, when he demands a sympathetic spirit in those who would study the history of religion. "We must have the religious ear in order competently to study phenomena of the religious order. How could the man who has no sense of the beautiful ever write the history of Art?"[1]

The story of the ministry of our Lord is a commentary on this law. There were men who saw no beauty in that stainless life, and heard no music in the words which fell from His lips. But how could the Pharisees, who were covetous, see any beauty in a life of sacrifice? or how could those, whose ambitions were listening for the intoxicating applause of men, delight in the melody of a life which sought no honour save the honour of doing good? How could the timidity of worldliness understand the courage which was ready to lay down its life rather than leave undone the Father's will?

The law is true: As we are, we see.[2] Our perceptions take the colour of our character. There are some things which the pure alone can see. The condition of the organism counts for some-

[1] "Proleg.," p. 32.
[2] See further illustrations in the Appendix, Note 4.

thing in the order of life. May it not be that the fullest revelation waits for us—not when we have the keenest wit, the quickest intellect, the farthest-reaching knowledge, but when we are likest to God? Only when we wake up after His likeness shall we be satisfied with it. Like only can understand like. The law abides always: *As we are, we see.*

3. The third law is the Law of Sacrifice. "*No pains, no gains.*"

In one sense this law may be said to spring from the former. Our inability to perceive is caused by fault or defect in ourselves. There is need therefore of some change in us in order that the fault or defect may be removed, and the power of vision strengthened. For this end we must sacrifice every hindrance. Reluctance to sacrifice is fatal. He that loves his life loses it. The principle applies to all spheres and all aims. The man who succeeds in his object is the man who takes pains, sacrifices his pleasures, his pride, his daintiness in the determination to win at all costs. It is a law written everywhere, that only in sacrifice is progress possible and success secured. The corn of wheat must die before the golden harvest can come. The bright flowing water yields its free spirit to the stiffening hand of a frozen death, but it is thus that it gains power to burst the rocks asunder; stern necessity drives men through the paths of pain on their way to the stronghold of power; sorrow, bitter and biting, has struck hard at the hearts of men, who learned to enchant the world with their music only after they were broken-hearted. Sacrifice is the law of progress;[1] and it must find its place in any religion which aspires to guide men, and win an abiding dwelling-place among them.

But it will be said—are not these three laws sufficient? The nature of man needs to be surrounded by pure and great thoughts, that it may grow pure by being purely shone upon. The nature of man needs to be cleansed, that it may perceive the high dignity and worth of the pure thoughts which are presented to it. The nature of man needs to bear the cross, if he is to be the pioneer of better things. If we have thoughts that are high to regulate our minds, sentiments which are high to prompt us forward, wills that are strong and ready to sacrifice whatever hinders our advance; have we not enough? True, these three are great laws; and in almost every religious system they find a place. Most religions admit the sovereign influences of ideas, and therefore provide their worshippers with doctrines.

[1] See Appendix, Note 5.

Most religions recognise in some way the need of a moral fitness in the worshipper. Most religions have acknowledged the validity and value of sacrifice in some form. But it is not every religion which has seen the need of another law without which the three of which we have spoken are strengthless. They may be able to bring man within sight of the goal, but not within reach of it: to reveal perchance what it is, but not to give the power to attain it. Like Archimedes, under the guidance of these laws we may ascertain that the world can be moved, but we have not been given the vantage ground from whence to move it. One thing they lack, and that is the element which completes and perfects sacrifice; without which sacrifice may be dazzling and brilliant as fire, but not as yet pure as the light. This lacking element will be understood by the fourth law of man's spiritual nature.

4. The fourth law, needed to complete the previous, and which I call the Law of Indirectness, is this: *A man cannot perfect himself in anything if he seek perfection directly;* for if he does so, the shadow of himself intervenes and spoils his work. Sacrifice, when it is sought as sacrifice, has a self-consciousness which mars its simplicity and spoils its moral force. When men preach self-sacrifice—

self-sacrifice as the moral force which can regenerate mankind—they forget that self-forgetfulness is essential to perfect sacrifice; a sacrifice, undertaken because sacrifice is noble, is alloyed with that self-regarding look which mars its beauty in the view of the soul itself. Sacrifice, which knows itself as such, is not pure sacrifice. Something more is needed, some impulse of enthusiasm, some inspiration of love, to lift it out of the level of self-regardfulness. The love of country, the love of home, the love of children, become consecrating powers precisely in this way. The patriot who dies for his country; the youth who lovingly tries to support his aged parents; the mother who rushes into the flames to rescue her child ;—follow impulses loftier than those of self-conscious action. Theirs is the impulse of pure love, which sees not the sacrifice, but the one object for which they are willing to dare and to do all.

The truth of this law may be seen in various ways. The man who aspires to be eminent in any special line has often to turn his back upon the direct road. The poet does not find poetry in making verse; he must leave this schoolboy trade; he must commune with nature, drink in her spirit, till the soul within him, fed with great ideas, seeks to express itself in song. The man whose mind is set upon merely being an artist seldom climbs high in his profession, except perhaps as a master of technical skill; for really great work he must have the soul of the artist, and the artist soul is nourished on more than the skilful handling of the brush and of colours. The orator is only great when he entirely forgets the arts of rhetoric and the tricks of elocution, and speaks as one possessed of a great theme, to which he burns to give utterance. Self-consciousness is the ruin of the highest powers in man; none reach the loftiest range but those who scarcely think of themselves as artists, poets, orators—but just know that there are thoughts and truths which cry within them for expression. Such men would say to the young aspirant for fame : If you would sing, or paint, or speak—go, fill your mind with great thoughts; think, meditate, till the fire of inspiration comes, till God begins to move, as of old, upon the teeming thoughts. When the fire has kindled, and speech is a necessity, then you may be what you will—for you are not thinking of yourself. Inspiration takes the place of self-consciousness.

The same principle is true in religious matters. There is a fatal self-consciousness. A man may wish to be a saint ; but he who, wishing to be a saint, strives to be a saint, will never, so striving,

become a saint. The fatal self-consciousness is there, as it was in Sir Percival :
" Thou thoughtest of thy prowess and thy sins.
Thou hast not lost thyself to save thyself."

Sacrifice seen to be right, and done because it is right, yet felt and known to be sacrifice, on the whole is a just and worthy thing. But sacrifice evoked by the inspiring love of some object, felt not as a sacrifice but as natural because needful for the sake of the object loved, is greater still. This it is which sets the smallest acts of love higher than the greatest acts of duty. Duty done is noble; but the highest duty, done merely as duty, stands on a lower plane than the smallest act of pure, generous, unselfish love. The one is of earth; the other is of heaven. The one is great in the realm to which it belongs; but the least in the kingdom of heaven is greater. This is recognised by universal human instincts. The generous and loving man is held in higher regard than he whose life is coldly correct. With all its blunders and mistakes the soul that moves under the impulse of high, generous love is pardoned and received; "she loves much; she is forgiven." Such a nature, having no thought of self, or of its own greatness or its own praise, is forgiven because of its nobleness. Love acts, like genius, because it must. It wears no pride, no self-pity on its face. It smiles at the lifted axe and the glowing flame, because it is love.

This is the truth to which J. S. Mill gave expression when he said, "Those only are happy (I thought) who have their minds fixed upon some object other than their own happiness; on the happiness of others, on the improvement of mankind, even on some art or pursuit, followed not as a means, but as itself an ideal end. Aiming thus at something else, they find happiness by the way."[1] This is the Law of Indirectness. This is the "siege perilous," in which only the pure-hearted can sit and find their joy, their power, the free possession of themselves and their lives, when they have flung self, and pride, and the desire of happiness away. This is the philosophy of St. Paul. He rehearses the record of his doings and his sufferings; yet how he scorns himself, as it were, in the doing it: "I have become a fool in glorying." (2 Cor. xii. 11.) Who that has known love recapitulates his sacrifices, or thinks of his greatest hardships, keenest sorrows, bitterest self-surrenders as sacrifice at all? Love knows no boasting, no language of self-praise; she is great, chivalrous, noble, self-denying, self-sacrificing, yet never knows herself to be these. This is the

---

[1] J. S. Mill, "Autobiography," ch. v.

bloom upon human actions, which, like the bloom upon the fruit, not only makes them beautiful, but protects them from invading evil. All deeds of self-sacrifice are consecrated only when the love which inspires them blinds the doer of them to their greatness. This I call the Law of Indirectness,[1] because the principle at the root of it is this, that the greatness is not found by one who seeks to be great. Eloquence is not achieved by one who seeks to be eloquent, nor saintship by one who seeks to be saintly. But power of every kind, intellectual and moral, comes best to those who seek not to be great, but only to be good.

As we think, we are. As we are, we see. Progress is through sacrifice. Sacrifice to be pure must be inspired by something higher than the desire to be self-sacrificing. If these four things be true—if these are principles which are constant in human nature, then it would seem to follow that any religion, if it is to be an abiding one, must recognize these Laws. The religion which has no message to the thoughts of men, or no appeal to the moral nature of men, or which ignores the high law of self-sacrifice, or seeks to establish self-sacrifice apart from some inspiration of love, will assuredly fail.

[1] See Appendix, Note 6.

Man cannot do without ideas, without morals, without sacrifice, without inspiring love. These four principles have their exaggeration; when undue stress is laid on the first, doctrinism becomes a fetish; when on the second, we get meagre moralism; when on the third, we have a cruel sacrificialism or meaningless asceticism; when on the fourth, we reach unpractical mysticism.

Such are the laws of man's spiritual nature to which, as it seems to me, religion must conform itself if it is to abide in perennial vigour, and bid defiance to the processes of decay. But laws, it must be recollected, are nothing in themselves; they are but the ordered expression of facts which underlie them, the formal statement of the methods in which inherent powers and qualities manifest themselves in action. Beneath the laws of human nature lie the qualities, the instincts, of human nature; it is these which alone produce the laws, and give them reality and meaning. Our next step must therefore be to examine what these spiritual instincts or properties are, of which the laws already mentioned are the expression; we shall thus be enabled to discern both the aptitude of the human heart for religion, and the essential elements which a religion must possess which can hope to be universal, and to establish its throne for ever among the children of men.

In the meantime, remembering that religion seems natural to men of every race, and that the laws of their spiritual nature have the character of permanence, we may believe that religion will not die. The heaven will be opened. Nay, was it not in the past also that heaven was opened? There was one Teacher who taught great and gracious truths which men's minds understood, whose character was bright and stainless, whose life was one pilgrimage of self-sacrifice, and the inspiration of whose career was love. Standing by His side, I think I can see heaven open and the angels of man's aspirations rising, and the angel of Divine love descending upon Him who was so truly Son of Man.

LECTURE II.

SOME ESSENTIAL ELEMENTS OF RELIGION.

One guarantee of the permanence of religion is the permanence of man's nature, and that permanence is expressed in certain spiritual laws.

It may be asked whether we cannot predict any of the elements which will be found in the religion of the future.

I.—It is likely that we can; for a large field of investigation is being opened up to us in the comparative study of religions. The history of religions may suggest to us the elements which the nature of man has demanded in religion.

II.—The elements which man's nature asks are three:
Dependence.
Fellowship.
Progress.
1. Two of these are indicated by Definitions of Religion.
2. All three are suggested by general considerations, but the evidence that they are, as a fact, demanded by mankind must be sought in the history of religions.

III.—The evidence on this point will be given by
Non-universal or minor religions.
Universal religions.
1. Hints of these elements meet us on the threshold.
2. The witness to them in some non-universal religions.
(*a*) The religion of Mexico.
(*b*) The religion of Israel.
(*c*) The religion of Greece.

The need of these three elements for man.

Lugubrious. They predict the decay of familiar faiths. "Christianity," they say, "is played out. The heritage of the future does not belong to her. Her shroud is already prepared. She may be decently buried."

It is not always wise to prophesy. There are modern Sauls who like to play the prophet's part, but who would be better employed in humbler avocations. Instead of prophesying, it is wiser to inquire whether we can ascertain what features of religion are likely to endure.

I.—Our first duty, then, will be to ask what are the sources from which we may glean facts likely to help us. The sources of investigation are, briefly, the past and the present. It is not by turning our eyes to the future that we shall best descry the first glimpses of the morning which is coming. Like the man who looked for the dawn and found its earliest tokens on the summit of the western hills, so, perhaps, we may catch our first view of the future by turning our glance on the past. But we must not gaze only on the past; we must look to the present also; the future is the offspring of both, and both are alive with interest and with teaching. The poet, indeed, speaks of the past as dead, and the present as living. There is a sense in which this is true, and, as the poet meant it, doubtless it was true. But there is a sense in which the past is never dead; a sense in which it is alive for evermore. The future is not the offspring of dead parentage, but of the past and present, which are both alive.

We must, however, notice some difficulties in the way of our investigation. There are, first, external difficulties. These arise from the number of religions, and from the variety of views and opinions concerning the definition of religion. The number of religions is legion, and they present strange and conflicting differences of features. Eastern and Western, barbarian and philosophical faiths compete for our attention; and at the same time the very definition of religion is not agreed upon. Religion, according to Kant, is morality; according to Mr. Matthew Arnold, it is morality touched by emotion; according to Fichte, it is knowledge; according to Hegel, it is freedom.[1] But if thus we are met by difficulties, we have the advantages derived from the progress which has been made in the comparative study of religions. In this way our investigation has been made easier. Our work is simplified by those who have opened up roads through hitherto impassable country. But it

[1] *Cf.* Max Müller, "Origin of Religion," pp. 14, 19, 20. Matthew Arnold, "Literature and Dogma," p. 16. See Introduction, p. xxxvi.

is here that we are conscious of difficulties which we may describe as internal, as they arise from the feelings. There is a feeling of contempt, and there is a feeling of distrust. Some think the comparative study of religions to be a danger and a mistake, others disdain it as nugatory and vain.

It may be true that many who study the religions of the past and of the present do so with inglorious aims; but, if religion be of any value, we ought to rejoice in every manifestation of interest shown in its history. Now, the distrust, of which we have spoken, arises mainly from the idea that to engage in such study is to ignore the special dignity of Christianity, and to place a divine revelation on the same level with mere human religions. This objection, if it be one, shows a strange perversion of mind. By the supposition, Christianity is different from other religions in that it is a divine revelation. If so, nothing, we should imagine, would be more welcome than the study which most reveals the difference.

It is, perhaps, more important to observe the strange and false view of life of which this distrust is a symptom. If we limited our thoughts to man alone, the comparative study of religions would be pregnant with interest: it would be like the reading of the great spiritual dream of the race. But if we believe in God, we must believe that every page of history will show His hand, and, most of all, that page on which is written the story of the way in which man has sought after God, and God has revealed Himself to man. If we believe in no guiding hand and no self-revealing Love in the past, and see in history only the vain struggles of man against the bars of his prison, then let us refuse, if we can, to study the history of religions. But if we believe that behind all life and the things which darken our hopes and perplex our thoughts, there is a Love which never fails, and a Wisdom which, though inscrutable, is wonderfully kind, then the story of the past must always have a surpassing interest for us; for, though it is the record of the struggles of man, it is more—it is the story of his education at the hands of that God who is Love. And what story could possess greater charm than that which tells us how man has looked for the knowledge of God; how the hand of God has from time to time lifted the veil, and let in the brightness of His presence upon the darkness of life? For those who thus realize God in life there need be no fear of any investigations which throw light, not merely upon the aspirations of men, but upon the power and wisdom of God.

There are others who despise the comparative

study of religions, not because they fear that irreverent hands may be laid upon sacred things, but because they feel a contempt for all studies which appear to them mere attempts to revive an interest in subjects dead or doomed to die. Religious history can only be interesting if religion be above contempt. Hard contempt is a state of mind no less unworthy of the student than selfish fear. Extremes meet here as elsewhere : the religionist and the scientist are at one. The religionist dislikes such studies, because he fears their results; the scientist dislikes such studies, because he thinks them worthless. But both these are unworthy tempers, contempt more so than fear, for contempt brings forth no fruit of knowledge or faith. It is easy, perhaps fatally easy, to allow a spirit of contempt to grow. When we open the door of our ark, and look forth upon the troubled waters of Life, we may, if we will, send forth as our messenger the spirit of criticism and contempt, but, like the raven, it finds its life in destruction and death, and can bring back no pledge of hope. It is only when the spirit which goes forth is the spirit of sympathy, gentleness, and docility that we can expect the olive branch of hope and knowledge to be brought to our doors. "Contempt," says a modern writer, "diminishes as we grow wiser." It is true.

Life, as we learn to know it better, is too sad, the faults of man are too pathetic, and, at times, are too noble to be treated with contempt; and, I think, when we have learned, through larger knowledge, both to distrust ourselves and to love our kind, it dies out altogether. Hence, we must banish the spirit of fear, and rise above the spirit of contempt; we must come to the study of the religions of the past with the spirit of those who desire to know, and with the belief that there is something to be learned in the record of man's struggles, if we are to gain anything from the study of the world, which lies in the hand of God. In this spirit we may reach the knowledge of those essential elements which have existed in the religions of the past, and which will probably be found in the religion of the future. We shall not despair to see the heavens open.

The field of investigation, then, is the history of religions, past and present. In these we must seek for those elements which give the essential features of any enduring religion. We must lay the evil spirits of distrust and of contempt which haunt our path. We have to seek for truth, and we must quit ourselves with docility and courage.

II.—Before entering upon the field of investigation, it will be as well to ask whether we can obtain from the definitions of religion any indication of the features we might expect to find.

1. From the definitions may be gathered two of these features, to which a third may be added. The first is Dependence. "The most primitive element which it (the theistic idea) contains is doubtless the notion of _dependence_ upon something outside of ourselves."[1] Thus Fiske writes; following Schleiermacher, who held that religion is a feeling of absolute dependence on God. Réville admits that Schleiermacher was right in believing dependence to be an integral part of religion.[2]

A second feature is Fellowship. Plato saw that religion was likeness to God, founded on a sense of kinship between the human and the Divine.[3] Schelling thought that it involved the idea of fellowship or harmony as opposed to any contradiction between knowledge and action. "The first meaning of religion is consciousness, the highest unity between what we know and what we do, which makes it impossible that what we do should contradict what we know; as the tendency of the spirit to be one with its centre —God, is morality."[4]

[1] Fiske, "The Idea of God," p. 62.
[2] See Introduction, p. xxxvi. *Cf.* Pfleiderer, " Philosophy of Religion," vol. i., p. 305.
[3] Plato, "Theæt."   [4] Schelling, "Werke," vol. i., p. 55.

II.] *of Religion.* 55

Strauss declared the ineradicableness of this idea of kinship: "In our inmost nature we feel a kinship between ourselves and that on which we depend."[1]

Réville's formal definition of religion emphasizes the same feature which I call Fellowship, for he says that "religion is the determination of human life by the sentiment of a bond uniting the human mind to that mysterious Mind whose domination of the world and of itself it recognizes, and to whom it delights in feeling itself united."[2]

These (and more might be added) are enough to show that in the minds of men who have studied the question—though following different schools of thought—both the idea of Fellowship and that of Dependence are among the essential features of religion. But to these two features I venture to add a third—Progress. This expresses belief in the forward and upward movement of creation, the belief in personal spiritual progress, and the conviction that not for ourselves alone do the wheels of time move forward, but that they bear all things onward to an age in which the children of men shall be blessed. My reasons for adding this feature are simple. The

[1] Quoted by Max Müller, "Origin of Religion," p. 3. *Cf.* Introduction, pp. xxxvii., xliv.

[2] Réville, "Prolegomena to the History of Religions," p. 25.

idea of Progress refuses to be excluded. The search for happiness, thought by some to be universal, involves Progress, for no definition of happiness seems so complete as that of Madame de Staël, who said, "Happiness is constant occupation in congenial work, with the full exercise of our powers, with a continued sense of progress."[1] If stagnation is misery, progress is happiness, and it can hardly be ignored in a religion which aspires to be abiding. Again, religion cannot be one with men, unless it be one with men's growth and progress. This, which is always true, will be found to meet with more ready recognition in an age like the present, when the interest in forward movements is so keenly felt by all classes. If, in some quarters, progress has been constituted a religion, we may well believe that religion must possess in itself an element of progress. Dependence, Fellowship, Progress—these are the three features which we believe to be essential to religion, if it is to prove a permanent power in the world.

2. The fitness and naturalness of these three elements will be seen on reflection.

It has often been said that the progress of the race resembles the growth of the individual from

[1] *Cf.*Aristotle, τὸ ἀνθρώπινον ἀγαθὸν ψυχῆς ἐνέργεια γίνεται κατ' ἀρετήν. Nicom. Eth., bk. i., ch. 7.

childhood to manhood. The analogy might be justified by argument: it is enough that it is accepted by Réville, who, in this, follows Voltaire. Now, let us look for a moment at what takes place in the history of the child. The first feature respecting child-life which strikes us is the infant's often quoted absolute dependence. From earliest days its needs must be supplied by another. This is the education by which it learns dependence. It cries for its food, and its little cry is one of absolute trust that the cry will not be unheeded. Dependence is its first idea. But as the child grows, and intellect develops, it passes from the stage of absolute dependence to what is at first partial, and then complete, companionship. He shares in the walks with his father. By-and-bye the prattle of the little child passes into the more thoughtful speech of the boy; and this, again, into the graver reflections of youth. The relationship which was once one of Dependence, has grown to be one of companionship also—that is, Fellowship is added to Dependence. But life has a further stage. With manhoood dawns ambition—the wish to exercise his powers in the great and moving world. The father shares those feelings, for, if the son is ambitious for work, the father is ambitious for the son. He would rather see him enter into the world, use his energies there, and become a living force, helpful in the advance of human life and human civilization, than selfishly keep him at his side for the luxury of his friendship and companionship. Thus the idea of Progress adds itself in human life to those of Dependence and Fellowship. The powers which have been won through Dependence and Companionship must be now used in Progress. We may take a second aspect of this analogy, and one which is, as I believe, closely allied to the development of religion. We may reflect on the way in which love grows. The love of the child is a love which is scarcely more than the consciousness of dependence, love which is drawn out towards those from whom it receives; but later, when what is more usually called love begins to declare itself, it is a love which desires companionship. The friendship of boyhood is dear; but it is soon followed by the love which seeks companionship in wedded life. And then comes that change which alters the whole position of man with regard to life. He is no longer one who merely depends on another; he has become the one upon whom others depend. The man has become the father, and thenceforward he feels that progress, whether for himself or for his children, is a feature of life which can never be ignored. Thus into the ordinary development of life, these three—Dependence, Fellowship, and Progress—enter as natural and familiar elements. It is not surprising that these elements should enter into religion.

Assuming, then, for a moment, that they are features of religion, we may note that none of them alone can constitute religion, nor can any one of them be ignored by religion.

Dependence cannot stand alone. Otherwise religion becomes a demoralizing force;[1] and this is easily understood, because if religion consist merely in dependence upon God, man tends to become weak, greedy or insincere; his needs and his desires are the main interests of his religion; the question of his moral and spiritual affinity to God does not necessarily arise; a religion such as this becomes open to the reproach that it is little more than refined covetousness. Jacob prayed at Bethel that God would keep him, and bring him to his father's house in peace; he asked mainly for prosperity and comfort for his material life. Viewed thus, he exemplifies religion conceived of as dependence; and had Jacob had no experience beyond that of Bethel—had not Penuel succeeded

[1] See Appendix, Note 7.

Bethel—he would never have outgrown the selfish timidity of his character.

If religion, viewed only as Dependence, tends to deteriorate character, it tends also to harm the race by weakening the springs of moral activity. Where Dependence is all, there is no need for effort in life or spiritual co-operation in worship; worship becomes a mechanical ritualism, and religion the parent of superstition.

But while Dependence cannot stand alone, it cannot be ignored, for it carries the idea of reliance, and reliance is needful in religion, for all who are conscious of weakness must depend upon the strong; and man is weak.

Neither can Fellowship alone constitute religion. A religion which inculcates Fellowship without a sense of Dependence becomes pantheistic, and is deficient in that reverence which the less feels towards the greater. Similarly, Fellowship without the necessity for Progress becomes a kind of spiritual luxury. The mystic, yielding to his emotion, longing to become one with the Deity, and to merge his spirit in the Great Spirit of All things, is likely to shut himself up from the more active duties of life. Intent upon the realisation of the union of his spirit with the Great Spirit of All, he forgets the union of his life with the brotherhood of the world, and the duties which he owes to men; he loses the sympathetic spirit of progress.

Fellowship cannot be ignored, for it is the satisfaction of that craving for harmony which is strong in human nature, which is felt as a desire for concord between our thoughts and the life which is outside ourselves; for the Divine synthesis, or the reconciliation between what is and what ought to be—the peace between our character and our conscience. It is that desire for inward harmony, which is, though not always recognised as such, the longing of the spirit for oneness with a higher law or higher life. It is seen in that wonderful and even mysterious desire, manifested in almost all religions, for atonement.

Nor can Progress alone be counted as religion; for the religion which consists solely in the recognition of the sacredness of Progress will not prove sufficient. Having no Dependence upon the Great Spirit of All, it will lack reverence. Owning no Fellowship between the human spirit and the Divine, it lacks that inwardness of life which has often proved to be the heart of religion. It becomes a moralism—often a moralism with Atheistic tendencies.

Again, Progress cannot be ignored. All life is felt to be sacred. The movement of the world is not to be regarded as outside the thought of God any more than it is outside the interests of men. And if this be so, the idea of Progress is inseparable from the complete religious idea.

Thus all three—Dependence, Fellowship, and Progress—seem to be needed. If these three elements fit the laws of man's spiritual nature, then it will be seen, from what we have said, that we cannot ignore them without the retribution of growing stagnant, and immoral, and even of losing grasp upon truth. Our ideas of God become unworthy, our ideas of man narrow, our powers of touching the world-life wither away. We become unwilling witnesses that true and complete peace is only found by man when his spirit is at peace with the world, itself, and its God.

III.—Hitherto we have only been dealing with the need of these three elements as attested by the nature of the case. We turn now to the history of religion, with the view of ascertaining what evidence we may gather concerning man's religious needs. At the outset, it may be well to consider what we expect and what we do not expect from the study of this evidence. We do not expect to find these three elements entering as essential elements into every religious system; but we do expect the several systems to show what, according to their history, man has required at their hands. The history of religion will thus reflect the essential needs of man; and we are to ask whether man's nature is constant in requiring certain elements to complete religion.

Religions have been divided into those which are universal and those which are not universal. By universal are to be understood those which have overlapped the borders of the country of their birth, and have proved themselves capable of ministering to men of differing races and lands; in distinction from those the history of whose life has been within the limits of the land which gave them birth. The consideration of those religions which are universal, and which are admitted to be so by the best authorities, will be dealt with in the next Lecture. In the present we shall only note the hints of any essential elements of religion which may be observed in what we may call the lesser religions.

1. At the outset we meet with evidence. Take the element of Dependence. The ancient mythologies are clear on this point. The needs of man led him to look upward to the heavenly powers. The forces of nature were in the hands of great Beings on whose bounty man depended. The rain must be implored.

The tempest and the fire must be deprecated. The gods must be propitiated. Man's earliest religious feelings are often the pathetic expression of his sense of Dependence on powers greater than himself. The sacred books of the East—the Vêdas and Mantras—carry evidence. Here we find prayer and praise; and the teaching that "the best road to the knowledge of God is that feeling of Dependence implied in prayer and praise." The worship of the Zulus and Khonds, described by Dr. Tylor, will further illustrate this:—"Among the Zulus, the sacrificer says, 'I pray for a healthy body, that I may live comfortably and thou, "so—and—so," treat me with mercy!'"[1] The Khonds, when offering a human sacrifice to the Earth-goddess, say: "By our cattle, our flocks, our pigs, and our grain, we procured a victim and offered a sacrifice. Do you now enrich us. Let our herds be so numerous that they cannot be housed. .... We are ignorant what it is good to ask for. You know what is good for us. Give it to us."[2]

The element of Dependence enters into all early religions. Can we as readily find among them

[1] Matheson, "Natural Elements of Revealed Theology," p. 220.
[2] Dr. Tylor, "Anthropology," p. 365. See Note 8 in Appendix.

the element of fellowship? Turn to India alone. The Brahman Pantheism taught that nature was the manifestation of God, and that man must blend himself with Him or it. This expresses the strong yearning for fellowship with the Divine.

The same element may be found on the threshold of Indian worship. "Nearly all the gods," writes Professor Max Müller, "have epithets applied to them which are derived from this Rita" (a word meaning road or path), "and which are meant to convey the two ideas, first, that the gods founded the order of nature, and that nature obeys their commands; secondly, that there is a moral law which man must obey, and for the transgression of which he is punished by the gods."[1] The first carries with it the idea of Dependence; the second expresses the necessity that man should bring himself into harmony with the will of the gods as expressed in nature; and in this we have an aspect of the element of Fellowship.[2] For the moment you say there is a *moral* law which man must obey, you express the idea that it is necessary for men to come into complete harmony with that moral law, and thus—seeing that the moral law is regarded as the expression of a divine

[1] "Origin and Growth of Religion," p. 243.
[2] See Note 9 in Appendix.

will—into harmony with the Divine Being. Connected with this is a large class of sacrificial ideas which imply the need that man should bring himself into oneness with the ruler or rulers of the universe.

2. In further illustration we may briefly note features presented by the lesser religions.

(a) The ancient religion of Mexico shall be our witness. When Fernando Cortez landed in Mexico, he found it inhabited by a people far advanced in civilization. Their irrigation was carried on by splendid aqueducts; "their streets were cleansed by day and lighted by night;" good roads, joining the important centres of civilization, were provided throughout the whole of the country, and a system of posts so complete that his landing was known in the most distant provinces within a few days of his arrival.[1]

Our interest lies in the religion of these people. Their worship exhibited the element of Dependence. The sun and the moon, the gods of fire, of the rain, of the storm, were regarded as beings upon whom they depended for health and food and comfort. They had grasped in a measure the idea of Fellowship. Their sacrificial system may illustrate this. Their rites were bloody; human victims were sacrificed by thousands.

[1] Réville, "Hibbert Lectures," p. 33.

Twenty thousand human beings are reported to have been sacrificed in thirty-four years. Yet we can hardly describe them as a cruel people, for side by side with such savage practices we find a tenderness and consideration for the sick and poor, which raised hospitals and infirmaries for their benefit. The self-contradictions of men are many; and it needs patience to understand them. We can only do so by seeking to discover what men are trying to say as well as what they do say. Many terrible words and deeds are but brutal and imperfect attempts to express some great and heartrending emotion. The explanation of these cruelties of the Méxicans may be found in some strongly-felt need. We notice that they not only sacrificed human victims, but they practised what we may call a religious cannibalism.[1] After they had given up the eating of human flesh as ordinary food, they would eat it at religious festivals; and there was a religious meaning in this. They felt the absolute necessity of entering into communion and fellowship with their gods. The victim was prepared for sacrifice; the priest plunged in the knife. He seized and tore out the bleeding and quivering heart, and flung it into the brazier to be consumed. The worshippers fed upon the

[1] See Note 10 in Appendix.

flesh of the victim, and, eating this food, they believed that they entered into communion with the god, for that the god had entered into fellowship with the victim, and that in feeding on the victim's flesh they became incorporated with the god. The same idea seems to have been present in their practice of asceticism. The idea of suffering entered into their religion and duties, and they mistook suffering in itself for the moral good which may come from suffering. They believed that suffering itself possesses an irresistible moral force. We may regard this as a crude conception, but we must realise that there is in it a certain nobleness, when we perceive a readiness to endure any pain, if thus they may enter into fellowship with beings higher than themselves. They desire to be one with their god, they desire also that the god may become one with them; and in their beautiful legend of the humming bird they seem to have grasped the notion that God may become incarnate, and that true kinship and communion may be established between God and man. In the Mexican religion, then, we have found the ideas of Dependence and Fellowship. Is there any hint of the idea of Progress? Among their numerous deities there was one god, Quetzalcoatl, elsewhere called *Hurakan*, from which, it is said, our word hurricane is derived. But this god is, in their estimation, more tender in his feelings, more beneficent in his influences, than their other gods. He is averse to human sacrifices. His breath is sweet and life-giving. Where he comes, beauty is spread over the face of the world, and all things smile. He bids the seasons appear with varying blessing. He sends the freshness and promise of the spring, and the warmth and brightness of the summer; he commands the fruits of the earth to come forth. All the sacrifices offered to this god are sacrifices of simple fruits and flowers, tender and beautiful as the god himself. Their faith concerning him is touching and sweet. He is one who sometimes leaves them, and their land is wintry and forlorn; in his absence they turn their eyes to the West and believe that he will return; not merely with the returning spring, but with the true summer of the world, bringing in his train the virtues of justice and kindness, and establishing the reign of the righteous in their midst.[1]

And what is this? It is more than a parable of the Seasons; it is the dream of a glorious future, the dream of that golden age which is the common heritage of many creeds. And herein we have an acknowledgment of

[1] Réville, "Hibbert Lectures," pp. 62-65; cf. pp. 38, 115, 224. See Note 11 in Appendix.

the element of Progress, and a witness that man is never satisfied with a religion which is one of Dependence or Fellowship only. There is a native philanthropy in the hearts of men which has its aspirations and yearnings, which dreams of an age of justice and peace, which prays for the progress of good, which longs to see the day of peace and goodwill among men. This spirit we have found, where we should hardly have expected it, in the Mexican religion.

(b) Take an illustration from Judaism. We may remind you that—as has been often pointed out and recently by one[1] to whom religious thought is deeply indebted—the idea of God, as revealed in the sacred Hebrew books, passes through three stages. God is first the God of Power—El Shaddai—rich in blessing, mighty in judgment. Here is the idea of Dependence. Then He is known as Jehovah, the Eternal, and Unchangeable, the "I Am" who knows the sorrows of His people, and in relationship with whom His worshippers rejoice. Here is the idea of Fellowship. Thirdly, God is known as the Lord of Hosts, Jehovah-Sabbaoth, the Lord whose presence is the guarantee of the national development and security of the people.

[1] Westcott, "Revelation of the Father," p. 6.

(c.) In Hellenism we may find hints of the same. In his appeal to Penelope's suitors, Telemachus takes three grounds. "Arouse," he says, "within yourselves a Nemesis, or moral sense; an αἰδώς, or a sense of honour, and regard for the opinion of your fellow citizens; and the fear of the wrath of the gods."

"These three principles," writes Mr. Gladstone, "were the three great pillars of morality." Nemesis was self-judgment by our inward law; αἰδώς was self-judgment according to a standard applied by others; and fear was the expectation of judgment by Divine law.[1] In other words, we see the element of Dependence in the recognition of the gods whose retribution is to be feared; the element of Fellowship in the recognition of the morality to which we are bound inwardly to conform; and the element of Progress in the recognition of the relationship which we bear to mankind at large.

Thus, in this rapid survey, we have seen how these three elements are demanded by the religious instincts of men. And the evidence of which we have spoken has been forthcoming. Generally speaking, we may say that these minor religions attest strongly the element of Depend-

[1] "Juventus Mundi," pp. 383-4. See Note 12 in Appendix.

ence; and not quite so strongly, but still sufficiently, those of Fellowship and Progress.

In the next Lecture we shall examine the greater, or universal religions, with the view of ascertaining whether these three—Dependence, Fellowship, and Progress—show themselves in the history of the larger, as they do in the history of lesser, religions. Dependence, Fellowship, and Progress—man needs them all. Placed in this little world, surrounded by much that is dark, man irresistibly looks upward; conscious of the power of thinking and willing, he looks within; linked by subtle and manifold ties to the millions who share with him the struggle of life, he looks around, not always to see sights which inspire hope. Looking around, and seeing the sorrows and failures of men, he is filled with pity; looking within, and finding his own weakness and helplessness, he begins to despair. The glances around and within are dark indeed; he must look heavenward, even though his eyes fail with looking upward. Though the heart and the flesh fail, God is the strength of his heart; and the glance upward becomes the look of faith. It finds utterance in the cry : " Oh God, Thou art my God." (Ps. lxiii. 1.) The glance inward becomes one of humility and awakens the cry : " I am not worthy that Thou shouldest enter under my roof;" (St. Luke vii. 6), and the glance around is no longer that of pity, ending in despair, but that of strong and hopeful love, which says: "I have compassion on the multitudes." (St. Matt. xv. 32.)

It is well to take these three glances—to look around with compassion to see where and how we can help the faint and hungry; to look inward for the wisdom which is born of self-knowledge; and to look upward that we may see that above the ladder of daily duty is the Lord God of all duty.

Upward, yet not upward only, lest we adopt an indolent faith, whose motto is: "All for us." Around, yet not around only, lest, forgetting God, we should rely only on self, and adopt the life whose motto is: "All by us." Around, yet inwards also, that we may learn all that needs to be wrought within us, and win the precious gift of true humility. Then, as from the sad glances, within and around, we turn our eyes upward once more, we shall see that, notwithstanding the darkness, Heaven is still open, and that the angels of God are ever ascending and descending; for, rightly understood, even the sighs, the self-judgments, and the aspirations of men are angels which lift them heavenward and bind them to God.

LECTURE III.

ESSENTIAL ELEMENTS OF RELIGION WITNESSED IN THE HISTORY OF THREE UNIVERSAL RELIGIONS.

The permanence of religion and the permanence of man's nature are correlated. There are certain essential elements demanded by man in religion. The main evidence on this point must be sought in the history of the three universal religions :

I.—Islamism in its history illustrates this demand. The original element in Islamism is Dependence. The Sufite movement is the demand for Fellowship. The Mo'tazilite movement is the effort after Progress.

II.—Buddhism in its original form attempted to meet the demand for Fellowship. Later developments show the demand for Dependence. The worship of the Buddha. The mulplication of Deities. The practice of Prayer. The element of Progress is recognized in the hope of a Future.

III.—Christianity in its history shows the reiteration in various ways of the demand of human nature for these three elements :

    (i.) The teaching of Christ.

    (ii.) The witness of history and controversy—

        1. To Dependence.

        2. To the need of Fellowship.

            (a) Montanism. (b) The struggles of Athanasius. (c) Asceticism. (d) Saint Worship. (e) Mysticism.

        3. To the need of Progress—

            (a) The Schoolmen. (b) The School of Nature.

    (iii.) The existence of parties as a witness to the need of Dependence, Fellowship, Progress.

Thus mankind in all periods has shown the need of three great elements in religion.

LECTURE III.

ESSENTIAL ELEMENTS OF RELIGION WITNESSED IN THE HISTORY OF THREE UNIVERSAL RELIGIONS.

"Hereafter ye shall see heaven open and the angels of God ascending and descending."—*St. John* i. 51.

THE position which we have reached is as follows. We have seen that there are reasons for believing that religion will survive; the grounds for this are to be found in the fact that man everywhere shows invincible religious tendencies, coupled with the fact that man's nature seems to be permanent. There are certain laws or principles of man's spiritual and moral nature which appear to be constant. These point to the permanence of man's nature, and also to the elements which the future religion must possess if it is to survive. Some idea of the form which the religion of the future is likely to take may be derived from the elements which appear to be essential. These elements are Dependence, Fellowship, Progress.

In proof of the need of these three elements we must turn to the witness of religious history. We found their need attested in the history of the Mexican religion. We saw hints of the same in the language of Hellenism, and in the religious conceptions of the Hebrews.

These, however, only touch the hem of the subject. The religious history of the world centres in those religions which are called universal. We can only make approximate guesses at the population of the world; but recent authorities seem agreed that three-fourths, if not four-fifths, of the population of the world will be found distributed among the three universal religions—Islamism, Buddhism, Christianity.[1]

We are about to interrogate the history of these three great religions, and ascertain whether we find in them evidence that the elements of Dependence, Fellowship, and Progress are essential to the completeness of the religious idea. One point needs, perhaps, to be made clear before we go further. We must understand what we mean when we speak of a religion as universal. We may recall the distinction pointed out by Kuenen. A religion may be regarded as universal, because as a fact it has shown itself capable of transcending the limits of the land of

[1] See Note 13 in Appendix.

its birth. But this by no means implies that it has within it the essential elements or qualities calculated to ensure its complete universalism. It is universal in fact—as Kuenen[1] would say— because it has shown itself more than national; whether it is universal in quality demands further investigation. This distinction is important, and it enters deeply into the drift of these Lectures, the aim of which is to ascertain what are the elements without which a religion cannot be said to be possessed of the quality of universalism, and then to ask how far the great religions truly possess it.

In the present Lecture our inquiry is whether the history of the three universal religions bears witness to the need of the three elements of Dependence, Fellowship, and Progress. In the next lecture we shall ask how far these three elements are native to the religions in whose history we have found them; for the three elements may appear in the history of a religion, and yet not be of its essence; they may be accretions, rather than developments; additions, and not evolutions; adoptions, not children born in its home; proselytes of the gate rather than children of the covenant. In this Lecture we are merely regarding the history of

[1] "Hibbert Lectures," p. 6.

these religions as attesting what are the elements which man demands in the faith which aspires to permanence. And our inquiry will show us that Dependence, Fellowship, and Progress are asked for by the spirit of man, whether we interrogate the story of Islamism, Buddhism, or Christianity.

I.—Islamism.

The figure of Mohammed loomed large and terrible upon those who saw him only through the fog which dread and ignorance spread around him. To them he was an object of horror against which anything evil might be said. He was the first-born of Satan, the dealer in black arts; his very name became an epithet of reproach. But, now the mists of prejudice have cleared away, we can afford to see the founder of Islamism in a fairer light. We can understand him better as we recall his traditional portraiture. A lithe and slender figure, broad-shouldered, and upbearing proudly his majestic head, crowned with dark, flowing and curling hair; an oval face bronzed by the sun; the nose, "the rudder of the face, the index of the will," strong and masterful; teeth brilliant as hailstones, and eyes bright as stars; soft, small, nervous hands: all made up a figure goodly to look upon. His peculiarities also are known to us: the deep blood-vessel on the forehead that darkened with passion; the strange egg mark between the shoulders, the so-called seal of prophecy; and the gracious gait, light and springing, as of one stepping downwards. Joyous he was and loving as a child, patient as a woman; ready now to romp with the children, to tell them stories, now to sit patiently in a foul dense atmosphere, nursing the sick child till it died with its head on his bosom; full of a sweet, soft courtesy which would not willingly offend by gesture or by manner; never the first to withdraw his hand from another's grasp, or to turn aside from another's converse. Altogether you would say a delicate organization, sensitive, passionate, responsive; drawn to a strange, sad love of solitude, yet longing for the solace and soothing of a woman's hand, and flying to her sheltering arms as to a safe place from the wild terrors which at times fell upon him. Briefly, he is a man with that mixture of qualities which Coleridge declared needful for the highest genius, that blending of masculine and feminine qualities which is called androgynous; full of contradictions with his timidity and his courage, his passionate indulgence and his wondrous modesty, his outbursts of cruelty and his patient tenderness; terrified at the weight of the task laid upon him, yet finding it impossible to shrink from it; hating conflict, yet preferring it to the inward torment of the spirit that, Jonah-like, refuses its errand; gaining in his self-surrender the power which was needful to weld others together, and to inspire them with that loyalty to God which was the essence of his teaching.[1] From this picture of the Prophet, we may, after allowing for natural exaggerations, understand him and his system better. Dependence is at the root of Islamism. This may be called its initial idea. It is seen in the very word by which the religion is described. The religion is not Mohammedanism. The religion is Islâm— submission. It teaches that man is of small account. In the view of the Prophet, God was all; the varied and grotesque divinities and saints which were brought into the worship of men, Christian or Pagan, were impertinences. Man could only be religious in a complete self-surrender; he depended wholly upon God; he was but a slave of the Most High, who owned him and demanded from him the most absolute service. All other divinities were usurpers, standing between the sovereign and his subjects; man was God's slave, no other could share that proprietorship, and to the sense of this relationship with the Creator the Prophet would

[1] See Note 14 in Appendix.

restore man. "Obedience to God and His messenger is the strength of the Moslem system."[1] "Man lives on content with himself, but he must one day return to his Creator and Lord and give account to Him. This is in a sense the material principle of the oldest faith of Islâm."[2] We can see that the principle of Dependence shows itself here. The exalted idea of the sovereign and sole God, and the necessity of the most complete obedience to Him, are the emphatic statements of this Dependence. Islamism starts with this as its essential idea.

We must note next its relation to the idea of Fellowship or communion, which is the second element we are seeking. The alien gods and intermediate divinities, the worship of saints and the devotion to shrines, were offensive in the eyes of the Prophet; they savoured of the usurpation which he denounced; they robbed God of His glory. But Mohammed thought more of the glory of God than of the needs of man. He seems to promise, indeed, the restoration of union with the Divine, but he practically makes no provision for it. His mind is full of God and God's greatness; God is the

[1] Art. in "Encyclopædia Britannica" on "Mohammed" by Wellhausen, p. 554.
[2] Ibid., p. 548.

Ruler, man is the subject; God is the Creator, man is the creature; God is the owner and arbiter of all, man is His possession, and must surrender to God's will and submit to His decree. The profoundness of his conviction of the one truth overshadowed the other needful element; and he forgot that the subject, the creature, the slave, had been made in God's image, and had a heart which asked for real fellowship with the Divine. Mohammed hardly saw this; the emphasis with which he affirmed the one truth made the realization of the fellowship of man with his Maker difficult, indeed impossible. The idea of God's greatness, and of the absolute authority exercised by the fiat of His will, dazzled the popular mind for a while, but it had the effect of seeming to push man very far away from God. True Fellowship was impossible; the link between the Creator and the creature was that of power on the one side and Dependence on the other; the idea of holiness which satisfies the ethical feeling, and the idea of love which captivates the heart, were wanting. No wonder that Fellowship seemed impossible.

But the after history exhibits a reaction, and shows eloquently man's desire for some nearness or fellowship with the Divine. The followers of Mohammed could not rest in the pure

Theism which the Prophet sought to preach, and on his death they commenced the worship of Mohammed, viewing him as a mediator still living and pleading with Allah; and Medina became, in sanctity, second only to Mecca. Nor was this all; the worship of Walis, or saints, quickly followed. The sense of the need of some points of contact between man and the object of his worship led to saint-worship. If a power high and great cannot minister to this strong yearning of man's breast, humanity will invent some other mode of bringing the Divine near itself. And this is what happened in the history of Islamism. It was expressed in the saint-worship of which we have spoken, but it found its most important expression in the movement called Súfism. Súfism is a motley phrase; it covers a wide area; but from whatever source it sprang, its significance is clear. The Súfite is the Mohammedan mystic. He realizes the double yearning of the human soul: the longing for reconciliation which springs from the conscience; the longing for Fellowship which springs from the heart. The splendid absolutism with which Mohammed invested his idea of God made direct Fellowship between the Creator and the creature difficult, for the creature was the slave of the Divine will; and there can be no Fellowship where the will is enslaved. According to the saint-worshipper, if man must have Fellowship with the Divine, let him have it with those who are nearest to the great God, seeing that God Himself dwells beyond the reach of human fellowship. But where shall this be found, if not with the Prophet and with those great heroes of Islâm who have been the highest servants of God? The Súfite, moved by the same yearning, took a bolder line and claimed man's right to go straight to God. These movements in various ways sought to supply the element of Fellowship. "If the mystic element," says Kuenen, "was almost entirely wanting at first, and if the pressure of the sense of sin was unrelieved, Súfism and the belief in the mediation of Mohammed himself and of the saints so assiduously honoured, filled up the gap."[1] This movement, or rather, element, is of importance; for in the eyes of many its presence in the heart of Islamism is the omen of its future advance. The only path in Islamism towards reformation lies in this doctrine of mysticism, is the language of one writer.[2]

The third element to be sought in the history of Islamism is that of Progress. Dogmatism is

---

[1] "Hibbert Lectures," p. 37.
[2] Mirza Kasem Beg, quoted by Kuenen, "Hib. Lectures," p. 45. See Appendix, Note 15.

prone to be jealous of this element. True theology understands that it has a place within her fold. The laws of God are in Himself: they can work outside the range of all human institutions, and they do not therefore end with the dogmas of any prophet, however great. Dogmas may express truth or they may not, but at their best they are no more than expressions of it: they do not originate it; they may reveal, but they do not create truth. The vice of dogmatism appears in its virtual denial of God, or, what is the same thing, the limiting of the range of His rule. A doctrine is true and living when it declares anything which is; but it must declare what *is*, not what merely may or might be. The glory of doctrinism lies in the capacity which it has for declaring what exists as an unalterable fact or truth; the sin of dogmatism lies in its attempt to pose as a final authority for the truth, and to limit the operation of the truth to the system which is conscious of and which formulates it. It is like the attempt of an astronomer to prove that the planets move by the laws of motion, only when his glass is upon them. Truths can never be invented: they can only be discovered. The dogmatist is, in this, different from the prophet. The prophet perceives and declares truth, which is true whether people hear or forbear, whether the prophet speaks or is silent; the dogmatist is one who speaks of truth as though it were his monopoly, and insists that nothing is genuine without the trade-mark of his firm upon it. But truth is of God, and God's truth remains whether we formulate it wisely or unwisely, or do not formulate it at all. The righteous Ruler of the world rules the world in righteousness, and works with the growing thoughts and endeavours of mankind. Religion must recognize this, if it is to live. Man asks for the presence of God working in all history according to right. Righteousness is of God wherever it is found. Submission to the will of God may be an element of religious life; the recognition of the righteousness of God's universal rule is needful for the religious life of mankind. The submission of my will to God's will may be a religious submission or not; but the submission of my will to a system which says it is God's will, and enforces rules without grounding them on principles of righteousness, is neither religious nor wise. This is proved even in the history of Mohammedanism; for in the morning of its history we find those who resented the hard doctrine of predestination, who asked for the recognition of ethical principles, who reverenced will in man and righteousness in God, and who could not acquiesce in blind and unconscientious surrender to God's will merely because He was mighty. It is needless to tell the story of this movement. It is enough to say that those who called themselves the upholders of God's unity and righteousness, and who, together with those who, resembled them in teaching, are called the Mo'tazilites, or Dissidents, flourished for a time; but, notwithstanding the patronage of some of the Caliphs, the day came when the so-called orthodox, unable to see the worthlessness of a religion divorced from righteousness, rose against the Freethinkers, as they were styled. "It was not in the God of the Mo'tazilites whose essence was righteousness, but in the God of orthodoxy, the Almighty, subject to no other rule than his own caprice, that they recognized their own and Mohammed's Allah."[1] The Mo'tazilites fell; but their influence is sufficient to show that, within the history of Islamism, the plea for the third element of Progress was put forward. The movement would have freed Islamism from difficulties of its own creation; it would have enabled men to recognise the width of God's work in the world; it would have opened their eyes to the revelation of God in nature; and in giving this

[1] Kuenen, "Hibbert Lectures," p. 49.

knowledge, it would have saved Islâm from the stagnation which has befallen it. "This is *true*," must ever be the voice of the prophet; "this *only* is true," is the voice of the fanatic and the dogmatist. The difference is slight: but the voice of the prophet is heard to the end of time, and the truth, which he declared, mingles with the flowing life of the world and keeps it pure; the voice of the fanatic is heard, and it calls up the spirit of frenzy; it wins a victory, it binds and imprisons its foe, but its mad temper is its destruction, for the bound victim pulls down its sanctuary and slays the faith of the fanatic in its ruins. Islâm crushed the life within its bosom, and so doomed itself to prolonged barrenness. But notwithstanding this, the history of Islamism has yielded evidence of the three elements of which we have spoken. Dependence was its point of departure; something to satisfy the instinct for Fellowship was demanded and conceded in its growth; and the element of freedom and Progress was demanded and refused in its history.

II.—Buddhism.

The second universal religion which we are to examine is Buddhism. Here we are on difficult ground, for the word Buddhism is used to describe diverse systems, which, even if springing from a common stem, have branched off in different,

III.] *The Three Universal Religions.* 91

nay even in opposite, directions; and, moreover, the authorities are not so harmonious as we could wish. But I shall hope to speak only of such points as seem generally admitted. Fortunately, it is not within the scope of our purpose to form any theory of Buddhism. Our task is humbler: we only seek to show the elements which arise in the history of this religion, as in the history of others, at the bidding of the voice of the heart of man. Yet here, too, at the threshold, we may stop for a moment, and glance at the scenes which revealed the dawn of this beautiful and pathetic faith. The mists are great, for the time is distant, and myth and fable are mixed with history; we can hardly trust ourselves to the guidance of historians, and we certainly shall not depend upon poets. Yet even if we reject all that is doubtful, the story is one of simple beauty and true devotion. The central figure from which the religion sprang is original and strong. I am not disposed to resolve Gautama into a sun-myth; and that for a reason which I shall mention later. It is enough, perhaps, to say that it needs a prophet to create a religion; and Gautama was the true prophet of Buddhism, and that being so, I would not rob him of one leaf of the crown to which he is entitled. There were beautiful souls in the days before Christendom, and in other lands besides the land of promise, and Gautama was one of these. We see him in his pleasant home with his fair young wife, Yasodhara, and his baby boy—his only son— Rahula. There is given to him the fourfold vision which is so deeply to influence his life. "Pictures of the impermanence of everything earthly presented themselves to him one after the other, in the form of a helpless old man, a sick person, and a dead body; and at last a religious mendicant with shaven head and wearing yellow garments meets him, a picture of peace and of deliverance from all pain of impermanence."[1] The struggle has come; the voice—which, heard and refused, grows faint and then ceases, but which, heard and obeyed, summons man to a life of enlarged power —is calling to him. The fragrance of the night is breathing over his palace; the calm of his home life is before his eyes; his wife and little one are asleep, and the wavering light of the lamp illumines those dear faces; but the crisis has come: the voice which calls him is obeyed, he goes forth into the darkness, and the light of his life seems quenched. The choice, the Great Renunciation, has been made. The path towards higher peace must be trodden. The way is rough, and the experiences are bitter; he endures

[1] Oldenberg, "Buddha," p. 103.

hardship, and loneliness worse than hardship. At last the light and the peace seem to come. Disciples gather round him; his journeys become marches of triumph; he is treated with honour; he gives rules to his order; he is entertained with hospitality; he over-eats himself on one occasion; he takes some boar's flesh, but he is too old for such things; the food is too much for him; he dies, and his grave is hidden by the flowers flung upon it by grateful and reverent hands.[1]

It is acknowledged that the early history of Buddhism is obscure; but the difficulties are less in regard to its doctrinal than to its historical aspects. It is clear, however, that in the earliest form of Buddhism we have the element of mysticism. The whole attention of Gautama is fixed on the idea of salvation, salvation from the weariness and pain of existence. "Salvation by self-control and love."[2] It is the effort to subdue and get rid of the thing which makes life a felt discord. It is, as has been said, a quietistic philosophy. It is the expression of the soul's longing to be free from the causes of conflict, and to find complete and undying rest. Indivi-

[1] According to Prof. Max Müller, B.C. 477. See Note 16 in Appendix.
[2] Rhys Davids, "Buddhism," pp. 41 and 149. See Note 17 in Appendix.

duality is the burden: each individual is like a bubble, disturbing the smooth and serene surface of the ocean of existence; the object is to touch the bubble and make it sink back into the great sea, and then there is peace. This is quietism; it is an expression of that element in religion which I have called the instinct of Fellowship, the wish to find the secret harmony of existence. It does not alter the essential drift of this instinct to say that Buddhism does not admit a supreme Being. The yearning is for the cessation of the sense of discord, which is one of the supreme pains of conscious life. This seems to me the very root of Buddhism, even though most divergent views of the Founder exist. It may be an exaggeration to say that Gautama was a great philanthropic reformer, showing a fierce scorn against the hateful laws of caste and proclaiming the natural equality of all men. It is absurd to represent him as holding a doctrine "which centred in the belief of a personal God."[1] It is not wise to ignore the drift which it takes in certain schools towards atheism and annihilation; but we need not exaggerate it[2] or attempt to

[1] E. de Bunsen, "Angel-Messiah," p. 48.
[2] See Max Müller, "Origin of Religion," p. 312.

argue away the spirit which breathed through his system: a spirit never base or mean; sad, but not wholly infidel—for sadness, even when it denies good, is often a most potent witness to it. There is, of course, the exaggeration of a reactionary in Gautama. The Brahman religion, from which he recoiled, had become literal, mechanical, unethical, unsatisfying to the earnest and thoughtful soul; ritual and dogmatism seemed to him outside real life; life was within; the man within must be subdued; the discord which made life a pain was the discord within; and when men came asking questions about a life to come, or the being of God, I can imagine his answering with a sad and persuasive earnestness : " I know nothing about a life to come; all things perish; and there seems an end of all; what can we know? why turn aside from what is certain, to what is, after all, but a perhaps ? I know not what comes afterwards; but this I know, that right must be right, and the control of self most noble, and whatever salvation there is must come through moral and not mechanical means; by self-mastery alone is salvation secured; this is the gate of the unknown Hereafter—this the end of the intolerable weariness and discord which the sense of existence brings." Whatever there is of latent atheism and declared agnosticism here, there seems to me to be at least the germ of that human instinct which craves for an inward harmony; an atheistic mysticism if you will —an agnostic quietism—but still a quietism and a mysticism which recognise that the pathway towards peace lies in the moral victory of self-control. It is the recognition of this element which leads Professor Rhys Davids to say that the Buddhist salvation consists in an inward change of heart.[1] Of course the phrase is open to the criticism that it is one which bears in our ears a distinctly Christian significance, and that to use it of Gautama's teaching may be misleading, as it may carry with it Christian ideas which are wanting in Buddhism. The remark is quite fair, as regards the phrase; but we probably shall not do justice to Buddhism (and why should we wish to do it injustice?) unless we remember that in the very heart of it, as Gautama taught it, is the thought, that "to obey is better than sacrifice, and to hearken than the fat of rams "— that to reform oneself, to gain the inward triumph of self-control, is better than crying, "Lord, Lord." " Not to commit any sin, to do good, and to

[1] "Buddhism," p. 40.; *Cf.* pp. 108, 109, 112.

purify one's mind, that is the teaching of (all) the Awakened."[1]

So runs the famous verse; and it does not stand alone—

"It is good to tame the mind,
Difficult to hold in, and flighty;
Rushing where'er it listeth;
A tamed mind is the bringer of bliss."

Or, again—

"One may conquer a thousand thousand men in battle,
But he who conquers himself alone is the greatest victor."[1]

The peace will come when the thirst and craving of the individual are at an end. The thirst, the grasping state of mind, the longing for things and even for life, must cease before rest comes; then the discord is at an end, for the universe is all, and the individual has sunk away and lost itself in the ever-flowing stream. Here is exhibited faintly the feeble but true germ of the element which I have called Fellowship; the sense of discord within creates a vague yearning for reconciliation, synthesis, death of self, loss of self in that which is

[1] "Dhammapada," verse 183, Sacred Books of the East, vol. x. The translation of Prof. Rhys Davids, "Buddhism," p. 62, is as follows:—
    To cease from all wrong-doing,
    To get virtue,
    To cleanse one's heart—
    This is the religion of the Buddhas.

[2] From the "Dhammapada or Scripture Verses," Nos. 35 and 103, quoted by Prof. Rhys Davids in "Buddhism," p. 129.

L

other than self. The weariness of individual life leads to a longing for that rest which is oneness with the order of the world, it seeks that central point where the world's fret and motion are not felt. There is a great truth behind this; but the history of Buddhism will show us that man asks more than the emphatic statement of one truth.

There is no faith in the world whose history is so remarkable as that of Buddhism, or whose varieties are more distinct. It is impossible to follow out the history of its branches, but we can glance at some, and note the significance of such developments as we meet. Buddhism is an exile from the land of its birth. If we would trace its growth, we must go North or South. We must see it in Ceylon, Siam, and Burmah; or in Tibet, China, and Japan. But between Northern and Southern Buddhism there is a lack of fraternal appreciation; they both claim to hold the sacred deposit of teaching, but the North claims to hold it in larger and fuller measure than the South; and it must be admitted that the great Vehicle, as it is called, belonging to the North is more elaborate and complex than the little Vehicle of the South. But there is one feature which is common to both, viz., the enlargement of the early faith, notions being added which indicate the cravings of human instinct.

Buddhism, in its primitive purity, is entirely lacking in the spirit of Dependence. It aims at the loss of self, but it is through self-control; and the self-control is achieved by self; there is no doctrine of Divine help, no dependence on another. But as we look into the features of Northern Buddhism, it is this element which, supervening, has changed its expression. The religion, which was one of emancipation and redemption through self-help, has become one in which reliance on another than self has made its appearance. Dependence is seen in the worship of the Buddha, which is a fact in the history of Buddhism; it is seen also in the reliance which is placed on Maitreya Buddha.[1] In some of the temples of Southern Buddhism a pure white image appears beside that of Gautama; this is the Maitreya Buddha—the future Buddha—who is called also Ajita,[2] the Unconquerable One, whose advent to this world is looked for, and on whose victorious help the Buddhist places his prospective reliance. In the Northern Buddhism the worship of future Buddhas, or Bodhi-satwas, has been carried further, and as early as A.D. 400 two Bodhi-satwas, named Manjusri and

[1] Kellogg, "Light of Asia," p. 120. Rhys Davids, "Buddhism," p. 200. [2] Ibid., Note on p. 200.

Avalokiteśvara were worshipped.[1] Manjusri is the personification of Wisdom and religious Insight; Avalokiteśvara is the personification of Power and Providence. But this was not all; later the god Avalokiteśvara was cleft asunder, and, while he remained the Protecting Providence, his Power was given to another, who was named Vajradhara, or the bearer of the thunder-bolt. These are illustrations of well known developments, and they tend to the strongest expression of the feeling to Dependence. One example will make this plain. When Fa-Hian was returning from Ceylon to China by sea a storm arose, and the ship was in imminent danger. The pilgrim was afraid lest the merchants should wish to throw overboard the sacred books and images to lighten the ship, and so, with earnest heart, he invoked Avalokiteśvara, and called upon all the Buddhist saints of China, speaking thus:—"I have wandered far in quest of religious books. Oh! by your spiritual power bring me back and let me reach my resting place."[2] This story carries us to China, where Avalokiteśvara is worshipped under the name of Kwan-yin; the meaning of the name is supposed to be "a being who hears or perceives the cries of man." The worship was brought by traders

[1] Rhys Davids, "Buddhism," p. 201, &c.
[2] Beal, "Buddhism in China," p. 110.

from Ceylon according to some authorities, and was introduced into China between the beginning of the Christian era and A.D. 200. "The idea of an objective worship," according to Dr. Beal, "is unknown to the early Buddhists .... but now we see an 'object' of worship introduced, and veritable worship and prayer offered to it. This *cultus*, then, is the result of a necessity felt by the worshippers, who could never rest satisfied with the adoration of a logical abstraction or an invisible presence."[1] In fact, whenever we look at the developments of Buddhism, we find the tendency to add the element of which we have spoken. Mysticism expresses a truth—the truth that men desire to

"Bury themselves, the whole heart wide and warm,—
In something not themselves."

But one truth, like one leg, is of little use; another leg, artificial if not natural, must be added, if any movement is to be attained; mysticism, as seen in Buddhism, was lame indeed; it expressed the desire for the annihilation of self, but it needed further the element of Dependence. Men would not only bury themselves in something not themselves, "they would belong to what they worship." It is not enough to wish to lose self, and with it the pain and weariness of existence; man wants

[1] "Buddhism in China," p. 123.

someone greater than himself on whom he can rely, and in union with whom the rest of his spirit can be found.

There is a third element for which we must look—Progress—the spirit which links itself with the welfare of the race. Dependence and Fellowship are not enough; the spirit of man desires to bind itself for good with the growing life of the world. This spirit shows itself in the dream of a golden age, in the faith of a better future for mankind. This element we have already seen was added early to Buddhist belief. There was a Buddha to come. The worship of the Buddha, the reverence paid to his relics, was not enough. Buddha, or Gautama, had vanished, and was no longer a power; men might invoke his shade and long for a share of his spirit, but strictly he was no longer a dependable personal help to them. "As the Buddha himself has reached Parinirvāna, has passed completely away, the pious Buddhist naturally turned with peculiar reverence and longing to those Bodhi-satwas supposed to be now living as angels in heaven, who are the present result of the Karma which will produce the Buddhas of the future."[1] The worshipper is turning to the future; he looks forward to the advent of future Buddhas; to the Maitreya

[1] "Buddhism," Rhys Davids, p. 200.

Buddha, of which we have spoken, the Buddha of power and the Buddha of love, who will achieve triumph in the world and vanquish sin.

When, then, we see the little white image of the Maitreya Buddha placed beside that of Gautama, we see a proof that man cannot rest in a faith which is defective in any one of the three elements of which I have spoken. He must have one greater than himself on whom to depend; and while he is ready to merge his own life in that great bosom of life where there is rest, he casts wistful eyes towards the future, and will believe in no religion which does not embrace the law of Progress as well as those of Dependence and Fellowship.

III.—Christianity.

It is not necessary to our present purpose to investigate attempts made to weaken the claim of Jesus Christ to be considered the founder of Christianity.. Our aim is only to see whether in the history of Christianity the same three elements may be traced.

(i.) We start with the life and teaching of Him who gave His name to the religion. We note that He exhibited a spirit of complete Dependence upon God. He seemed to turn instinctively to His Father—" Father, save Me from this hour," was His cry. (St. John xii. 27.) " I knew that Thou hearest Me always," was His expression of trust. (St. John xi. 42.) His refusal to turn stones into bread was the same spirit of trust shown practically.

He lived in Fellowship with the unseen God. Communion with Him was the breath of His life, He had no thought in life sundered from what He believed to be God's will. "I came, not to do Mine own will, but the will of Him that sent Me." (St. John vi. 38.) "My meat is to do the will of Him that sent Me, and to finish His work." (St. John iv. 34.)

He realized a Progressive order ; He looked forward ; He never seized the present at the cost of the future. The glory of to-day will not compensate for the loss of to-morrow. When the heart of the people was set upon making Him a king, He would not take the crown, for His heart was set upon securing the golden age for them and for all mankind.

His teaching touched the same notes. He taught the principle of Dependence. He taught men not only that they might safely depend upon the power of God, but that they ought to rely on the love and wisdom of Him whom He revealed to them as their Father. His teaching was, "God cares for you—you may trust Him. Consider the lilies. Behold the birds. The Father of all will provide for His children."

He taught the principle of Fellowship. If men

were taken out of the dust, they were akin also to heaven. God was Father. They were children. This relationship made communion and intercourse between God and man possible. He Himself was the witness and guarantee of this fellowship. His prayer was "That they all may be one, as Thou, Father, art in Me, and I in Thee, that they also may be one in us." (St. John xvii. 21.) But the harmony between God and man must be inward and spiritual: for as out of the heart springs the evil, so in the heart must be the good; there the Divine order must rule: "the kingdom of God is within you." (St. Luke xvii. 21.)

He taught the principle of Progress. He taught that the individual man ought to merge his interest in the common good. His life should follow the law of the Divine life, and become a perennial beneficence. "Give, and it shall be given you—that ye may be the children of your Father which is in heaven." Life's advantages—the gifts and talents bestowed upon men—were to be used in helping forward the purposes of God. The talents or the pounds entrusted to men were to be laid out in the great mart of the world's good.

In the life and teaching of Christ we thus note the existence of those three elements of Dependence, Fellowship, and Progress.

(ii.) We shall find them appearing in the History of Christianity, to which we turn, be it remembered, with the view of observing what are the tendencies of man in the matter of religion. Not always nor everywhere in the history of the Christian Church shall we find perfection either of creed or of character. It is a dream to imagine the Church infallible, or always alive to the higher interests of mankind, and appreciative of their deepest needs. She has been often blind to one or other of the three great elements of which we have spoken. Her history is the history of many mistakes, misapprehensions, and exaggerations. We can admit her faults. She is not without spot and blameless. But we deprecate the too ready sneer at her blunders, and the ungenerous triumph over her failures. The reason is simple, and should disarm shallow and easy criticism. Christianity has not always been fully comprehended. We may even ask, Has Christianity ever been thoroughly understood? Her noblest sons and her keenest-minded disciples have missed some truth, or forced it into exaggerated importance. It is not everyone who has marked her bulwarks who has been able to set up her houses; nor have those who have seen the beauty of Mount Zion's situation been always able to understand that she is the joy of the whole earth.

But the mistakes and struggles revealed in the history of Christianity have their value. They serve to teach us caution, as we learn that men are weak and slow of heart. They also serve to exhibit with conspicuous clearness the spiritual needs of humanity. The struggles of the faith in different ages are often the efforts of men to affirm a truth with which man could not part. Those who have struggled to affirm it have often done so in one-sided and exaggerated fashion; but they have been the means of restoring a lost truth, or an element needful for the completeness of religious life.

1. The history of Christianity has given emphatic witness to the need of Dependence. The exaggeration of this truth has given rise to constantly recurring controversies.

We are not surprised at the early development and domination of this one element. The soil in which the seed of Christianity fell was favourable to a rapid growth of the idea of Dependence. We have seen that Roman Paganism largely rested on a belief in the powers of the gods, whose aid could be invoked by mere obedience to routine worship. The need of the harmony within was not felt. The ideas of the Roman world were not favourable, I imagine, to the cultivation of deep spirituality. The Roman Empire was a great manifestation of strength of character and gifts of organization. I do not think that anyone will consider it to have had any virtue for fostering the deep spiritual capacities or evoking the tender sympathies of men.[1] Subtle or profound thought, the loftier flight of creative genius, the culture of the inward life, the appreciation of what may be called spiritual experiences, even allowing for some splendid exceptions, are not to be reckoned among the special features of the Roman world. Order, discipline, the sense of responsibility to one central power, are more akin to its spirit. The political atmosphere tended to foster those elements of religion which were related to Dependence rather than those which belong to Fellowship. There was a colour of Imperialism in all its thoughts, and this gave to its religious conceptions the predominant hue.[2] There was a profound sense of divine power; there was but little idea of divine nearness.

We must not be surprised, then, if the teaching which grew up under the shadow of Rome took as its background the profound sense of God's power and greatness. We should expect that those elements of Christianity which lay stress on the deep and mystical union between the spirit of man and God should be comparatively lost sight of.

[1] Lecky, "Hist. of European Morals," vol. i., p. 167.
[2] See Appendix, Note 18.

2. But this could not be for long, if man's spirit desires Fellowship as well as Dependence. The thirsty soul will cry out for the living waters. This is what we find. The cry is a shrill one, but it expresses a real need.

(a) It is heard in Montanism. Men began to ask whether the door between themselves and God had been closed, or if the river of life which had flowed in Apostolic times had been cut off. The movement which is called Montanism covered great varieties of thought, but it certainly included men who claimed for themselves direct and immediate intercourse and communion with the God of their life. It gave expression to the thoughts of those who could not believe that there was no longer any open vision, and who craved for the tokens of God's presence and the witness of His Spirit. We are not at present concerned with the errors or extravagances of Montanists. We are only pointing out that they attempted to give voice to the claim of man for conscious fellowship with God, and for a continued revelation of His nearness and gifts. Rightly or wrongly they believed that the Church of their day had lost sight of a truth, or had substituted a lifeless form for a living force. The movement affirmed that Dependence was not enough for man—that he must have Fellowship also. It was allied with errors which were grotesque and absurd; it excluded from its view large portions of life; it was narrow and one-sided. But those who affirm a forgotten truth are usually one-sided; and we shall miss the meaning of history if we refuse to see the grain of truth buried in the abundance of chaff, or to hear the cry of real distress among the clamours of madness or folly with which it mingles.

(*b*) The demand for Fellowship to which Montanism gave somewhat incoherent expression finds a clearer utterance in the mouth of Athanasius. Arianism would have been impossible, had not one-sided conceptions of God grown up in men's minds. The infinite greatness of God is a truth which, if it stands alone, confuses, because it dazzles the mind. Transcendent greatness is soon thought to be unapproachable. If the infinitely great cannot be approached by the infinitely little, it seems no less true that the infinitely little cannot be approached by the infinitely great. The counterbalancing truth of the eternal kinship between the infinitely great and the infinitely little is forgotten. God and man can meet, because there is a Divine sonship. Arianism forgot this truth, and its forgetfulness led it to attempt a retrograde movement. It was a reversion to earlier and less universal conceptions. It was a reversion, as has been said, to Jewish Theism, and Semitic dependence.[1] Union between the Divine and the human was considered impossible. Only by a long chain of divinities and powers linked to one another by subtle gradations could God hold intercourse with man. The system thrust God far away from man. The fundamental idea was greatness, not nearness— dread, not devotion. It was, to use the words of Dr. Allen, "a symptom that the popular Christianity was shifting its basis from love to fear."[2]

Conceptions like this are tokens of the growth of Imperialism in Christianity. The conception— though fatal to any religion aspiring to universalism —was one which could be well understood and appreciated in the world that then was. The great Empire which shadowed and subdued the world was, in the eyes of millions, a natural and fit emblem of the realm of God. But it was a conception which the better natures and clearer minds resisted as destructive to the growth of the faith, and incapable of satisfying the heart of man. Athanasius, in resisting Arius, was a champion of the faith. He was no less an assertor of the rights

[1] *Cf.* Max Müller, "Origin of Religion," p. 313.
[2] Dr. Allen, "Continuity of Christian Thought," p. 88.

and liberties of man. The Son of God has consecrated human nature by becoming Son of Man. Union with the Divine was not merely possible to man; it was a reality, based on an eternal fact. Whatever imagery might be used to describe the relationship between God and man, the soul of man could not, in its truer moments, call Him Emperor; for God had revealed Himself as Father, and had proved His kinship with man in the Incarnation. Athanasius stemmed the tide, and checked the retrograde movement of his day; but he did more, he gave voice to the cry of humanity for a religion, which supplied the element of Fellowship as well as that of Dependence.

The victory which Athanasius won has been established in the later history of Christianity. There have been teachers who have revived the conception of a distant and unapproachable God, or who have had a fondness for investing their thoughts of God with fancies derived from arbitrary Imperialism; but their influence has been limited, and their misconceptions have been presented in alliance with other and compensating doctrines. The fatalistic teaching, which is found in certain predestinarian schools, and which shelters itself under the names of Augustine or Calvin, is an evidence, however, that the tendency has not disappeared. We need not be surprised; the element of Dependence is essential to the religious idea, and there will always be those who exaggerate its importance at the expense of other equally essential principles. The exaggeration may win a following; it may found a sect; it will never establish a religion which is universal, for it cannot satisfy the heart of man. Its existence, however, and its constant recurrence in the history and controversies of the Christian Church, are proofs that man is alive to the need of that element of religion which we call Dependence.

But the need of the element of Fellowship has been no less clearly seen. The controversy with Arianism was the evidence that man is not content with a religion which is one of chill Dependence. The Council of Nicæa acknowledged the claim of man to union with the Divine. The reality of that union was affirmed and guaranteed in the doctrine that the Son is of one substance with the Father.

(c) The craving for Fellowship finds its witness also in the asceticism which marks the history of the Church. In asceticism there was much which was alien to Christ's teaching, and which has been rejected by the purer branches of Christ's Church. But with the faith of the ascetics we have no direct concern. Our aim is only to notice the spirits breathes in the words and deeds of these teachers and thinkers. Elements of mysticism mingle with the utterances of Catholic devotion, no less than with the fervour of sectaries. The Albigenses in France, the sect of the Holy Spirit, the Petrobrusians, the Apostolical brethren, and the Waldenses have been recognised as possessing common aims. And these aims were directed towards the realisation of the idea of Fellowship. "These movements, however diverse in aspect, were yet alike in their aim to realise a closer relationship and communion between God and man, and to seek for God within the soul, rather than at a distance from it without." [1]

The thirst of these souls was shared by thousands who were never reckoned as separatists, but who found vent for their thoughts and feelings in less conspicuous or more prudent ways. Local accidents or political exigencies have had their share in canonizing some and condemning others, who were seeking to find the same God or to affirm the same truths. It is not our duty to touch on the differences which made one mysticism orthodox and led to the condemnation of another; we have only to note that the heart of humanity cannot be silent. It demands Fellow-

[1] Dr. Allen, "Continuity of Christian Thought," p. 207.

ship in its religion, and we can hear its demand in the history of Christianity; in St. Bernard and St. Bonaventura—in the mystics of Germany—in Eckart, Tauler, Nicolas of Basle, in the company known as the Dear Friends of God in the Oberland; in the Quietists, in Molinos, Fénelon, and Madame Guyon. It is easy to see the mistakes of the mystics; it is not difficult for ingenuity to ridicule them, or orthodoxy to denounce them; but it is acting like the deaf adder to stop our ears to the voice which they raised, witnessing to the quenchless desire of humanity, and demanding that religion should supply not only a Divine power, but a Divine presence; not only Dependence, but Fellowship.

3. Progress is the third element. Does the history of Christianity show that men were eager to have this also in their religion? Illustrations of this element spring up from various and unexpected quarters.

(a) It has been the fashion of some to ridicule the schoolmen with their fine-drawn subtleties and their dexterity in playing upon the "fringe of great questions," but few great movements are without some nobler aim than mere hair-splitting. Scholasticism will be found to contain within itself a purpose greater far than that of amusement with verbal subtleties. It is the witness of man's wish to establish a fundamental harmony between theology and the nature of things. The schoolmen were in a sense rationalists, they were the advocates of the necessity of intellectual harmony. In principle they were hostile to the devotees who were content to believe without demanding a reason. If this be so, we have here evidence in the history of the Church that men were alive to the need of reconciliation between reason and faith. The claims of culture and knowledge are admitted.

(*b*) Another indication of the element of progress is to be found in the recognition that nature is of God and has something to teach. This conviction enters deeply into man's heart, and is found in the bosom of Christendom. "You will find something far greater in the woods than you will in books. Trees and stones will teach you that which you will never learn from masters." The words are St. Bernard's. "The book of nature is equal to the whole Scripture," was the thought of Raymond of Sabunde.[1] These are examples of the spirit which is allied with the spirit of progress.

The development of art may show the same. Landscape painting was little esteemed in the early days of mediæval art. Michael Angelo's drift of thought is towards man rather than towards nature; Leonardo da Vinci, in his treatise on

[1] Dr. Allen, "Continuity of Christian Thought," p. 344.

painting, replaced man in the bosom of all created forms.[1] The sanctity of art, as well as the art of sanctity, was recognized. The religious helps, which spring from natural beauty and brightness, were perceived and welcomed. New joy and new love arose in men. "The one," says Mr. Ruskin, "who loves nature most will always be found to have more capacity for faith in God than the other." And the love of nature, whether in its aspect of flowers, or field, or sea, or the forms of man, becomes essential to the growth of human thought and is recognized as such in the Church.

But of all the illustrations of the recognition of the element of progress in the bosom of Christianity, the strongest is supplied by that truth which, though sometimes obscured, was never wholly lost sight of, viz., that all good gifts are of God: that the man who thinks, the man who discovers, the man who invents, the man who paints, the man of science, equally with the man who preaches and prays, is one of God's workmen, with a capacity to be used for the welfare of man and to

[1] "Michel Ange lui-même meprisait tout ce qui n'est pas de l'homme. C'est contre ce point de vue de l'Eglise que s'élève Leonard de Vinci, dans son Traité de la Peinture ; relevant de sa déchéance l'univers visible il replace l'homme au sein de toutes les formes de la creation." Quinet, "Les Révolutions d'Italie," chap. viii.. quoted by Dr. Allen, "Continuity of Christian Thought," p. 346.

the glory of God. Whenever such a faith is held, antagonism to progress becomes impossible. When the Tabernacle of God is reared in the wilderness of the world, the hands which rear it are not only those of Moses and Aaron, but those also of the Bezaleels of the times.

(iii.) One further set of examples may be allowed as we turn our attention to the history of religious thought in the Church of England. There are, if I mistake not, evidences that the claims on behalf of these three elements— Dependence, Fellowship, and Progress—have received emphatic illustration in her story.

There have been recognised in the Church of England two, or to speak more correctly, three great schools of thought. If we look dispassionately at the relationship between these schools of thought, we may observe how they tend mutually to correct one another. In one school much is said of man's weakness and inability, of himself, to turn to God. There is a Calvinistic drift underneath the tide of such teaching. The emphasis is placed upon what God does for man; thus prominence is given to the element of Dependence. Another school meets this by reminding us that man holds a power and a responsibility in his own hand; that in the use of the means of grace he may grow full of grace.

But, again, this latter school in turn teaches Dependence. It says that in baptism a gift of God is bestowed apart from subjective conditions. To this the former school applies a corrective, when it urges the need of conversion. There must be, it says, a personal apprehension of grace; man himself must feel and know and co-operate with God, and enter into conscious Fellowship with Him. And thus does one school supplement the teachings of another.

Again, one school of thought teaches Dependence in the form in which it proclaims the Atonement. The great Atonement for sin has been made. That is enough for man. He has but to look and live. The other school brings Fellowship into prominence when laying more stress on the Incarnation than on the Atonement. Thus these two schools of thought are not so much mutually antagonistic as mutually complemental.

But the third element, Progress, is not left without witness. The duty of giving emphasis to this element seems specially to have devolved upon a third school of thought. Christianity does not appear to this school as it does to that to which the individual aspect of religion is of supreme importance, nor yet as it does to the other school, to which the sacramental system and corporate life are the essential features; it appears rather, as showing that the paramount office of the Church is to work out those practical questions which relate to the social life and general progress of humanity. In its view the Church owes duties to the health, joy, and culture of the world. In this we have witness to the element of Progress.

Thus, whether we look at the history of Christendom or the history of our own Church, we find witnesses on all sides to the three tendencies of which we have spoken. Christianity bears witness to the fact that men will have in their religion the elements of Dependence, Fellowship, and Progress.

The result, then, of what we have said is briefly this. Religion is likely to be permanent, because man's nature is permanent, and the constancy of man's nature has been seen in the permanent character of what we have called its spiritual laws. Religious history shows that the three ideas of Dependence, Fellowship, and Progress are demanded at some time or other in the history of all religions. It remains to be seen what religions, if any, can really and fitly supply these three.

Meanwhile we must rest here: we have found thus much at least—man's need of Dependence, Fellowship, and Progress. Dependence is necessary, for we are weak and God is strong. Progress is necessary, the ladder is set, its foot is upon earth, it must be climbed, it goes upward ever. The end is glorious, and reaches unto God. Yet the ascent is hard, and man is ever lonely. But, behold, we are not alone. As we climb, heavenly Fellowship is ours. The divine sympathy and love are as the angels of God, and never leave the side of the struggling, the climbing, the heaven-seeking children of men.

LECTURE IV.

THE RELATION OF THE THREE UNIVERSAL RELIGIONS TO THE ESSENTIAL ELEMENTS OF RELIGION.

The question now assumes another form. Hitherto we have been asking what elements man demands in a religion. We have now to ask how far any religion has the native power to meet this demand.

With the view of answering this question, it is needful to examine:—

I.—Islamism.
   1. The element of Dependence is natural and indigenous.
   2. The element of Fellowship is found to be an artificial growth.
   3. The element of Progress has no natural home.

II.—Buddhism.
   1. Fellowship akin with its earliest features.
   2. Dependence demanded in later developments: North India, China.
   3. Progress recognized. Maitreya Buddha.

III.—Christianity.
   The three elements originally present:
   1. In the teaching of Jesus Christ.
   2. In its theological drift.
   3. In the teaching of Apostles.

Thus Christianity alone of the three universal religions possesses originally and indigenously the three elements of religion which the History of Religions shows that man's nature demands.

LECTURE IV.

THE RELATION OF THE THREE UNIVERSAL RELIGIONS TO THE ESSENTIAL ELEMENTS OF RELIGION.

"Hereafter ye shall see heaven open and the angels of God ascending and descending."—*St. John* i. 51.

THE reasons for thinking that religion will be permanent in this world strengthen as we consider them. Man's nature is permanent. The principles of his moral and spiritual being are intelligible and constant. In addition to this, we have seen that the history of religions exhibits man's nature as habitually demanding certain elements in his religion. If the religion offered for his acceptance does not supply them, we find that they are sooner or later added, as though man could not do without them. This shows that the nature of man is constant with respect to his religious instincts. It shows also that the religion which ignores these elements cannot hope for permanence. These elements are, as we have seen, Dependence, Fellowship, Progress.

We are thus led to another and a crucial question, on the answer to which depends the future of the great religions of the world. This question is: How far do the religions which aspire to be considered universal possess in themselves the power of satisfying these demands?

It may be well to recall the distinction which must always be kept in mind between the emergence of these essential elements in the history of a religion, and their existence as originally part of the religion itself. No doubt demand will create supply. If man wants in his religion Dependence, Fellowship, Progress, these will appear sooner or later. But there is an enormous difference between the system which has added certain elements to satisfy a demand, and the system which naturally and originally contained such elements. It is a difference resembling that between a demagogue and a statesman. It is the difference between astuteness and honest genius. In a religion, it is the difference between spurious and real universality.

Three religions stand before us reckoned as universal. We have to ask whether the universality which they possess is apparent or real, whether it is in their history only or in their quality also. Their apparent universality is admitted. They have outgrown the land of their birth; they have been accepted in other lands and by other races; they have gathered into their fold children of other climates and people of other habits. But the question which follows is this: Is the supremacy which they have gained fairly won? Is it due to the possession of native and original qualities which meet the needs of man? Or has it been won by the addition of qualities, alien from their original natures, and added to save them from perishing? They have the form of universality; have they its spirit?

The elements which man has persistently asked for have been at least three: Dependence, Fellowship, Progress. The history of religions appears to show that unless a religion possess, not as an after-acquisition, but as an original inheritance, the power of supplying these three, it cannot aspire to permanent or real universality, for it has not the spirit or quality fitted for the work.

The question then takes this form: Are these three elements, in the religions which are apparently universal, found in them as afterthoughts or politic additions, or are they found in them as native elements, legitimate and natural developments from the germ-principles of these religions? It is needful that this should be clear to our minds. It is like asking whether the flowers which are found on a particular plant have been tied there, or whether they grew there. It is like asking whether the features in a work of art are the spontaneous expression of the thought of the artist, or merely the clever arrangement of a needy man who consulted the public taste.

We may ask, then, Are these elements in a religion additions or growths? are they supplied in consequence of outward pressure, or are they the result of inward tendency? If the answer to this question be,—These elements are native, indigenous, the lawful development of the germ-principles of the religion; then, so far, the religion fulfils the condition of real, essential universality. If the answer be—They were added, they are alien from the original drift of the religion; then the universality of such a religion is only apparent. It lacks the quality, though it may possess the form, of universality: for if these elements are added to satisfy the demands of men, then their presence is not an evidence of the original greatness, but of the original poverty of such religion; they show not the power of the religion to help man, but the power of man to modify the religion.

On the other hand, if these elements are found in a religion, and are seen to belong to it originally and essentially, then it would seem that such a religion has a native fitness to meet man's needs. Such a religion carries in her bosom the life which blesses man and secures her own immortality. Such a religion may go forth in much sorrow, sowing her seed with tears; but inasmuch as she carries forth seed of that bread by which men's souls are fed, her harvest is assured, and with full gladness and abundant sheaves she will rejoice hereafter among the sons of men.

Our task now is clear. We have to take up once more those three religions whose universality is apparent, and examine them afresh with the view of ascertaining how far they possess these three elements—Dependence, Fellowship, Progress—not as accidental and super-added, but as essential, original, native qualities.

We shall take them in the order in which we considered them in the last lecture.

I.—Islamism.

1. We have already seen that the element of Dependence is supplied by Islamism. It is admitted that this element belongs to its very

essence. Islamism would not be Islamism without this quality, for it is the religion of dependence. Submission is the whole of Mahommedanism.[1] To lose this idea would be to drop the keystone out of the arch of its structure; it would be the breaking down of the bridge which it sought to build between earth and heaven. The ladder by which man climbs towards Paradise is the ladder of dependence and submission. Islamism is surrender. The element of Dependence is essentially in Islamism.

2. Is the element of Fellowship there also? Historically it is present. We have seen that a mystical element began to show itself among the followers of Mahommed. This mystical tendency covers and embraces the element of Fellowship. Man yearns for more than the sense of his dependence upon one greater than himself; he asks for the sense of the nearness of one who is kin with himself. The worship of the Walis or Saints is the expression of this yearning. Greatness does not satisfy; omnipotence appals; fitness and kinship are more attractive than arbitrary and irresistible might. If man cannot creep into the heart of God, he will crouch close under the shadow of those who seem to him godlike. He will worship the heroes, and rain tears

[1] See Note 19, Appendix.

upon the shrines of saints, and invoke their aid, feeling sure of their sympathy. The Súfite movement exhibits in bolder form the same tendency. It supplied a sense of nearness by saying that men might go straight to God and that God was One who felt with them and fought for them. So the missing element of Fellowship was supplied in two ways. On the one hand men had looked up to God with wonder and awe; but they could not feel the beating of the divine heart in sympathy with their own: that was too much to expect; Allah was too great a monarch for that; therefore the sympathy, which the conception of God failed to convey, was sought in the Prophet or the Saint. On the other hand the Súfite movement, teaching gentler thoughts of God, grew and became popular because it also met a want in human nature.

But it was not an indigenous plant. It arose because man wanted it; it did not spring spontaneously out of the heart of the religion itself. It is using far too mild an expression when we say it was not indigenous. It is far more exact to say that it was alien from the original spirit of Islamism. Those features, which give evidence of the craving of man for fellowship with the divine, are features which had no place in the religion as it came from its founder's hands.

Take Saint-worship. In the reverence paid to Walis or Saints, in the worship given to the Prophet, the mystical feeling found expression. But such a movement was out of harmony with the original faith. The adoration of the Walis "might lead us to regard it as a product of Islam itself. But, as a fact, it is far from being so. It is rather a protest against the very religion in which it occupies so prominent a place. The Moslem seeks what his faith withholds from him, and seeks it where the authority which he himself recognises forbids him to look." Again: "If it is only in this form that Islam can satisfy the demands of the pious soul, then it has become a religion of the world in the teeth of its own proper nature."[1]

Take the reverence paid to sacred places. The disposition from which this proceeds is akin to the impulse to Saint-worship. But this reverence for holy shrines is as alien from the original faith as is the worship of the Walis. The Ka'ba was reverenced, but its veneration "is in such glaring contradiction with the Moslem's otherwise pure conceptions of God, that a reconciliation can only be effected by the most far-fetched theories, and even then imperfectly."[2]

[1] Kuenen, "Hib. Lect.," pp. 43, 45.
[2] Sprenger, l.c. ii. 346, quoted by Kuenen, "Hib. Lect.," p. 32.

Take Súfism. Súfism exists in the bosom of Islamism; but she is like Israel, a stranger in the land of Ham; she is tolerated, but the son of the bondwoman cannot be co-heir with the son of the free woman. "The Moslem who makes terms with Súfism thereby gives his own religion a certificate of poverty, and the true Súfite is a Moslem no more."[1]

We need scarcely be surprised at this. The conception of God presented by Islamism will account for it. Islamism is a Deism. God is infinitely great, dwelling afar off, removed by His majesty to an immeasurable distance from His creatures. "Mohammed pointed the world to the solitary majesty of God, but he left it a solitary majesty; he did not bring the object of his reverence into union with the human soul." Parallel is the conception of man: man is a slave, the mechanical executor of God's will, finding "his highest goal only in absolute submission to a will he cannot resist, and may not try to comprehend."[2] This conception excluded mysticism, for "Deism and mysticism"[3] it has been truly said, "cannot really go together." We cannot

[1] Kuenen, "Hib. Lect.," p. 46.
[2] Matheson, "The Growth of the Spirit of Christianity," vol. i., p. 336.
[3] Kuenen, "Hib. Lect.," p. 46. See Note 20 in Appendix.

find the element of Fellowship naturally in Islamism. It is there, but not as a daughter born in the house. It is there as a historical fact, but it is of alien, not of native growth. We must admit, therefore, that Fellowship is not an indigenous element in Islamism.

3. Can we find there the element of Progress? Our first impulse would certainly be to answer "Yes." Memory and imagination are at hand ready to paint the glories of the culture and civilization which have flourished under the shadow of the Prophet's name. We cannot forget all that has been said of Arabian Science. Side by side with the conquerors came the teachers. Victorious in Africa and Europe, they brought gifts of surpassing value in their hands. We cannot ignore the venerable walls of Cordova and the great stream of knowledge which flowed throughout Spain, carrying with it fertilizing power, and regenerating the intellectual life of Europe.[1] We might acknowledge that from the middle of the eighth century to the middle of the thirteenth there were not merely great thinkers and scholars in the Moslem world, but that its average culture and intelligence were in advance

[1] See Bosworth Smith, "Mohammed and Mohammedanism," p. 287, 2nd Ed. *Cf.* Matheson, "Growth of the Spirit of Christianity," pp. 342-345.

of those of Christendom.[1] We do not undervalue the services rendered to civilization under the rule of certain princes who held the faith of Islâm.

Thus then, as a historical fact, Progress was fostered at periods of Mohammedan ascendency; but this does not show that Islamism allied itself naturally and sympathetically with the progress of the race. This question is one of great and present interest. No apology is needed for giving it as full consideration as our time will allow. One thing is clear. The relation of Islamism to Progress was not always one of sympathy. How is it, we may ask, that the earlier years of Moslem rule do not show any intellectual movement? Under the auspices of the first four Caliphs and under the guidance of the Omayyads, there was no zeal for culture, no thirst for knowledge, no desire of progress. Intellectual life drooped. Whatever growth and knowledge existed, withered at the touch of Islamism, like vegetation beneath the fiery breath of the desert.

[1] M. Renan, "L'Islamisme et la Science," p. 4. "De l'an 775 a peu pres, jusque vers le milieu du treizième siècle, c'est-à-dire pendant 500 ans environ, il y a eu dans les pays musulmans des savants, des penseurs très distingués. On peut même dire que, pendant ce temps, le monde musulman a été supérieur, pour la culture intellectuelle, au monde chrétien."

But, when the sovereign power passed from Arab to Persian hands,[1] a change took place. The throne of the Moslem world was moved eastward, and its sceptre was wielded by the Abbasids. When new conditions are followed by new results, we can hardly refuse to admit the probability that the new conditions have contributed to the new results. The land to which the Moslem power came was a land of culture. Unlike the Arab, who was destitute of all the instincts of higher civilization, and changeless as his changeless deserts, the Persian welcomed knowledge, loved science, and kept alive his intellect. It was on the soil of Persia, and under the rule of intelligent princes like the Abbasids, that the forward movement took place. That is, under Persian, rather than Moslem influence, civilization and knowledge began to flourish. Euclid, Galen, and Ptolemy were translated, and became the heritage of the eastern lands. There arose great thinkers, among whom Alfarabi, Avicenna, and Averroes reached the front rank.[2] Astronomy and

---

[1] It will be understood that this paragraph only refers to the questions of culture and progress. The question of corruptions of the faith of Islam in Persia is distinct. According to Mr. Bosworth Smith, "in no nation in the Mohammedan world has the religion less hold on the people as a restraining power" than in Persia —" Mohammed and Mohammedanism," p. 290, 2nd Ed.

[2] Renan, " L'Islamisme et la Science," p. 10.

algebra were studied, a fresh development of chemistry took place, the theory of distillation was reached, and, as some think, the invention of gunpowder belongs to this epoch.

We cannot argue *Post hoc, ergo propter hoc*. We cannot say that because culture and civilization advanced after the rise of Islamism, therefore the advance was due to Islamism. But we may, perhaps, argue,—*ante hoc, ergo non propter hoc*—we may plead that if before the rise of Moslem influence there was a cultivated soil in Persia, therefore the advance was probably due not to Mohammedan but to Persian influence.[1] Are we then to consider the state of the case to be this: to the Arabs culture was nothing; to the Persians it was much? The transference of the Faith from the one soil to the other was the transference of religion from a soil which was unlikely to develop culture to a soil which was pre-eminently likely to do so. It dwelt then in a country open to a twofold stream of thought and culture from the West and from the East. Influences reached it alike from India and from Greece. Are we to assign, therefore, the whole of that culture to the soil? Are we to conclude that Islamism as such is actually hostile to culture? The answer of Renan is that what we

[1] See Note 21, in Appendix.

are accustomed to call Arabian science, "because it is written in Arabic, is, in reality, Greco-Sassanidean; or, more strictly, Greek, for the fertile element of it springs from Greece." The answer may be challenged on the ground that it does not sufficiently recognize the influences which came from India; but few will challenge its accuracy as regards the Arab. But if not Arabian, might it be called Moslem science? Did the religion of Mohammed reach forth a fostering hand for its progress? If the race of Mohammed was heedless of culture, was the faith of Mohammed equally so? The answer is a sad one. The growing culture only "won from the orthodox Moslem his malediction." "Islâm persecuted philosophy and science."[1]

Progress has always had to fight against timid conservatism and hot-house religionism, against ignorance and self-opinionatedness. Hence it is a fair question to ask: Was the persecution and opposition to culture the work of an individual or of a party, or was it of the very tendency of the faith? The answer of Renan is that in treating science as an enemy, Islamism had only been consistent.[2] Notwithstanding this opinion, some may be tempted to ask: "What is there in

[1] "L'Islamisme et la Science," pp. 11 to 16.
[2] *Ibid.*, p. 20.

IV.] *Three Universal Religions.* 141

Islamism hostile to science?" Are there dogmas, held to be of the essence of Mohammedanism, which make the maintenance of the faith inconsistent with the spirit of Progress? The doctrine of the uncreated Koran, which is accepted by orthodox Islamism, affirms the changeless infallibility and, in most uncompromising form, the verbal inspiration of the sacred book.[1] This foolish dogma necessarily creates a collision between the creed of Islâm and the growing life of the world of thought. But it may be suggested that the faith of Islâm could freely surrender this ossified idea of inspiration without damaging the essential elements of her creed, and so become free to welcome those discoveries which reveal the unity of the world, the unity of the race, and the unity of nature. But even were this possible, which it is not, for the doctrine of the uncreated Koran forbids it, there still would be wanting a real link between the faith of Islâm and the spirit of culture and progress. It is not enough that a religion which aspires to universality should be passive towards culture—it must at least be sympathetic. But in Islamism there is no encouragement to culture. It offers no benediction to the student of nature; it speaks no cheering words to the

[1] See Note 22 in Appendix.

pioneers of progress. God is far away from human life; His sovereignty too august to heed the arts and thoughts of men. He is great, we are little; it is as vain to study His world as to try and understand His ways. The answer of the Caliph, when Sir H. Layard asked information respecting the population, commerce, and history of Mossoul, may illustrate this:—"What you ask," he said, "is both useless and harmful. You know much which does not interest me, and what you have seen I despise. Will greater knowledge improve your digestion, and can your wandering eyes discover Paradise?"[1] Whatever springs from such a faith is cut and dried, barren and limited. It has no sap, no seed of future life in itself; and its impotence is the more apparent, when we find behind it the conception of a God, who does not care to touch dead things to make them live. The inspirations of God cannot be claimed for man's art and science, man's songs and implements. He has bestowed inspiration once, and it lies within the covers of a book, and there is no inspiration for the working or for the thinking sons of men, to consecrate thought and dignify art. Man may paint,[2] and sing, and study, and

[1] Renan, " L'Islamisme et la Science," pp. 21, 22.
[2] As a fact Islamism discourages painting. See Note 23 in Appendix.

discover ; he may explore and explain the wonders of God's works ; he may alleviate by his discoveries the burden of life ; but it is not by a divinely-given wisdom he has done these things. God takes no delight in such things. It is little wonder that a hopeless fatalism has become a part of the creed of the Moslems.

The movement commenced by the Wahhábites,[1] who have been called the Puritans of Islamism, has, in the opinion of many, reasserted the purest and most essential features of the faith of the Prophet. Under their auspices the dogma of the uncreated Koran reigns supreme. Commenting on the phrase, "Puritans of Islam," Kuenen says : " The comparison is not unjust. But whereas no serious historian would ever dream of simply identifying Puritanism and Christianity, Wahhábism really is Islâm itself— Islâm, the whole of Islâm, and nothing but Islâm."[2]

The conclusion, then, seems to be this : Islamism has been, and still is, a great power in the world. There is much in it that is calculated to purify and elevate mankind, at a certain stage of history. It has the power of reclaiming the slaves of a degraded

[1] *Cf.* Bosworth Smith, "Mohammed and Mohammedism," p. 315, 2nd Ed., and Kuenen's " Hibbert Lectures," p. 52.

[2] " Hibbert Lectures," p. 52.

polytheism from their low grovelling conception of God to conceptions which are higher:[1] it has set an example of sobriety to the world, and has shielded its followers from the drink-plague which destroys the strength of nations. And, in so far as it has achieved this, it has performed a work which entitles it to the attention of man, and no doubt has been a factor in God's education of the world. But when we come to the wider question, and ask whether Islamism possesses those elements which will qualify her to stand the crisis of the future, and to emerge from its trials as a religion fitted to guide the future of humanity, to satisfy the demands of man's heart, and to be considered universal in gift and quality, we are bound to answer "No. It can teach man reverence and service. It can meet his instinct of dependence; but to minister to the higher needs of man, it is powerless." For the spirit of man, when it cries aloud in its agony, "Oh, that I knew where I might find Him! that I might come even to His seat!" (Job xiii. 3) Islâm has no answer. For the cry of him who asks that our fair world with all its beauty shall be regarded as a thing growing up under the inspiring hand of God, Islâm has no sympathy. It is like one

[1] Bosworth Smith, "Mohammed and Mohammedanism," pp. 161, 308, 2nd Ed. See Note 24 in Appendix.

of those countries in which the verdure is luxuriant, the flowers are of glorious colours, and the birds soar over our heads resplendent in plumage and majestic in flight; but where the flowers lack fragrance, where the birds lack song, and where the homes of men are not. The mirage-fever of the desert is upon us; we dream of water, we wake to thirst; we think of shelter, and we wake to yearn for the shadow of a rock in the weary land. Such faith can never be universal; it provides for Dependence, but not for Progress, and it supplies no link of Fellowship between the spirit of man and the Spirit of God who made him.

II.—Buddhism.

We have seen that the history of Buddhism exhibits all the three great elements—Dependence, Fellowship, Progress; but we have to ask whether these elements are indigenous and native products of the soil of Buddhism.

1. We shall take first the element of Fellowship. It is well to take this first, because the fundamental ideas of Buddhism, if allied to any of the three elements, seem to me to have some kinship with what we have called Fellowship. Buddhism, indeed, does not recognize that communion with a Personal God which the word Fellowship implies; but it must be remembered that, under this word, we include that group of feelings and

desires which make men cry out against the burden of life, whether of sin or of sorrow; which prompt the yearning to be rid of self, and which crave for that inward harmony which is, though not always recognized as such, the longing of the spirit for oneness with a higher law or higher life. This instinct, even when God is denied, is the unconscious desire of the soul for Him. It finds expression in quietism or mysticism, and, strange as it may seem, its presence may be traced in theories which place the ultimate goal of humanity in absorption or annihilation. Something akin to this is possessed by Buddhism, and, in one sense, lies at its very root. The Buddhist, like the quietist, yearns for the calm, equable, painless, passionless life; he longs to be free from the tyranny of desires which disturb him here. Only thus can true insight come to him. Thus he may reach the Nirvana. For this purpose life must be a sacrifice. A life of righteousness is higher sacrifice than oil and honey. It is higher still to become a monk, refusing joy and seeking repose; higher still, and highest of all, "when he obtains deliverance, and gains this knowledge,—I shall not again return to this world. This is the highest perfection of all offering."[1] The quietistic spirit, which speaks in

[1] *Cf.* Oldenberg, "Buddha," pp. 173, 174.

such words, appears also in the teaching, that it is not by right views, nor by traditions, nor by virtuous works, that purity is won, but by becoming what Buddha was, and endowed with insight.[1]

Desire, unrest, pleasure, are the tempters; they disturb or make impossible the true life. Buddha sitting under the tree, resolved not to quit it till he has attained the knowledge which makes free, is the picture of the quietist; he is the type of all those who have longed to reach that inner harmony which is peace. As far as the element of fellowship expresses itself in the longing for inward or self-rest, it exists in the very soul of Buddhism, though its expression is often given in a crippled and mutilated form. The soul longs for harmony and rest in itself. The God of peace indeed is not there. But the voice of the soul of man demanding Fellowship is heard in Buddhism, though Buddhism failed to perceive that the longing for inward peace is the longing for harmony with the higher law, or in other words, Fellowship with the Divine.

2. Is the element of Dependence supplied naturally by Buddhism?

As a fact—so we have seen—the element of

[1] *Cf.* "Sutta-Nipâta," translated by Fausböll. Sacred Books of the East, vol. x. p. xiv. pp., 160-1, 62, 212.

Dependence is present and recognised among Buddhists. Wherever Buddhism holds sway, we shall find expressions and tokens which only spring up when there is a felt need of some one greater and stronger than self on whom to rely. There is a constant and pathetic acknowledgment of this need in the prayer-wheels which revolve in Buddhist Temples, and in the sacred ribbons, which, among the branches of the trees in Burmah and Tibet, wave in the breeze and raise their silent cry, "Ah, the jewel is in the Lotus," *i.e.*, as Prof. Rhys Davids explains it,—the self-creative Force is in the universe.[1] Most of the great movements in the history of Buddhism have tended to restore to man the God whom he had lost, and to give him back One on whom he may rely. As a matter of history the element of Dependence is present; but does it belong to the essence of the Buddhistic creed? Our answer is only too plain. It is an addition, not only independent of Buddhism, but at *variance with the essential features of original Buddhism.* This is easily seen; the relation of Buddhism to previous beliefs will make this clear.

Professor Rhys Davids tells us that the noblest teachers prior to the rise of Buddhism believed "that there was something far higher than the

[1] "Buddhism," pp. 210, 211.

right performance of sacrifice; that the object of the wise man should be to know, inwardly and consciously, the Great Soul of all." But when Buddhism arose, it swept away the whole "Great Soul Theory." "For the first time in the history of the world, it proclaimed a salvation which each man could gain for himself, and by himself, in this world, during this life, without any the least reference to God, or to gods, either great or small." "God is in us, the seed eternal is within all," was the saying of the Brahman. "No," is the reply of the Buddhist, "all is transitory; gods and men alike pass away."[1]

Parallel with this is the fact, generally admitted, that the looking to Buddha for deliverance, and the offering of prayers to deities or Bodhi-satvas for help, were all of later growth. Again, mark another feature. Buddhism is a religion, but it is a religion almost wholly without recognised theological dogma.[2] I say without recognised dogma because no philosophy or religion has existed, or can exist, without dogmas, at least unconsciously held. But a religion which pretends to do without theological dogmas must exclude the idea of Dependence. When-

[1] "Hibbert Lectures," pp. 28, 29; see p. 209, *et seq.*
[2] Réville, "Prolegomena of the History of Religions," p. 203. Kuenen, "Hib. Lect.," pp. 283, 284.

ever Dependence, or the sense of reliance, on a greater than ourselves is admitted, a creed, concerning that greater one or thing, is sure to follow. But in Buddhism there is such a shrinking from dogma, that, on many of the questions which most deeply touch human life and destiny, it refuses either to affirm or deny, or even to affirm that it refuses to affirm or deny.[1] The element of Dependence, therefore, cannot be native to Buddhism.

3. Is the element of Progress indigenous to this religion? has Buddhism any natural link with the advance of the world, and with the growing order of human life? We saw, indeed, in its history a recognition of the idea of Progress. Some hope of a golden age grew up, and found expression in Buddhism. But this is the growth of a later time; it does not belong to its essence. Interest in life, the strong enthusiasm which fills the souls of those who believe that the ages are leading up to a golden year, the delight in the powers and forces which manifest themselves in the world, are entirely wanting in the original and orthodox Buddhism. Such a spirit is optimistic, but Buddhism is a pessimistic quietism. Quietism in Christianity has been blamed, because it turns its face away from human progress; but what

[1] See Note 25 in Appendix.

shall we say of the quietism of Buddhism? How can we hope to amend a life, which is radically bad, by the aid of a system which teaches that man's highest aim should be to escape from life? All that has been said against the ascetic and non-worldly attitude of Christianity might be urged with additional force against Buddhism. It is full of the strong, sweet, pathetic compassion which looks upon life with eyes full of tears, but only to turn them away from it again, as from an unsolved and insoluble riddle. On this point let us listen to those who can speak with authority.

Réville writes:—"Buddhism, born on the domain of polytheism, has fought against it, not by rising above nature in subordinating it to a single sovereign spirit, but by reproving nature in principle, and condemning life itself as an evil and a misfortune."[1]

In the same strain, Kuenen writes:—It has "turned away from life and is blind to its significance and its worth."

It has, according to the same writer, no natural function to deal with evils, against which more hopeful creeds are wont to contend. "Its mission is not to root out what it holds to be deadly errors or to proclaim precious truths, nor, in the first instance, to contend

[1] "Prolegomena of the History of Religions," p. 98.

against moral evil, or to build up a society in which righteousness and peace shall dwell. It seeks not to convert, but to *rescue*,—to rescue from delusion and desire. The moral life is not its end, but its means."

Similarly he tells us that Buddhism has its purpose, but that purpose is not allied with the spirit of progress. Buddhism has helped "order and discipline; but has it ever supported a people in its endeavours after progress, in its recuperative efforts when smitten by disaster, in its struggle against despotism? No such instances are known. And, indeed, we had no right to expect them. Buddhism does not measure itself against this or that abuse, does not further the development or reformation of society, either directly or indirectly, for the very simple reason that it *turns away* from the world on principle." [1]

Buddhism is not the religion of progress, if, as Oldenberg tells us, it has no message for the classes which most need upward help and encouraging impulse :—" For the lower order of the people, for those born to toil in manual labour, hardened by the struggle for existence, the announcement of the connection of misery with all forms of existence was not made, nor was the dialectic of the law of the

[1] " Hibbert Lectures,"pp. 203, 284, 281. See Note 26, Appendix.

painful concatenation of causes and effects calculated to satisfy 'the poor in spirit.' 'To the wise belongeth this law,' it is said, 'not to the foolish.' Very unlike the word of that Man who suffered 'little children to come unto Him, for of such is the kingdom of God.' For children and those who are like children, the arms of Buddha are not opened."[1]

It may be urged that these views scarcely do justice to Buddhism. We are willing to admit that there is much of high and beautiful moral teaching in the Dhammapada. In it great truths are taught of gentleness and self-control. Wrong-doing and violence are rebuked. The love of self is to be cut out like an Autumn Lotus. The way to inward rest is open to all. Pity, sad and earnest, for the weakness and sorrows of life, lifts up her voice in Buddhism. Under its auspices Asoka, "the first liberal king in India, ruled as a man of the people and for the people." But for all this the voice of Buddhism sounds like the voice of Pity without hope. Its sweet pathos cannot compensate for the lack of that robust faith whose word is Forward, and whose martial music stirs man to go in and possess the Land of Promise.

Hence we see that Fellowship, as a scanty thing, robbed of its joy and personal communion,

[1] "Buddha," pp. 157, 158.

may be found in Buddhism; but of Dependence upon any but self, there is none; while Progress towards a goal of gladness and fuller life is outside its range. This religion, so beautiful and so sad, cannot therefore wholly satisfy man. There are moments indeed in which we are all Buddhists. When life has disappointed us; when weariness is upon us; when the keen anguish born of the sight of human suffering appals and benumbs us; when we are frozen to terror, and our manhood flies at sight of the Medusa-like head of the world's unappeased and unappeasable agony; then we too are torn by the paroxysm of anguish, and would flee to the Nirvâna of oblivion and unconsciousness, turning our back upon what we cannot alleviate, and longing to lay down the burden of life, and to escape from that which has grown insupportable. "Save me from this hour," is our cry.

That hour must come,—if it has not come— to all, except the hardhearted, who never suffer; that hour must come when you find yourself beneath the weight which has rolled down upon you, and bruised and broken you: when the spirit and the life cry out against contending any more— it must come, for Buddhism represents a phase of universal human feeling. Then, when it comes, remember, that natural as is the cry, "Save me from this hour" (St. John xii. 27), it is higher to resolve "The cup that My Father hath given Me, shall I not drink it?" (St. John xviii. 11.) "I must work the works of Him that sent Me." (St. John ix. 14). It is better to forget self than to wish to rescue self, better to face duty, than to shrink from it; better than giving way to despair is it to press manfully on across the wilderness of life, though as yet the land of promise be all unseen; for such pilgrims, even in the desert, streams will break forth and glory will shine from their crown of thorns.

III.—Christianity.

We turn to Christianity. Are the three elements here? Are they indigenous? We saw that, as a matter of history, they were present. But the history of Christianity is a history of controversies; and those controversies are viewed by the many, either with indifference or with indignation, and by the few with interest, as having a significance far beyond the subjects in debate. Wise people will read in them indications of the drift of human thought and feeling, and the interpretations of life given in different periods of the world's history; and more, they will regard them as witnesses to the desire to preserve some principle which is felt to be needful, though often its breadth and fecundity are not fully realised even by the combatants themselves. Human nature, indeed, knows more than it can consciously express. The contest over trifles, thought to be contemptible, may be sometimes sublime. It can never be contemptible when we hear in it the voice of a soul in agony, lest it should lose something which it feels to be needful to its life. The instincts of humanity are often right, even when clamouring unreasonably. The contest to the outsider may seem to be a contest for a straw, and even the combatants can hardly explain their own earnestness. But when the struggle is surveyed by the daylight of after facts, it will be found that the blind instinct was often a true one, and that men were striving to preserve something which neither they nor humanity could afford to lose.

In the light, then, of the three elements of Dependence, Fellowship and Progress, let us look at some of the controversies of Christian history. The crude and novel dogmas, which have been regarded as heretical, have often been the expression, lame and incomplete, of those who strove to place emphasis on some forgotten or ignored truth. In emphasising a truth they have exaggerated it, and in exaggerating it have lost sight of some equally-needed truth.

Patripassianism affirms Fellowship, for it expresses its belief that God can be one with human suffering; but in affirming Fellowship it tended to destroy Dependence, and was opposed by the Church, because the Church felt that Dependence upon One above the reach of human infirmity, strong where man was weak, was needful as a refuge for the human soul. Arianism, while seeking to bring God nearer, in reality thrust Him further away. It declared, in fact, the impossibility of God becoming man, of God being able to feel the touch of human infirmity, or the throb of human sorrow; and Arianism was opposed, because it tended to destroy the element of Fellowship. By an opposite route Docetism and Gnosticism reached the same result, weakening the sense of Fellowship between the human and the divine. The same is true of Sabellianism. The Son and the Spirit were made unreal, and consequently humanity appeared less and less capable of working out the Divine purpose in the world. We are not surprised then to find that, the true ground of Fellowship being obscured, a Pantheistic tendency soon made itself felt in Sabellianism.

In the heresy taught by Paul of Samosata, there is an absolute tendency to revert to Deism, that is, to the theory of a distant God. Hymns distinctively Christian were suppressed by him and the Psalms of Judaism put in their place. According to him, Christ was not a revelation of God Himself, but merely a man who became God.[1] He thus impaired the sense of Fellowship between the human and the divine of which the Incarnation is the expression. In later times Calvinism, in its assertion of the supreme sovereignty of God, again remarkably emphasised the spirit of Dependence; but it tended to weaken the sense of Fellowship, and to strangle the power of Progress. Mysticism was the exaggeration of the element of Fellowship, but it tended also to reduce the personal greatness of God, to weaken the sense of reverence, and to withdraw Him from the progressive life of the world. Humanitarianism in the Church affirmed the element of Progress, but it often did so at the expense of the elements of Dependence and Fellowship.

Thus in the history of the Christian Church, through controversies and inward conflicts, the three elements have made themselves manifest.

But are they indigenous, belonging to the very heart of essential Christianity? If I can show you that they are present in the first teachings of the Founder—if I can show you that they are intertwined in the earliest conception and form of the

---

[1] See Art. in Christian Biog. Dict., "Paul of Samosata."

Christian faith, and also are enforced by His immediate followers, then it seems to me that we may conclude that these three elements were essentially, radically, and originally present in Christianity. We have in a measure dealt with this point.

1. Take the teaching of the Founder in the Sermon on the Mount. The need of Dependence is enforced. Look up to Heaven, and see the birds of the air—your Heavenly Father feeds them; look around and see the flowers—your Heavenly Father clothes them: you are of more value than they. Learn to depend on your Father in Heaven.

The element of Fellowship is present also. The beatitudes, with which the Sermon opens, express this, for they affirm that the true blessedness of man is to be found in communion with God, and that there must be an ethical similarity between God and man. This is the true fellowship of the kingdom, "Blessed are the poor in spirit, blessed are the peacemakers, blessed are the merciful." (St. Matt. v. 3, 9, 7.)

Again, the element of Progress also is to be found. The theories which Christ lays down touch human life. Man is not to alienate himself from the life or the needs of his brother men. He has to give largely and liberally; to throw himself into the system and order of the social life around him, and to render the duties and services which his country lays upon him. " Whosoever shall compel thee to go a mile, go with him twain." (St. Matt. v. 41.) "If smitten on one cheek, offer the other; if asked, give; if defrauded of thy coat, surrender also thy cloke; if wronged, forgive; if persecuted, bless." What mean these, and kindred expressions, but this—do not separate yourselves from the normal interests of life, remember that you owe something to the humanity with which you are connected? That is Christ's teaching. Or, if I wanted to have it summed up in a single phrase, I would find it in that utterance, "Be ye perfect, as your Father also is perfect" (St. Matt. v. 48), for in it He combined the three ideas, Dependence, Fellowship, Progress. You have a Father. Here is Dependence. You must be perfect as your Father, for there must be spiritual resemblance between God and man. Here is Fellowship. And if we want Progress, what according to Christ is the character of that Father after whose perfection He bade men strive? He is One who is working ceaselessly for man's good. He scatters His rain upon the evil and the good, and sheds His sunshine on the just and the unjust. If then you take your life and powers into the world, give as your Father gives, use your energies and your capacities as your Father

IV.] *Three Universal Religions.* 161

uses the forces of the universe, associate yourself according to your measure with your Father's purpose and work—then the whole of your being and energy becomes identified with the onward movement of the great world in which God has placed you. There is Progress. Or take the Lord's Prayer. Thus pray we to our Father, "Give us this day our daily bread." There is Dependence. "Forgive us our sins." There is the cry for Fellowship; for sin is the dark shadow which comes between us and God. "Thy kingdom come, Thy will be done on earth." (St. Matt. vi. 9-13.) There, in the earnest yearning for the golden age of humanity, is Progress.

Or take some of Christ's parables. Man is as a lost sheep, sought by the loving Shepherd. What picture more fitly conveys the sense of our Dependence? Man is also a prodigal son, who can return to his Father's heart and his Father's home; and what more beautifully conveys the Fellowship that is possible between man and God? Man is as one entrusted with talents or money, to be laid out so that the Lord may receive His own with usury; and here the teaching is that man has no right to use powers and opportunities for himself alone; but that his duty is to expend all for the welfare of humanity, for the good of the race, which is

P

the desire of the Lord of all. He is to be a worker for Progress.

2. The same features are found in the earliest conception and form of the Christian faith.

The Benediction, with which St. Paul closes an epistle,[1] carries the same thought. His benediction is of grace, love, and communion; we depend upon God, we are united with God, and we can labour with God. And as the Church has seen in this benediction the doctrine of the Trinity, we may pause to ask whether this doctrine, so strange, so inscrutable, yet which has been deemed so essential in Christendom, may not, in the nineteenth century, acquire a new and a deep significance as an emphatic mode of expressing elements of truth which men cannot afford to lose. Its mysteriousness might have hindered its acceptance, but the conviction that it enshrined a fact, in which alone man's highest spiritual aspirations could be satisfied, was so strong in the Christian conscience that the doctrine has prevailed in spite of its mystery. For what is it that, after all, by a strange providence, has caused it to enter into the very heart of Christendom? What is it which has given to it its fulness of meaning? I answer, its conception of God. Say what you

[1] 2 Cor. xiii. 14.

will about creeds, the glory of them lies in their conception of God; and it is precisely here that the splendid power of Christianity to minister to the triple need of mankind is found. It revealed One upon whom you may depend, for it called Him God the Father, and it said His name was Love. It taught us of God the Son, that it might reveal to us the absolute fellowship which subsists between God and humanity. It taught us of God the Holy Ghost, and it said there is not a virtue, nor a grace, nor a talent, nor an intellectual faculty, nor any power of genius, which is not the gift of that Spirit. The gifts of statesmanship, and of magistracy, the opportunities and talents of prophecy and foresight, the power of working miracles, the creation of sympathy and compassion, they are all the gifts of that one Spirit, and are in seven-fold measure distributed throughout the world. Intellectual gifts, far-reaching keenness and sober sagacity; moral gifts, of courage, truthfulness and love; physical gifts, strength of body and endurance, are instruments in the use of which the world's progress and culture have been secured; but according to the Christian system, and according to its doctrine of the Holy Spirit, they are all of them gifts from God Himself, and teach us that the progress of the world is as dear to God, as it is needful to man, and that whether man wields the gifts of magistracy, of poetry, of prophecy, of discovery, whether he be statesman or artist, evangelist or theologian, he is one who has been raised up by God, and fitted by the gifts of the Divine Spirit for carrying out the will of God in the progress of the world.

3. Every apostle witnesses to the three elements of which we have spoken. St. John tells us that his Master said, "I am the Truth and the Life." (St. John xiv. 6.) When the disciples longed to see the Father and be satisfied, the answer of Christ was that the Father could be seen in the Son, or that He, upon whom men could depend, was the One also who had entered into fellowship with them. When the disciples asked how the Divine Presence could be manifested to them and not to the world, Christ answered that, in the progress of the holy life, through holy obedience, the inward divine fellowship would be realized; the Father and the Son would tabernacle within the spirit of man, and the light, which is never seen on land or sea, would abide in constant hope in the heart of the faithful man. St. Paul's teaching exhibits the same features. He speaks of one God and Father of

all on whom all creation depends. The idea of Fellowship he expresses thus: "I live; yet not I, but Christ liveth in me."[1] But he also recognizes Progress. "I reach forward." "I press on."[2] There is something towards which we are growing. We shall all come to the perfect man.[3] The groaning creation travails,[4] and reaches forth its lame hands; but it yearns for the better era when Progress shall be perfected, when men shall have reached the climax of their growing life, when they shall be manifested as sons of God. Similarly the doctrine of the Incarnation exhibits these three elements also. The Word was God—therefore a surety for our Dependence. The Word was made flesh—there is the Fellowship between the Divine and the human. The Word dwelt among us—there is the guarantee of human Progress. The doctrine is the witness not only that God becomes man, but, as the ancient creed has it, that the humanity is taken into God.

Dependence and Fellowship will be admitted, I think, to be indigenous and native elements in Christianity; Progress is the only element upon which doubt is likely to be cast. Kuenen says that the attitude of religion towards asceticism is

---

[1] Gal. ii. 20.   [2] Phil. iii. 12, 14. Old and Revised Version.
   [3] Ephes. iv. 13.   [4] Romans viii. 22.

always the test of religion.[1] But Christianity never favoured that asceticism which expressed its abhorrence of matter as such. Indeed, in this sense Christianity is not ascetic. If in Christianity we find such asceticism, that asceticism is not native to Christianity. For Christianity has declared that every good and perfect gift is from above—that the earth and its fruits, the dust from which man is born, earth's tabernacles in which the Divine spirit dwells, are not unclean, but holy. For since Christ wore human flesh, none can say that the flesh is unclean, and none can say therefore that the fruits of the earth are in themselves unholy, or that anything which tends to beautify and brighten our earthly existence is outside the range of Christianity.

Christianity was championed by men who identified themselves with the great and progressive life of the world. The indignant protest of Tertullian illustrates this. "We," he said, "are not those who live naked and self-exiled in the woods. We are one people with you. We do not shrink from your life. We are found in your forum, in your market places, in your baths, in your shops, your bridges, your inns, your fairs; we served as soldiers with you and as sailors with you, we were merchants with you, we

[1] "Hibbert Lectures," p. 288. See Note 27, Appendix.

practised the same arts and contributed to the same public works."[1] The conception, which underlies such a protest as this, is the sanctity of human thought, consecrated in the gifts which the Divine Spirit had given to man. I look to Islamism, and I find there a conception of life which is different. Whatever we have to do, that the will of God assigns us to do. As with Casabianca, standing on the burning deck, the hour of fate has come, and fate has come in this wise. *Kismet.* I must meet it. That spirit breeds heroes, I think, and when a man realizes that his life is in the hands of a Power greater than death, he does confront his foes more bravely. The soft pathos of Buddhism almost seems to become a girlish thing alongside the stalwart heroism of Islamism, and yet both are features of life. The dignity and courage displayed by the followers of the Prophet are not in themselves ignoble things. But when I look at Buddhism stooping in pity over the sorrows of life, I cannot call the heart of compassion an ignoble thing. These religions are as ladders, and they go up to God, and the angels of God will support those who seek to climb them. But when I ask whether these fulfil all the conditions which humanity demands in an universal and abiding

[1] Apol., cxlii.

religion, I am bound to say "No." They do not satisfy our sense of Dependence; or they only give us a crippled feeling of Fellowship, and they bar the way of Progress. But in Christianity these conditions are fulfilled—they are all here. Dependence: for God is love, and mercy is His attribute; Fellowship: for He has identified Himself with human sorrow; Progress: for the advance of the world and the development of all its beauty and glory, its present culture and future power, are but expressions of Divine life and energy in the world. The ladder disappears, and in its place stands the Son of Man saying : "There are ladders that lead to God, but it is weary climbing, even though angel hands should help you." With Him are the angels of life and of love; over His head the heavens open; upon Him descends visibly the symbol of life and the prophecy of power. The heaven is open, and the angels of God are ascending and descending. They are most clearly seen, and heaven is most fully open where He stands, who is the Son of God and the Son of Man—most truly Son of God, because most truly Son of Man.

LECTURE V.

RELIGION AND MORALITY.

It being admitted that Religion is natural, two questions may be raised; whether Religion is (1) necessary, (2) ethically helpful to mankind.

Taking the latter first, this Lecture is occupied with the relation of Religion and Morality.

Ethical efficiency may be taken as a test of Religion.

I.—The question considered as one of Fact.

   (i.) The Fact is that the influences of Religions on morals have been not wholly evil or good, but mixed.

   (ii.) The interpretation of this Fact.

      1. The results of Religion due to more than one factor. Man a factor, no less than Religion.

      2. Examination of this factor. Religion never sown in virgin or passive soil.

      3. Evil may result from man or from religion.

II.—The question considered as one of Principle.

   (i.) The statement that religious principles are immoral.

      1. The statement is ambiguous.

      2. The statement confuses Religion with its shadow —Religionism.

   (ii.) The principles of Christianity in relation to morals.

      1. Christianity in principle hostile to Religionism.

      2. The consideration of three charges of demoralising influence.
        (a) Orthodoxy preferred to morals.
        (b) Sentiment preferred to conduct.
        (c) Energy diverted from the world-life.

   (iii.) Conclusion with regard to Christianity.
      Its principles embrace all life.
      Its orthodoxy is the highest morality.

Conclusion.—Religion gives a sort of Eternalism to Righteousness.

LECTURE V.

RELIGION AND MORALITY.

"Hereafter ye shall see heaven open."—*St. John* i. 51.

THE position which we have now reached is clear: that religion will exist in the future, because religion is natural to man, and man's nature is permanent. We have noted also that man's religious nature demands certain elements. Further, in Christianity we find essentially and originally the supply of these elements. Judged on the grounds of fitness, Christianity possesses qualities which render likely the continuance of her power. But here we meet another question. It may be conceded that religion is natural, but it may be asked, "Is it so certain on that account that religion will live on?" Must we not dispose of another question first, and ask, "Is religion necessary?" "Does it serve any indispensable object? does it achieve anything which cannot otherwise be achieved? Is humanity dependent on it to such an extent that it cannot do without it?"

It may be said, that we can secure by other means everything that it was thought religion only could safeguard. Scientific moralism for instance will prove a sufficient guardian for morality without the aid of religion. Further it may even be urged that history shows that religion is not the guardian of morality; on the contrary, it has been declared that religion is a demoralising force in the world, and that consequently the strongest of existing religions is destined to follow other extinct faiths to the dim shades of death, leaving its place to be taken by the growing conscience of mankind.

There are, in a view of this kind, two points. First, religion, it is said, is needless, because we have a fitting and dependable substitute for it; secondly, religion is a demoralising force in the world. Our business is to consider these two points, and it may be convenient to take the latter first, and that for a simple reason: If the latter be true, it becomes needless to discuss the former, for that which is demoralising may fairly be considered to be needless. It has indeed been maintained that the question of morality must not be allowed to settle the value of religion; because religion professes to deal with something which is higher than morality, and therefore the necessity for religion might exist, even although it could not be claimed as a moral factor in the world. There is an element of truth in the theory; this will be seen later; but for the present, we may admit that the ultimate test of religion is ethical efficiency. Far higher—if I do not misread the signs of the times and the moods of men's thoughts—far higher than the question of miracle or prophecy, lies that other question of the ethical force at work in the world; and if it can be shown that religion is a demoralising influence, the question is ended, and there is no need to ask whether it is necessary or not. But is religion a demoralising force? There are some who reply that it is. You have only, they say, to look back upon history to see cowering under the shelter of religion, great crimes, blind ferocity, fierce fanaticism. The so-called " ages of faith " were ages without mercy, without morality. Further, it has been said that not in its history alone, but in its very principles religion is demoralising. Religion, it has been urged, prefers orthodoxy to morality, lays more stress upon sentiment than upon conduct, and bids men secure heaven rather than do their duty upon earth. It teaches men, therefore, to be eager about eternity but careless about the present, and to withdraw from the world forces which might have been used there for the welfare of mankind; and thus religion, by misdirecting the energies of human nature, proves itself injurious to the moral development of mankind.

We shall first take up the historical aspect of the question. In dealing with this my answer is twofold. First, the fact is not altogether as it has been stated, and, secondly, the true interpretation of the fact is different from that which has been advanced.

I.—The unqualified statement, that the influence of religion is demoralising, is not verifiable in fact. The statement, if it means anything, means this, that all religions have been demoralising forces. Facts, it is said, support this. Look at the massacres of so-called heretics and unbelievers, the tortures which have been inflicted on the pioneers of progress in the name of religion, the tyrannies which have been permitted, the immoralities which have darkened even Christian countries. And men are disposed to quote with approval the old indictment which has been made against religion by Lucretius,[1] and to exclaim against the flagrancy of the wrongs which it has impelled men to perpetrate.

[1] De Rerum Nat., i., 102.

(i.) It is well for us to consider the real aspect of these facts. The truth is, the influences exerted by religions are neither wholly good nor wholly bad. It is easy to show religions whose influences have been evil, and religions whose influences have been good. If on the one side we cannot forget how religions have degraded the thoughts and affections of men, if there dwell in our minds the car of Juggernaut, the terrible hecatombs of the Mexican religion, the fires of Smithfield, the massacre of St. Bartholomew, and the tortures of the Inquisition, we can on the other side speak of the earnest sighing after righteousness of men like Zoroaster,[1] of the chivalry and heroism which have beautified Christian lives, of the devotion of Elizabeth of Hungary, of the heroic self-sacrifice of the monk Telemachus in the Coliseum, in our own day of Father Damien among the lepers, and of the myriad stories of those who in every age and every clime under the banner of the Cross have shown themselves to be the true servants of humanity.

Taking all such facts into account we are perfectly prepared to answer, that the true, sensible, and reasonable statement of the case is this, that the influences of religions cannot be reasonably said to be either wholly bad or yet wholly good;

[1] See Note 28, in Appendix.

they produce mixed results. This is the judgment of those who have impartially studied the question. Réville says: "Morality has suffered from religion; it has also enormously gained." " Sometimes morality is in advance of religion, sometimes the reverse."[1] Hallam says :— " Beyond every doubt, the evils of superstition in the middle ages, though separately considered very serious, are not to be weighed against the benefits of the religion with which they were so mingled."[2] So, too, M. Renan, speaking of the ages of faith, says of Christianity, that "It evolved order, hierarchy, authority, obedience from the voluntary subjection of wills: it organized the crowd; it disciplined anarchy. What effected this miracle, which astonishes us quite otherwise than pretended infringements of the laws of physical nature? It was the Spirit of Jesus, strongly grafted into His disciples; the spirit of sweetness, of self-abnegation, of forgetfulness of the present; that unique pursuit of inward joys which kills ambition; that preference boldly given to childhood; those words perpetually repeated as from the lips of Jesus, 'And whosoever will be chief among you, let him be your servant.' (St. Matt. xx. 27.)"[3]

[1] "Prolegomena," pp. 64, 84.
[2] "Middle Ages," vol. iii., chap. ix., part i., note (1848.)
[3] "Hibbert Lectures," p. 159.

Even prejudiced writers are ready to admit the same. One who has touched with a very partial and partisan hand on the ages of faith, frankly acknowledges that to Christianity must be ascribed one supreme achievement—an unequalled power of cultivating saintliness of character.[1] But to grant that any religion is capable of creating saints is to grant that religion is a power for good. It is a power for good, for we must measure a man's life by his capacity for influencing others. The moral and intellectual worlds are, like the world physical, worlds of plains and valleys and hills; and the power of filling the valleys with water comes ever from the heights. When men eminent in intellect rise high above their fellows, they become the water-sheds, so to speak, of intellectual culture; when men become great in saintship, they pour forth energies which, like the waters which run among the hills, flow down to baptise and invigorate the world. There is a power in saintship which, as an influence for good, would go far to compensate the seeming evil which has flowed from many a creed. Hence the fact is, and I claim for the moment no more than this, that the results of the religious influences in the world are mixed results.

[1] J. Cotter Morison, "The Service of Man," p. 197.

It is not a fact that they are an unmitigated evil, but it is a fact that the results are partially good and partially bad.

(ii.) The true interpretation of this fact may be perfectly consistent with the view that religion is a moralizing factor; or, in other words, before we blame religion for those immoralities which the history of religions displays, it is fair to ask whether they may not be due to some other cause. There is, surely, some reasonableness in this suggestion.

1. When more causes than one are at work, to attribute the effect to one of them exclusively, without further investigation, is confessedly illogical. The case may be found mirrored in the language of a domestic quarrel, wherein you find the father and mother in absolute antagonism to each other upon the origin of the passionate nature of their child, and each says to the other, "This is the fault of that terrible temper which you know belongs to *your* family." It is surely not the way to deal with a result like this, to say that it is solely due to one cause. If C is the resultant of A and B, the evil in C may be due to A or B, or to the combination of both.

The laws of growth illustrate the same truth; when the farmer looks upon his harvest and finds it faulty or scant, he knows that the defect may be due either to the quality of the seed or the quality of the soil, or to some incongruity between them. So it is with the moral facts of which we have been speaking. If religion can be illustrated by the seed, humanity is the soil, and the results which have been spoken of may be due to religion which is the seed, or to humanity which is the soil, or to a combination of both.

2. We may examine in this case the soil—that is, humanity. No seed of thought or action sown here is sown in a virgin soil. Beneath the surface are latent seeds, the energies, the ideas, the thoughts, the feelings, the prejudices and the hopes of past ages. Other seed has been sown there in times gone by. Other harvests have been reaped from the field, and seeds which have failed to fructify hitherto, may, when the warmth of the new day begins to be felt, spring up and mingle with the new seed which has been sown. The poppies will be mingled with the corn; the tares with the wheat. There are customs existing among civilized, intelligent, and Christian people which are only the relics of a once vigorous Paganism. We hang up mistletoe at Christmas, and we forget we are only carrying out a Druidical ceremony. We toss our pancakes on Shrove Tuesday; but we do not mean to sacrifice to heathen gods, and yet we are following a Pagan

custom. The very days of the week may remind us that we derive, as it were, a substratum of ideas from other religions than that of Christianity. So true is it, as Renan says, "that almost all our superstitions are the remains of a religion anterior to Christianity, and which Christianity has not been able entirely to root out."[1] The new growth in any field cannot free itself from contact with earlier sowings. The soil itself is charged with energy, and in it linger seeds which may spring up with power; and to argue that the harvest is the result of the new-sown seed is to show yourself deficient in historical instinct.

3. But again, the soil is not merely the human nature of yesterday, it is also the living humanity of a particular age. Every new movement deals with a humanity which is a living aggregate. We speak sometimes of humanity as if it were a dead thing, and forget that it is possessed of personal force, will, passions, prejudices, and strong powers of self-assertion. When a truth is sown among men and women who have passions and wills of their own, its task is not light and easy; its results cannot be calculated with that certainty which belongs to things material. When the chemist goes into the laboratory, the elements with which he deals

[1] "Hibbert Lectures," p. 32. See Appendix, Note 29.

are passive ; but the reformer and the religious teacher encounter elements which are by no means passive. Every one of the beings, amongst whom his work is cast, has life, is moved by feeling, is stirred by prejudices, is capable of strong and passionate resistance. The temperance reformer has to contend with the passion of self-indulgence, the man who preaches greater activity has to contend with natural apathy, the philanthropist has to fight against the selfishness of the world; and if religion bids men sell what they have and give to the poor, she finds that the selfish heart of the hearer takes up arms against her. If she preach the Cross, she finds that the flesh shrinks from it. If she bid men gird up their loins and live like men, she finds that the spirit of slumber is strong among them. It is to be remembered that resistance to religious teaching is always possible. It is calmly said in the nineteenth century—for notwithstanding our boasted knowledge, we are sometimes ignorant of theology—it is calmly said in the nineteenth century, "The latter [*i.e.*, grace in contrast with evolution], as emanating from Almighty power, can no more be arrested or withstood by imperfect development in the race, than by moral degradation in the individual. At least, that is the theory."[1] I do not know—

[1] J. Cotter Morison, "The Service of Man," chap. vi., p. 147.

there may have been sects and small bodies of men who have held such a theory as that,—but I never knew any reasonable Christian who held it. Jesus Christ did not hold it, for He taught in His parable of the sower, that men could receive or reject the good seed sown; and that the world was free to be saved or to perish, when He left that great unanswered question—" When the Son of Man cometh shall He find faith on the earth?"[1] Certainly the followers of Jesus Christ never held it, for there is St. Stephen's indictment against men, "Ye do always resist the Holy Ghost."[2] Certainly St. Paul never held it, for he warned men lest they should "quench the Spirit."[3] And even if religion desired to hold it, I venture to say that she could not do so without suicide, for the idea of coercive grace is destructive of faith. Where would be the glory of any creed which was able to sweep away a man's convictions like a whirlwind that sweeps the surface of the earth, and which called that conversion which is only desolation? The destruction of individual will, the denial of the power of man to resist his Maker, is the negation of the possibility of religion. Therefore, when you are dealing with the souls of

[1] St. Luke xviii. 8.   [2] Acts vii. 51.
[3] 1 Thess. v. 19.

men you are no longer dealing with passive and obedient material; you have to reckon with caprice, passion, self-will; and it becomes unreasonable and unfair to charge the immoralities noticeable in religious history wholly upon the influence of religion.

Again, it is unfair to charge the inconsistency of the professors of religion on religion itself. No impartial man would declare that Islamism permitted intemperance, because he observed drunken Turks in the streets of Constantinople. It would be unfair to say of any Eastern creed that it sanctioned cruelty to the brute creation, because some Orientals were found ill-treating animals. No person would charge science or medicine with intolerance, because the Royal College of Physicians once excommunicated Dr. Geynes for impugning the infallibility of Galen.[1] So also, when we hear of the immoralities which have darkened and disfigured the history of Christianity, we should not, because men "lived like Pagans and believed like Christians," charge this looseness of living upon the religion which they professed. We shall rather adopt the impartial tone of Rousseau, and say that this contradiction between profession and practice does

[1] *Cf.* Dr. Munk's "Roll of the Royal College of Physicians," 1878, vol. i., p. 62.

not "prove that religion is superfluous, but that very few people are religious."[1] Or, we shall say, with Montesquieu, the assertion that religion is useless because religious people have been wicked, is about as absurd as to say that law is useless because it is sometimes broken.[2] Religion must reckon with the passions, the appetites, and the covetousness of man. The condition of the soil is not wholly favourable to the life of the seed. The harvests of which we complain may spring from the weakness and wickedness of men, and not from the worthlessness of religion.

But, further, if religion suffers from the influence of past superstitions and present passions, it suffers also from the faults of those who teach it. The best religion is not always administered by those who are infallible in judgment or in morals. We admit that religion has often been laid open to ridicule by those who have misinterpreted its meaning, misused its power, and distorted its doctrines. But as it would be unfair to judge science by the weakness of its exponents, so is it unfair to judge religion by the weakness, intel-

[1] Emile, tom. iii., 199, quoted by Croslegh, "Christianity judged by its Fruits," p. 140.
[2] Esprit des Lois xxiv., p. 2. Ibid., p. 137.

lectual or otherwise, of religious teachers. The treasure is always in the earthen vessel. The light is enclosed within a lamp, and the beams which shine upon our faces are not always pure light, but light changed, perhaps partially absorbed, by the medium through which it passes. "Religious ideas," says George Eliot, "have the fate of melodies, which, once set afloat in the world are taken up by all sorts of instruments, some of them woefully coarse, feeble, or out of tune, until people are in danger of crying out that the melody itself is detestable."[1] But the original music is beautiful as ever. Nothing can mar its glory; yet, when we heard the song from the lips of the costermonger, or produced with the nasal twang of the street singer, we were ready to denounce it as execrable. This really means that we recognise how cruel a thing it is, that what is noble should be debased by false or feeble interpretation.

The historical aspect, then, of the question is this: it is not true that religions act wholly as demoralising forces. The results vary, and the variety of the results may be due to the quality of the soil into which the seed has been cast.

II.—But the second accusation is that the essential principles of religion are hostile to

[1] "Janet's Repentance."

morality. If this be so, then, although the result may be partly due to the passions of men, yet religion herself cannot be wholly exonerated from blame. Our question, therefore, at present is this: Are the *principles* of religion thus hostile to morality?

(i.) 1. It is well nigh ludicrous to ask such a question when we consider the ambiguousness of the word Religion. Religions are as various as philosophies, and some, in their principles, are moral, some immoral, some neutral. Réville writes: "As we rise in the religious scale the relation between morality and religion comes into operation." "Religion," he says, "desires to realise the synthesis of the human spirit, and of the superior spirit whose existence and sovereignty man believes that he discerns in the world."[1] There is nothing intrinsically and specially moral in this. In seeking it, religion might use means which morality rejects. Every religion must be tested by its principles.

2. Further, there is a thing which is found near religion, but which must not be confounded with religion. There is a great shadow which follows every movement in the world, and troubles it. Such a shadow waits upon religion; I shall venture to call it religionism. It is an

[1] "Prolegomena," pp. 95, 201. See Introd., p. xliv.

absolute foe of all morality, and of all true religions. It is to religion. what charlatanism is to science. Its source is not difficult to seek. There is a strong wish, amongst men of a certain type, to avoid the difficulties of existence and the labour which belongs to it; to win without conflict; to get credit for learning without burning the midnight oil; to gain the prizes of life without the strenuous labour which merits them; to grasp the crown without the lawful striving. Such men are to be found, and doubtless we have felt the temptation ourselves. We love the applause, we scarcely love the needful toil. We love the prize, we shirk the examination, and we feel how true it is, that we all desire to produce results by short and labour-saving methods. Mr. Ruskin speaks of giving the angels barrel-organs to make their music easier. There are some, who are not angels, who would be willing to turn the handle all their life long, if only the world would take them for musicians. In every walk of life this spirit appears. Medicine is followed by quackery as its shadow, art by trickery which strives to produce effects by an imposing arrangement of curtains, screens and lights. The great speculators, who make haste to grow rich, are examples of the way in which men seek to reap harvests before they have borne the burden and heat of the day. Learning has had its shadow; the pedant is the parody of the scholar. We are not surprised that a temper, which is thus universal, should show itself in religion. Religionism is the shadow of religion. It makes itself a home in all religions, in Buddhism, in Islamism, Judaism, and Christianity: its effect is to *de-ethicize* religion.

In some religions it early shows itself, for they are little better than religionisms at the outset. In others, affinity of temperament makes its development easy, for they have already a predisposition towards religionism. An example of this is supplied in the old religion of Latium. Prayer was a magic formula producing effect without reference to the moral disposition of the man who prayed. In worship, "the exact observance of the rites compels the Deity, who, if the petition be presented in proper form, has no inquiry to make into piety or the feelings of the heart." This is witnessed by M. Renan.[1] Eastern religions show the same spirit. Buddhism in its earliest and purest form tried to shake itself free from ritual, but in later Buddhism we find the prayer-wheel, *i.e.*, a kind of mechanical method of winning the result, which, under the nobler conception, could only come to those who

[1] "Hibbert Lectures," p. 13. See Appendix, Note 30.

were morally fit for it. In Islamism, the pilgrimage to Mecca is supposed to produce high privileges and almost magical results. Zoroaster cried out for righteousness, and yearned to see in nature symbols of the highest truth; but the degraded forms of Sun-worship and Fire-worship were those shadows of his teaching, which took the outside of the thing for the whole. In Judaism the same spirit is seen. When Moses lifted up the serpent in the wilderness, a great power of healing went forth to the people. The serpent on the pole expressed the fact, that there was a power to heal greater than the power which smote, and man's faith grew strong and the deadly wounds lost their power. In later ages it became the intrument of sheer charlatanism. The brazen serpent was worshipped, incense was burnt to it, it was a symbol no more; it was a fetish. In the same way, in the earlier times, the ark was the sign of the Divine presence; but in a more degenerate age the cry was "Let us fetch the ark, that it may save us."[1] Rather than purify their own lives and reform their own habits and realise God once more in their midst, they thought that by some mechanical expedient they might gain the victory, without having

[1] 1 Samuel iv. 3.

the moral courage to produce within themselves the true means of success. Christianity in its history shows examples also. There the worship of system took the place of reverence for Christianity. Men grew more anxious to gain adherents to the system, than converts to its spirit. They were content with submission without conviction. Multitudes were driven wholesale into the Dneiper for baptism at the sword's point. The spirit of the bigot and the charlatan was abroad. In a later period there were missionaries who used in worship heathen idols to which they had given Christian names.[1] Their action was like that of the man who takes a novel of Zola's, binds it, and backs it with the title "Moral Philosophy." He has changed the cover, but not the book; it is easy to alter names; it is difficult to change characters. An indolent religion is content with superficial results, but thereby it betrays a spirit of religionism and not of true religion. This is that spirit which turns everything high and sacred into a fetish. There are people who treat their Bible as a fetish. They read their chapter, as they call it, they care not to understand it, nor to perceive its truths. There are others who make the Holy Communion a fetish. They attend or

[1] See Appendix, Note 31.

assist at a celebration as if it were a charm, but they fail to repent and reform their lives. The same spirit is seen when the Christian ministry is degraded to the level of a priestcraft; when the hysterical cries of excited and not over-responsible people are accepted as evidence of a deep religious change; when the easy utterance of a few stereotyped phrases is allowed to pass instead of the noble argument of a regenerated life; when apathetic and mindless attendance at certain ceremonial acts is permitted to stand as a substitute for conviction of spirit and reformation of morals; when the Church is venerated and her work neglected; when the machinery is everything and the fabric nothing; when the great end of all religious systems is forgotten in the eagerness to preserve some unimportant details of imaginary orthodoxy. Wherever this spirit shows itself, there we find that shadow of religion which I call religionism; and wherever this shadow exists, there we are prepared to admit that the tendency of the religion thus debased is towards demoralization. It matters not with what high and holy truths the teacher may have been entrusted, if he become religionistic, and is not anxious for the moral elevation of his hearers, he confuses the issue and lowers the aim of his religion; he insensibly and unconsciously degrades the moral tone of the people amongst whom he ministers.

Religionism then is demoralising, but religion is not necessarily so. The religionistic spirit lowers the moral tone; and one of the safeguards of the moral influence of a religion is to be found in its freedom from the religionistic spirit.

(ii.) 1. Genuine Christianity has no affinity with this demoralising spirit. In essence it is antagonistic to it. Our Lord's teaching was in contrast with the religionistic teaching of His age. The religionistic spirit spoke on this wise: "It is expedient for one man to die,"[1] *i.e.*, we must preserve our system by the sacrifice, if need be, of an innocent life. Or, "let us call down fire from heaven,"[2] *i.e.*, let us destroy those who withstand our teaching and our progress. Men actuated by this spirit vainly thought that they did God service. In contrast is the language of Christ. He will hear of no unrighteous counsels of expediency. He says, "Why even of yourselves judge ye not what is right?" (St. Luke xii. 57.) To those who would call down fire from heaven He says, "Ye know not what manner of spirit ye are of." (St. Luke ix. 55.) Upon His followers He enjoined the duty of leaving

---

[1] St. John xviii. 14. [2] St. Luke ix. 5.

unmolested those who did not receive the faith; they were to leave unharmed the tares which, alas, were mixed amongst the wheat; they were to show kindness to the unthankful and unholy, and to exercise gentleness and benevolence even towards those who persecuted them. He insisted upon right actions, and refused the easy substitutes of sentiment and profession. A man's religion must be, doing, not hearing only, if it is to be founded on a rock. The Apostles taught in the same strain. Circumcision was nothing. The man whose character was moulded by the power of religion, and whose life was purified by it, was the man of true religion. St. Paul believed in the faith which worked by love. St. James would recognize no faith that did not show itself in action. St. John taught that only the love which showed itself in loving thought, in loving word, and in loving deed, could guarantee the reality of religion. Impartial witnesses attest this truth. "Christianity," says Réville, "derives its chief strength from the beauty of its morality."[1] Similarly Mr. Lecky writes: "Unlike all Pagan religions, Christianity made moral teaching the main function of its clergy, moral discipline the leading object of its services, moral dispositions

[1] See "Prolegomena," p. 84.

the necessary condition of the due performance of its rites." [1]

The history of Christianity attests the same. Ambrose withstanding Theodosius, because his hands were stained with blood, Chrysostom preaching at Constantinople, bore witness to the truth of that sacred utterance, "If I regard iniquity in my heart, the Lord will not hear me." (Ps. lxvi. 18.)

2. (a) We can now meet the three accusations of which we have spoken. Orthodoxy, it is said, is preferred to morality. True, the religionist prefers it. Orthodoxy and ceremonial are put by him above the Religion of Life. But Christianity, the Christianity of Christ, reverses the order. "I was an hungred," said Christ, "and ye gave Me meat; thirsty, and ye gave Me drink." (St. Matt. xxv. 35.) And when He speaks of these actions of love, those to whom He speaks are surprised. These men might not have been orthodox, intellectually or ceremonially, but the orthodoxy of their lives is clear, and it is that which Christ honours. Right thinking is indeed of importance to men, as we have shown in dealing with that law of man's spiritual nature, "As we think, we are." To believe rightly, to believe

[1] Lecky, "Hist. Morals," vol. ii., p. 2. See App. Note 32.

that life is governed by love and not by evil, to believe that we are not alone in our struggles or left to despair, but that there is a power to help men towards a righteous and loving life, is essential to a true Christian feeling. Rightly used it is a help and not a hindrance to morality; but in the view of our Lord no orthodoxy will atone for the lack of the spirit of obedience and love.

(b) The second accusation is that religion prefers sentiment to conduct. The religionist may do so, but Christianity does not. Here the words of Christ are again familiar. He warns men of the folly of crying out, "Lord, Lord," if they do not the things which He commands. (St. Matt. vii. 21.) "If ye love Me, keep My commandments." (St. John xiv. 15.) But whilst Christianity says that sentiment must not be preferred to conduct, Christianity itself insists upon sentiment, *i.e.*, upon the truth that religion must have root in the feelings of man. Christianity is justified in this. A true feeling of attachment, and a loyal sentiment towards morals are essential to true morality. But while Christianity insists on this truth, she no less discountenances the notion that feeling or sentiment can be an adequate substitute for obedience.

(c) The third accusation is that religion withdraws energy from the life of the world. Under its influence it is said men become ascetics, and forget to be patriots. Mr. Lecky has said that Christianity withdrew energy from the world because it was deficient in civic virtues.[1] The answer shall be given by M. Renan. Speaking of Christianity, he claims its universality as "one of the causes of the greatness of the new religion. Humanity is a many-sided, changeful thing, urged this way or that by opposing desires. Country is great, and holy are the heroes of Marathon and Thermopylæ. But, nevertheless, country is not everything here below. We are men and sons of God, before we are Frenchmen or Germans. The kingdom of God—that eternal dream which will never be torn from the heart of man—is the protest against all that in patriotism is too exclusive. The organization of humanity, with a view to its moral improvement and its highest happiness, is a legitimate idea. But the State understands, and can understand, only the organization of egotism. . . . . But it is not

[1] "Ascetic Christianity decisively diverted moral enthusiasm into another channel, and the civic virtues, in consequence, necessarily declined." "Patriotism itself, as a duty, has never found any place in Christian ethics, and strong theological feeling has usually been directly hostile to its growth."—"History of European Morals," vol. ii., pp. 142, 145.

enough. . . . To him who belongs to a great race, self-devotion is as natural as egotism, and religion is the organization of self-devotion." [1]

Christianity was not wholly oblivious of the considerations of patriotism, but its arms embraced men of every nation; the brotherhood to which it looked forward was not the limited brotherhood of any one race, but that of the world of redeemed humanity. But I am not afraid to admit the indictment. If it be an indictment against Christianity, that she weakened national feeling because she yearned for universal brotherhood—I plead guilty to it, and if the nineteenth century will not find herein a triumphant vindication of Christianity, I have done—I can say no more.

A similar indictment is made when it is said that on principle Christians prefer the unseen to the seen. It is as if men, so thinks a modern writer, were so much attracted with the thought of the distant land to which they are going, that they are perfectly heedless of the preparation for the voyage which is to take them there.[2] The illustration may be answered by another. The keen realisation of the unseen, so far from rendering a man regardless of the

[1] "Hibbert Lectures," p. 30.
[2] See J. Cotter Morison, "The Service of Man," pp. 90, 91.

things seen, intensifies his view of their importance. The recognition of larger purposes gives force to present opportunities. The general who surveys the country through which he is to lead his army in battle, will mark the outline of its hills, the length of its roads, the undulations of its valleys, with keener eyes than the mere holiday traveller, because he has an end in view which is unseen by the ordinary world. In the same way the man who sees beyond the things present, who believes that all things move forward to some far-off end, will measure at their true value the significance and importance of apparently insignificant things below. He sees the temporal glorified in the light of the eternal.

(iii.) But, further, there is a spirit in Christianity which consecrates life, and which makes men see, if they will, that everything is holy. There is a narrow Christianism which does not realise the sanctity of all life, and which can only see good when it can be uttered in religious phrase. But the Christianity of Christ is higher and deeper than this. The Christianity of Christ says it matters not how insignificant man's occupation may be, if only it be righteous, and helpful to others. The difference lies not in what men do, but in the spirit in which they do it. The sculptor or the poet, the statesmen, the lawyer or the writer, may carry on the work of God as well as the priest or the preacher. All life is claimed by Christ, and every vocation in His esteem is great and worthy.

We maintain, then, that Christianity is in the highest degree an ethical religion. Its morality goes deep; it sinks beneath the surface and asks for the heart; it claims man's conduct; it demands that his sentiments should be pure, and his actions truthful. Its morality is deep and strong. Its orthodoxy is its highest morality; for its orthodoxy is a desire to be like God, and to realize that the aim of our life is to grow like unto our Father which is in Heaven.

Our conclusion on the whole is this. It is a fact that the influences of religions, speaking generally, are mixed. This arises partly from defects in the soil of human nature, which do not give religion fair play, and partly from the imperfection and feebleness of the religions themselves, which lay them open to that disease which afflicts all religions, even the best, and which I have called religionism. But as regards Christianity, there is nothing demoralising in its principles. Christianity is a fact in the world, and she affirms that morality is not a mere passing shadow having relation only to the conditions of this world, but something which has a corresponding reality in the eternal world. She tells us, that beyond the morality which we see, there is an eternal righteousness. She teaches us to look deep, and see the spirit within the form, the soul within the body of things. It is as when one looks into the face of a great leader either of science or of letters. We marvel at its force, and are conscious of its fascination. The physiognomist tells us that the breadth of the forehead, the prominence of the brow, and the keenness of the eyes, mean qualities of intellectual power and cultivated habits of observation. He reads in chin and lip perseverance and the power to endure. But others look at the same face and read deeper. They see the human history there. They read in that brow not merely intellectual strength, not merely indomitable energy, but the tragic story of a soul which in its pursuit of knowledge would not make its judgment blind, but was content to bear all the taunts of men rather than forego what it believed to be true. In that compressed lip they read of the soul that can suffer, and also of the heart that can love; behind the outward they read the inward man. We feel then, that behind the face which fascinates us there is the inward man, the true man, greater, more fascinating in the tragedy of his life, than even the outward man could express. In some such fashion religion points us to the principles and powers of which morality is but as the visible countenance; she affirms those eternal principles of which righteous conduct is but the expression; she says that behind the trite legalism of our morality there is an eternal righteousness and an eternal holiness. Where morality gives rules, religion points to principles; where morality speaks of duty, she speaks of the love of duty. Religion and morality are one in pointing out that there is a ladder from earth to heaven, and that it must be climbed; but while morality can see no more than the ladder, religion can see the angels on either hand. Morality can behold only the clouds into which the ladder goes, but religion can anoint our eyes to see that in the open heaven above its summit stands the Lord God Almighty.

LECTURE VI.

THE NECESSITY OF RELIGION.

Religion being natural to man, and having capacity as a moralizing factor, the question meets us—Is religion necessary? Is there, in other words, any adequate substitute for religion?

I.—Morality must be preserved.
  (i.) The indispensable elements of real morality.
  (ii.) The connexion of these elements with
    1. The laws of man's spiritual nature.
    2. The needed elements of religion.
  (iii.) Danger of moralism; the shadow of morality.

II.—Proposed substitutes for religion:
  (i.) Three considered as substitutes.
    1. Knowledge.
    2. Altruism.
    3. Drift of the world, or evolution of morals.
  (ii.) The defectiveness of scientific moralism in relation to
    1. The dark side of life.
    2. The unfit and the unfortunate.
    3. The deeper side of man's nature.
  (iii.) The indebtedness of social sentiment to religion.
    1. As a fact in history—Influence of religion.
    2. Ethically—the ideal set up.
    3. Sociologically.

Conclusion—Religion seems necessary to men.

LECTURE VI.

THE NECESSITY OF RELIGION.

"Hereafter ye shall see heaven open."—*St. John* i. 51.

THE result of our thoughts, thus far, is as follows. Religion is likely to survive, because religion is natural to man, and man's nature, as far as we can see, is permanent. Various religious ideas have grown up in the world; they have passed through vicissitudes; they have been modified by changes; but most persistently man has insisted on the presence of these elements— Dependence, Fellowship, Progress. Christianity alone has shown itself to possess all three elements, naturally and originally.

Christianity may on this account be reckoned as the flower of the religious idea. Judged therefore from a mere human standpoint, we should say that the chances of survival are on the side of Christianity. Whatever modifications of the religious idea are likely to occur in the future, Christianity embodies, in all probability, the conceptions out of which the religion of the future will grow.

But other questions press upon us. Religion may be natural, and the religious idea supplied in Christianity may be the most congenial to human nature, but it does not follow that religion is always needful to man or helpful to morality.

The charge that religion is demoralizing, we have seen to be one which needs to be put in another form, unless we wish to confuse ourselves with ambiguities. The statement is such that no student of the history of religion will for a moment consider it to be even rational. It has more rhetoric than reason in it, and may be justly suspected.

To-day this other question meets us: Is religion necessary? Can man do without it? It may be true that it is natural to man, but time and education combine together to make it possible for man to do without many things which were necessary for him in his earlier growth. Man outgrows the cradle and the nursery. To say that a thing is natural does not carry with it the presumption that it will be *always* necessary. But besides this, it is also suggested that there is something better in the world at present to supply its place. Religion may have been necessary in the earlier ages of man's history,

The Necessity of Religion.

but is it necessary now? Have we not acquired a knowledge of nature which enables us to dispense with the aid of religion in the future? Now, when we ask that question, it seems to involve yet another—Is there in the world an adequate substitute for religion? It is essential to our purpose to consider this; for unless there is a substitute, and an adequate substitute, we cannot say that religion is unnecessary.

I.—This, then, is our subject : " Is religion necessary?" On all sides it is allowed that what is wanted is a guide and influence which will call out all that is best in man, and be capable of forming the highest and truest type of character. For morality, in its widest and best sense, is the order of what is needed to constitute true character in man. It is not enough to provide a feeble moralism in lieu of a sturdy morality. The substitute for religion must be a force sufficient to educate completely and perfectly the human character.

(i.) For this end it must be able to develop the three elements which all agree are needful —conscience, intelligence and will. We must have the conscience to tell us that there is a right; the intelligence which enables us to perceive what is the right; and the will, that is the strength to resolve, " I must do this." In other words, a character is not perfect unless it is sensitive to right, clear in thought and firm in action. It may be well to cite some independent authorities in support of this triple analysis. Mr. John Freeman Clark tells us that what is needed is a sentiment of right and wrong, an idea of what is right, and the effort to achieve right.[1] M. Paul Janet describes the three things which are needful as " Good, duty, virtue."[2] The sentiment that there is a good is what is perceived by conscience; the idea of what is duty is grasped by the intelligence; and when the right is followed by a firm act of will there is virtue. Dr. Martineau says there is a distinct preference for the higher principle over the lower, which constitutes conscience.[3] And this seems to me to involve the three things of which we have spoken: firstly, the perception that there is a higher principle; secondly, the sense that we ought to be at one with that higher principle; and thirdly, the choice of it, which involves will.

(ii.) *a*. Now these three elements, which go towards the maintenance of the complete human character, correspond with the laws of man's spiritual nature. There must be affinity or sympathy of nature on our part with the thing which is higher, in order that we may perceive its loftiness. This

[1] " Self Culture," p. 195.   [2] " La Morale," p. 1.
[3] " Types of Ethical Theory," vol. ii., book ii., ch. ii., § 7 & 8.

is only another statement of the law that "as we are, we see." But, again, the mere sentiment that it is higher is not enough. There must be an intelligent recognition of it also. There is need of perception as well as sympathy, and this corresponds to the law—"as we think, we are." The third law is sacrifice, but every effort of will to carry out what we feel to be right is of the nature of a sacrifice. Every exercise of the will means a determination of victory over some hindrance or foe.

(*b*) It may be seen further that these three elements correspond with what we have been speaking of as the three needful elements of religion. For Dependence arises from the recognition of that which is higher (and in most cases better) than ourselves. Fellowship is the feeling which desires to be in accord with that high and righteous will. And, thirdly, Progress, which is impossible without effort, corresponds to the exertion of our will which, as we have seen, has the nature of a sacrifice. These three imply conscience, intelligence, and will. A true and perfect morality can never exist without these three elements. Briefly, then, what seems to be true is this : if morality is to be preserved, it must be in the frank recognition of all that morality involves. Man is only a perfectly moral being when he has

s

sympathy with goodness, intelligence to perceive his duty in regard to it, and will to achieve it. Sympathy with goodness is needed; for a series of moral actions done without moral sympathy does not make a man truly moral. But, again, a moral being must have thought: he must not only feel that there is a duty, but he must know wherein that duty lies. He must have, that is, not only an affection for right, but some intelligent comprehension of it. Possessed of a conscience, but not of thought, he would scarcely be able to play his part in the world in which right often depends upon the even balance of various considerations. And, again, he must have will, for if he be incapable of exerting a determining influence over his own actions, he can hardly be called a moral being. For if there be no power of choice, there can be no blame or praise.[1] These three things must be reckoned with by any substitute for Religion, for no system will be sufficient which does not recognise man in the completeness of his being.

(iii.) It is all the more important to notice this, seeing that there is in the realm of morality a shadow corresponding to that which we saw waiting on religion. This shadow we shall call Moralism.

Let me ask you to notice the difference between

[1] See Appendix, Note 33.

morality and its pale shadow. What we have first to examine is the case of an action, good externally, but not accompanied in its performance by any sympathetic appreciation of goodness. Let us suppose that the action in itself is good, and that the world looking upon that action merely on the outside, approves of it. Let us suppose that it has been achieved by the exercise of thought and will. Here, two conditions are fulfilled—the right is perceived and acted upon; but there is no inward sympathy with right as such. Such an action is moralistic rather than moral, for it has not been prompted by the sentiment of goodness. The sentiment of goodness, if I may translate it into other words, means that the inward feeling is in sympathy with the moral object pursued. Hence a man may pursue an object with outward energy all his life, while goodness has never dwelt in his heart as a welcome guest. His actions may win wide approval and applause. He may give a large contribution to a charity, but it does not necessarily follow that he has any of the sentiment of goodness which seems to be indicated by his liberality. There may be other motives at work. He may know that his munificence will come under the notice of royalty, and that some reward or distinction may follow. The world applauds the action, but in its heart condemns the man. Far differently the world judges of an action like that of Casabianca. Whatever may be our opinion of his wisdom, we feel that he was heroic. We render him a homage of sympathy and approval which we refuse to the self-seeking person who serves his own ends under the cloak of charity. Thus, where inward sympathy with good is lacking, though there may be outward moralism, there can be no true morality.

Again, an act may be wrong and the motive right, yet it may be an act of moralism rather than morality. A high end may be sought, there may be even an enthusiastic desire to maintain what is good, yet the action may merit condemnation because evil in its method. A man may feel an impulse to good, yet he may display unscrupulousness in his mode of promoting the good. Care to do no wrong when seeking to do right is essential to the highest right. No action is perfectly moral that does not show self-control as well as self-exertion; and no man can safely act on the impulse of even the highest sentiment without the safeguard of moral judgment. When, through attachment to a cause which, in their consciences, they believe to be high and good, men are prepared to employ unworthy or impure means, their good motive does not excuse them.

Their conduct is not the conduct of pure morality. There is nothing which tends more rapidly to demoralise a man's character than the determination to defend a cause which he believes to be right, by means which he knows to be wrong. To do this is to play the game of life, but not by the laws of life. It is taking unlawful power into our own hands; the higher morality would say, "Do right, and leave the rest." Virginius had a high motive when he plunged the dagger into his daughter's heart. Charlotte Corday was impelled by a generous impulse when she struck the tyrant in his bath. Simon Peter might have pleaded a good and chivalrous purpose when he drew his sword against the servant of the high priest. But perfect morality tells those who wish to work right by ways that are not right, that they have missed the meaning of right. There is another and a better path to take. "Put up thy sword into the sheath," is the language of the highest and the best. Unrighteous weapons are not needed in a righteous cause. To do evil that good may come, merits a damnation which is just and right. The shadow takes the place of the reality; and moralism overthrows morality when men sacrifice right means on the imaginary altar of right motives.

Thirdly, moralism exists where there is a

want of a co-operating will. The subjective merit of actions is to be measured by the effort of will required to accomplish them. Some men are born with an aptitude for virtue. Moral actions are more difficult to some men than to others. The merit of the action, therefore, is not to be measured so much by the action itself, as by the effort which the man makes in order to perform it. Submission is easy to the docile, hard to the impatient. There is more merit, therefore, in the patience of the eager man than there is in that of the naturally submissive. This may explain how it is that morals may be high while virtue is low. For if men live amid surroundings of high morality and up to the level of those surroundings, their moral life is high, but virtue, that is, the energy and effort of will, is not greatly taxed. It is the remembrance of this which determines our interest in certain characters. We see no difficulty when a man like Richard III. acts strongly and firmly. But the spectacle of Hamlet believing that he ought to do a strong and terrible thing, yet conscious that he is infirm of purpose and feeble in will, fills us with measureless pity. We see that there would be merit in the strong self-exertion of a Hamlet, while the same action would be meritless, because effortless, to a Richard. It has been said that the grace which would be sufficient to make St. John a saint would hardly do more than keep St. Peter from knocking a man down. In other words, self-restraint in St. Peter would be a greater virtue than in St. John; and hence, if it could be shown that a man had inherited all the best moral qualities, he yet might be a man of less vigorous morality than one, who with corresponding disadvantages, was deliberately and consciously striving after right. True morality, then, demands the exercise of will, the exercise of judgment, the exercise of sympathy. Without these, morality dwindles into moralism. Deficient in will, it has no virtue; deficient in self-controlling judgment, it is passionate; deficient in sympathy, it is hypocrisy. This will explain what we mean by moralism.

All are agreed that morality must be preserved; but what is wanted is not moralism but morality. In other words, the character of man as a moral being must be nourished, and this, in the three particulars of which we have spoken. Any substitute for religion will be found inadequate which does not recognise sentiment, intelligence and will.

II. (i.) We are now in a position to examine the proposed substitutes for religion. These may be arranged under three heads—the power of Knowledge, the sentiment of Altruism, and what we may call the Drift of the world.

1. First, let us take Knowledge. Science, it is said, will adequately safeguard morality. We must ask what this means. It cannot mean that science, which is only organised knowledge, is capable of guarding morality. Some men tell us that our theology is incapable of guarding our morals, and theology which is only the organised knowledge of religion, is in this sense of the nature of a science. All the Apostles taught that, in this sense, theology could not preserve morals. There is an unquestionable value in organised knowledge; it helps us to perceive more clearly what our duty is by making what we know more readily applicable to the details of conduct.

But the argument goes far beyond this. It is claimed that the diffusion of knowledge will enable us to live more truly moral lives, that is to say, that all the mistakes of the past have been due to ignorance; and the theory is urged in one celebrated book, that the progress of the world is due solely to knowledge.[1] I am perfectly prepared to grant—and I do not suppose any one who studies the moral history of man with an impartial mind will do otherwise than admit

[1] Buckle, " Civilization," see Appendix, Note 34.

—that to the progress of knowledge we owe clearer conceptions of what our duty is. For instance, we have gained a knowledge of sanitary matters; we know now what our duty is. If the citizens of a great town allow the sanitary conditions to remain imperfect, there is blame to them, because knowledge is within reach. Or again; we have learned, through political economy, that indiscriminate charity does more harm than good, and hence we have had impressed on us the knowledge of our duty to exercise inquiry and wise judgment before we follow the impulse of our charity. All this is true, but while knowledge has given us information concerning what our duty is, it has not in the least altered the original principle of duty. Take the case of a landlord who has upon his estate cottages which are not fit for human beings to live in. Their condition is absolutely at variance with the laws of health. That man, indeed, is bound now by the possession of knowledge to put them into a sanitary condition. But why is he bound to do so? Because there is a principle anterior to that of knowledge to which he owes allegiance, and that principle is the duty of caring for his brother man. But the knowledge of the sanitary condition of the houses did not create his duty towards his brother man. The old Baron, who knew nothing whatever about sanitary laws, was just as much bound to do his duty according to his light as the landlord of to-day. Knowledge does not create the obligation of duty, though it does create sometimes a knowledge of what our duty is in particular cases; it helps our powers of judgment, and in that degree it may extend the field of duty. It is the same with regard to charity. The political economist tells us that indiscriminate charity is bad. We are ready to concede it; but the new knowledge that it is so does not alter one whit the great original principle which, in the conscience of man, tells him to be kind to his fellow-man. When our ancestors gave their alms to the beggar or the cripple on the road, they were following the instincts of their conscience to do good, just as much as the man who now goes to the proper authorities and institutes an inquiry. It is perfectly true that this latter man is wiser than the former; but he is no better man for that. Good and bad, better and worse, turn not so much upon the knowledge, but upon the original motive by which a man determines his actions, and increasing knowledge can only give us clearer ideas of the most effectual way of doing our duty. It cannot give us any new principle of duty. Knowledge thrusts upon us responsibilities, because it increases our opportunities of duty; but no knowledge, under heaven or beneath the earth, has created our sense of duty. It cannot create that sympathy with goodness without which the best moral actions are but pale moralisms. Hence, knowledge standing alone cannot afford an adequate substitute for religion.

2. The second substitute for religion is the theory of Altruism—the theory, that is, that men's actions may be governed by the sentiment which desires to serve humanity. There is truth and glory in this. Here we get something of the sympathy with goodness, which was lacking under the guidance of mere knowledge. Here is something deeper and higher than the theory that the diffusion of knowledge will protect morality. It is higher because it does set up an ideal of life for men to aim at. It is deeper because it seeks to move the heart and waken the sympathies of men. But can it be accepted as a substitute for religion? First, it is doubtful whether this Altruistic sentiment is strong enough for the task. The egotistic or selfish tendencies are strong and real; their strength is admitted by those who have no great sympathy with religion. "As a general rule," says Büchner, "these principles" (that is, philanthropic ones) "only make them-

selves felt where the good or the interest of the individual as such is not in question, whilst, wherever this is the case, social egotism has no bounds, and recoils before no deeds."[1] In the same way Comte admits that active life is essentially egoistic, and sympathy only possessed of feeble energy.[2] It will thus be seen that there is a doubt whether the Altruistic sentiment is alone strong enough to hold its own against the selfish impulses of men. But, further, supposing that the Altruistic sentiment superseded the selfish, yet it will not secure morality, for the ultimate force to which it appeals is public opinion. And public opinion, though it is a great power, is not a moral power, as Dr. Martineau has reminded us.[3] The principle of Altruism will, no doubt, win its way in the world; in the future it will be universally recognised. The happy days for which the poet has yearned, and for which faith has laboured, will assuredly come. Though we may doubt with the doubt that is born of declining years, the vision of Hope will yet be realised. But when that vision is realised, it will not be through the unaided sentiments of man—the holy

[1] "Man," translated by W. S. Dallas, p. 161.
[2] Quoted by Dr. Martineau, " Types of Ethical Theory," vol. i., p. 466.
[3] *Ibid.*, vol. i., p. 468.

city of universal brotherhood is a city whose builder and maker is God.

3. The third substitute for religion is the great Drift force. Let us see what it means. It means that the accumulated experience of past ages has created our social instincts, and will continue to do so in a constantly improving way, so that the weight of the past is a continually growing force for moral good in the world.

Man began his career in a struggle for existence. He soon found that the interests of the community were essential to the individual welfare, and now the morals of to-day bear witness to the vast growth of common interests which possess a kind of instinctive force over the conduct of men. "The impulse of human nature," says Büchner, "towards movement and progress is so considerable that it attains its object even under the most unfavourable circumstances,"[1] thus arguing that we may fairly leave the morals of the future to this wide and powerful drift.

Conscience according to this theory is the product of social factors.[2] Conscience, like every other power or faculty of man, has been evolved in the progress of the past.

There are many who feel immense dread of such

[1] "Man," p. 159.
[2] See Appendix, Note 35.

a theory as this; they can recognise the theory of evolution in things physical, but any theory of the evolution of conscience appears to them fatal to the very life of religion. But there is no need to be afraid of truth, and if it can be shown that conscience has been evolved, it is the part of religious and wise men to accept it. It is of course far from true that this has been proved, but, even were it proved, it would still leave the first germ of conscience unexplained; for the theory of evolution is a theory of method, not a theory of origin. The evolution of the moral sense does not explain the origin of it, any more than the evolution of the world explains the origin of the world. Evolution is merely the name for a mode in which the forces of life and nature show themselves at work. A Divine power would still be found in conscience, were it subject to a law of evolution, just as there is none the less Divine power in nature by reason of the evolution of nature. Moreover, there is a truth in the theory of moral evolution, there is a power constantly at work in the world, a power not ourselves, which makes for righteousness, as Matthew Arnold would say.

The point we have to deal with, however, is not whether there is a truth in this theory, but rather whether this drift or tendency offers a fitting substitute for religion. I scarcely think so, for the morals thus formed would rather be moralistic than truly and completely moral. We must refer to what we have already said: viz., that to preserve perfect morality, we must keep alive sympathy with higher right, perception of the right, and the effort of the will in achieving that right. But if man's morals are formed merely by slow inherited tendencies, which have been born into him by the past, the credit and merit of moral life disappears. For, I may ask, am I more moral than my ancestors? True, the influence of my surroundings may have raised my moral conduct above that of my ancestors. My morals may be better, but my morality is not necessarily greater. It is needful to remember that virtue may be high, though morals are low; virtue, I mean, in the sense of the conscious exertion of moral force. The real virtue of a man's morality consists in the energy which he shows in rising above a conventional level. The men and women who rose above their age and exhibited grand pictures of sturdy energy towards the right were moral heroes in their time. But the morals which do not rise above the level of the age scarcely express any virtuous morality at all. If, then, the progress and growth of moral life be left to the influence of this drift force, we may see higher morals from age to age, but we need not necessarily see greater or more real morality among individual men. We do not yield admiration to those characters which owe their beauty to influences with which their will did not co-operate. We may acknowledge a certain goodness, but it lacks greatness when it is sundered from will. Greatness consists largely in the exercise of will. A man is great when he is able to impress his will on others. It is thus that Napoleon and Cromwell are great. A man is great and good when he is able to impress on others his passion for right and his sympathy with good. But if the only force at work be what we have called the drift force of the world, then we see not our tokens; there is not one prophet more. The light which shines from the prophet's face is no longer the light of heaven—the only light which he has to give to men is the light which he reflects from their countenances. Nothing is left for us to admire when we find that brilliant deeds of self-sacrifice are only due to the pressure of irresistible tendency; hope also dies, for conflict is useless, effort is needless and vain. The bad is bad, the good is good; but the bad cannot become good—man is as he was born; hope dies. The race may be growing better, and in long ages hence, it may climb into regions of a purer morality, but meanwhile it is vain for the individual to wrestle with the terrible inheritance of evil, or hope to snatch, in the improvement of his own character, a victory from the resistless force of social influences.

These three alleged sources of morality—Knowledge, Altruism, and the Drift of the world, can hardly, therefore, become adequate substitutes for religion.

(ii.) But it is needful to go further, and to notice the deficiencies of these substitutes. It is not too much to say that there are whole realms of man's life which are left untouched by them. We shall notice three defects.

1. The dark side of life is not sufficiently reckoned with. The theory that all things will inevitably grow good, narrows our vision of life, and promotes an easy optimism which is soon followed by demoralising indifferentism. What it sees is the growing good, and it sees only the good. It forgets that men may be passion-led and self-interested.

Advocates of this theory resemble Timon of Athens. The banquet of life is spread, the guests are assembled, and they, being noble and generous themselves, believe that all who are gathered at the table are noble and generous also. But the

T

time comes when the dark and shabby things of life begin to show themselves: meanness and selfishness are found at the table as well as generosity and nobility. Soon comes the penalty of not looking facts in the face, and of not recognizing the dark as well as the bright side of men's nature. Timon, finding himself deceived, is determined to discard all faith in humanity. With wild ravings he insults the friends who are still true to him. He who has refused to believe evil in any is now incapable of believing good in any. It is a dangerous thing to stake the whole of our life and happiness upon the belief in the absolute and entire goodness of humanity. Such optimism is followed by indifferentism, if not cynicism. This reliance upon the moral drift theory fosters the visionary hope, against which Mr. Herbert Spencer warns us. "A visionary hope," he says, "misleads those who think that in an imagined age of reason, which might forthwith replace an age of beliefs but partly rational, conduct would be correctly guided by a code directly based on considerations of utility."[1]

Again, is it wise to ignore one dark shadow of life—the tendency to deterioration? It is not my province to lay down any opinion on the theory of reversion to type. But there can

[1] "Study of Sociology," p. 306.

be no question that there are in the history of man what we may call ebullitions of animalism constantly taking place. It is time, says Letourneau, that man was told that he is animal in every fibre and particle of his being.[1] Those who are acquainted with the history of aboriginal races know well what this means. The "boundary boys" in Australia seem to be periodically seized with an irresistible desire to return to savage life, and after having posed as the dandies of the colony, they frequently drop back into wild, if temporary, savagery. It is a fact that men are governed by their passions and their feelings, and no theory is likely to work which ignores this fact. We are beginning to see that for the victory of goodness in man we need more even than sentiment, perception and vigour.

We may well recall the caution of Mr. Spencer against assuming " that men's beliefs and actions are throughout determined by intellect; whereas they are in much larger degrees determined by feeling."[2]

2. There is no message for the unfit or unfortunate. There are some born unfit to cope with life, or to struggle against the weight of inherited tendencies. The proposed substitutes

[1] " Sociology," p. 450; *cf.* Büchner, " Man," pp. 75, 108, 130.
[2] " Study of Sociology," p. 307.

for religion offer little help to these. They are as they are—change is impossible. Unfit to take their part in the world, they must just be allowed to die out. The unfortunate hear no words of tenderness from this theory of drift. The world may be moving forward towards a bright goal, but the weak must be sacrificed; their lot is to die, crushed beneath the wheels of the advancing world. To bid them ask philosophers for a scientific solution of their position, is to bid them despair. Mr. Cotter Morison trusts that the day is coming when the artizan will peremptorily refuse to share his crust with the eight or ten children of his brother artizan, because his brother artizan ought not to have married.[1] But what about the children— the victims of this folly—are they guilty? These sheep—what have they done? It seems to me that when we begin to apply such philosophy we forget our charity. Life, indeed, will improve; we are at one with the thinkers who believe this, but we cannot forget those men and women who in life's march have dropped out of rank, and we ask for them a better verdict than that they must perish. Humanity cannot always stretch its own arms wide enough to shelter the feeble and the unfortunate. It wants One who will not cast away the broken reed nor quench the smoking flax.

[1] "The Service of Man," Preface, p. xxix.

3. The deeper side of man's nature is not met. The substitutes for religion have no answer to the two cries of the saint—the cry against sin and the cry after God. But these cries cannot be ignored, the realization of sin is widespread and deep; and it is most deeply felt where men's lives have been purest, and their aspirations after holiness greatest. Those who have seen the vision of God can never be self-complacent; a noble discontent is theirs. The cry over wrong and the cry after God come loudest from the lips of the best. Is there no meaning in the voices of yearning and lamentation which are lifted up by David and St. Paul, by Augustine and Fénelon? Is there no reality in the cry of the soul athirst after God? "My soul thirsteth for God, for the living God." (Ps. xlii. 2.) To tell men that the answer to these cries is to be sought in cold and philosophical moralism seems like offering stone to the soul that is asking for bread. The fact that no growth of a humanitarian moralism can do away with a distinct religious need in man is admitted by Mr. Spencer. "However dominant may become the moral sentiment enlisted on behalf of Humanity, it can never exclude the sentiment, alone properly called religious, awakened by that which is behind Humanity and behind all other things." "No such thing as a 'Religion of Humanity' can ever

do more than temporarily shut out the thought of a Power of which Humanity is but a small and fugitive product."[1]

(iii.) These defects are fatal to the theories which we have been examining. But suppose for the sake of argument that we accept the theories of scientific moralism and Altruism. Christian people, in one sense, will not deny the hope they hold out. They believe that the earth will be full of the knowledge of the Lord as the waters cover the sea. They believe in a golden age. They believe in a new city whose foundations will be strong, and whose walls will embrace a regenerated society, whence sin, sorrow, and death will be excluded. They believe as much as the most splendid theorists of to-day in the happy era to which the world is tending. So far there is agreement. But when we seek to know the power which is destined to achieve this change, and we are told that it is the accumulated social sentiment and drift of humanity, we have a right to ask what are the forces which form this sentiment and drift power. These forces are not merely physical, but intellectual; and not intellectual only, but moral; and not only moral, but religious, for the humanity of to-day is the product of all the influences of the past. Religion

[1] " Study of Sociology," p. 311.

itself is one of the factors which has been at work in the creation of the social sentiment.

The world could not be as it is without the influence of the past, and the various religious thoughts and sentiments in different parts of the world have all had their share in the formation of the present. Renan notices an example of this when he calls our attention to the fact that the worship which Rome has spread abroad in the world is by no means that of the old Jupiter Capitolinus or Latiaris; still less the worship of Augustus or of the Genius of the Empire; "it is the worship of Jehovah." "It is Judaism," he says, "in its Christian form that Rome has unconsciously propagated."[1]

1. In the same way it would take a treatise to show how largely men's thoughts have been influenced by the teaching of Gautama and by the enterprise of Mahomet. No person describing the movements of the world could afford to ignore these men who have so largely coloured the thought and habits of succeeding generations. And the Christian may fairly claim that from the life and teaching of Jesus Christ there have spread influences into the very heart of humanity, which, even were Christianity as a recognized religion to disappear, could never be obliterated

[1] "Hibbert Lectures," p. 16.

from the life and the sentiments of the human race. But further, the power of Christianity may be observed in this, that it has been able to influence the world, not so much by opposition as by a magnificent power of absorption. Take for example the two rival philosophical tendencies of stoicism and epicureanism; we might study these with the air of critics who desire to find out defects, but we prefer to read them with the wish to discover their good elements. Epicureanism, in its best aspects, was a protest on behalf of the beauty and the gladness of life; it was not the gross and sensual thing which we associate with the word in the present day. It was the endeavour to win the happiness of life by the exercise of a prudent moderation; it did not turn away from the good things of existence, but it taught men to use them. Stoicism, not unlike Buddhism, turned away from life's gladness and sternly urged as a virtue the necessity of self-control. The happiness of life, according to the Stoic, is to be found within; the happiness of life, according to the Epicurean, may be found without. It is clear that there is an element of good in both teachings. Christianity, possessed of that wondrous magnetic force which could draw the good out of every system, came into contact with both philosophies, and reconciled what seemed opposing elements. While teaching men that gladness might be found within, she taught also that God had given men all things richly to enjoy. By such processes Christianity enlarged her power, and diffused her influence among men. Such influences have entered into the consciousness of the world, and have tended to create the faith and the habits of mankind; they have been what we may call ethical factors in the formation of human thought and feeling as it is to-day. To talk of doing without religion is to talk of ignoring the rich inheritance which already belongs to men, whether they will or not. It is as if a banker were to declare that he would not be indebted to the accumulation of capital and credit which has been gathered in the earlier days of the firm's existence. It is precisely the possession of that capital and credit which enables him to do business so successfully as he does; he may attribute his success to his quickness or his sagacity, but his quickness and sagacity, unaided by the possession of capital and credit, would soon bring about disaster. It is in the same way difficult to calculate the influence, on the ethical life of humanity, of that moral capital which has been accumulating in the world through forces which have been largely religious. Is it wise, we may ask, even were it possible, is it wise to destroy them?

2. The same thought may be illustrated when we note the ideal which faith has set up before men. Various ideals have claimed men's attention; the world's history may be read as a history of the struggles between competing ideals of life. If we ask what ideal has after long ages of conflict prevailed over all others, we find that victory belongs to the ideal set up by Christ. To be such as He was, to live a life like His, to resolve that the guiding star of our being shall be the law, not of self-indulgence, but of self-denial, not of self-assertion, but of self-sacrifice, is the ideal of life which is now approved by humanity.

Heine dreamt that he saw the gods gathered at their banquet. Goblets of heavenly wine were before them; they drank and lived at ease, till the door was flung open, and there came tottering in a pale-faced figure, panting, and bearing the weight of a large cross, which he flung down upon the table. The faces of the gods turned pale, and slowly one by one they vanished away. The dream recognised that there was an ideal of life higher than that of strength, or wisdom, or joy, and that this ideal alone could survive. Before the majesty of the ideal of sacrifice, all must bow. Every creed that did not realise this in its morality was doomed to perish. Self-sacrifice has come to be recognised as the highest moral law; Altruism is but another name for it; the ideal is recognised and accepted. But the ideal was set up by Christ. The German poet saw that He, whose hand put down the gods of might and wisdom, and taught the victorious power of sacrifice, was none other than the Christ who both taught and lived the life of loving sacrifice.

The ideal then set up by Christ has survived, and every year has added to the recognition of its strength. This, too, is a factor which has had its share in moulding the thoughts and characters of men; it is part of that reserve capital by which the world can stretch forward to greater enterprise in the future. Still more remarkable is the fact that, in setting up this ideal of life, Christianity anticipated the ideal which is now recognized as the *highest* ideal for man. The unconscious witness to this among the assailants of Christianity is most striking. Büchner tells us that "our present state of culture has already long since left far behind it all and even the highest intellectual ideals established and elaborated by former religions."[1]

And what is this lofty ideal which has outstripped the ideals of religion? We can give it from the same authority. "The only correct

[1] "Man," p. 219.

and tenable moral principle depends upon the relation of *reciprocity*. There is therefore no better guide to moral conduct than the old and well-known proverb: 'What you would not have done to you, that to others never do.' If we complete this proverb with the addition: 'Do to others as you would they should do to you,' we have the entire code of virtue and morals in hand, and indeed in a better and simpler form than could be furnished us by the thickest manuals of ethics, or the quintessence of all the religious systems of the world."[1]

The reader of the Gospels will be amused at this language. Here is a man declaring that the very principles which Christ laid down are better than all that can be found in the thickest manuals of ethics, including, we venture to suppose, his own writings, and the quintessence of all the religious systems of the world. The Christian asks no more startling vindication of his position than this which is offered by Professor Büchner. When Auguste Comte sought to condense his teaching into a single maxim he could find no better than the words of the Lord Jesus, "It is more blessed to give than to receive,"[2] but he is apparently unaware of the source from which he

[1] "Man," p. 211.
[2] "Discours," p. 216; Acts xx. 35.

is quoting. It is not too much to say then that by the admission of those who are not favourable to Christianity, the ideals set up by Christ are precisely those which are acknowledged in this age of culture to be the highest and the best. A standard of life which is proclaimed as the discovery of to-day and the climax-morality of the ages was displayed to the heart of humanity two thousand years ago. And since our Lord lived and died this ideal has been working amongst men. Wherever Christianity has been preached it has been proclaimed. The wealth of such ethical teaching has been invested over and over again in the great market-place of the world, and it seems strange to deny to the Lord of this teaching that which is His own, and to withhold from Him the usury of that glorious and unselfish success which is to be found in its universal recognition at the hands of the best and the most thoughtful of men.

3. The truth is that the religious factor cannot be got rid of; it is part of the history of the past, and of all men the sociologist will admit this to be the case. The power of the religious sentiment, the force of the moral ideal, have been transmitted from generation to generation. The religious influence is in the blood of humanity, it has ennobled men, even though they have been

unconscious of the source of such ennobling. It is vain to attempt to falsify the pedigree of humanity, or turn back the stream of its history. It is too late to think of withdrawing the capital out of which the moral greatness and moral riches of the world have been created. It is impossible to ignore the supreme power of religion and the large share which religious thoughts and feelings have had in the formation of the characters of men and of the life of humanity.

To conclude, we have asked whether religion is necessary, and whether we can find an adequate substitute or power which can preserve those sacred things which have hitherto been considered to depend almost entirely upon religious influence. We have seen that of the various substitutes proposed, none can be accepted as satisfactory. To rely upon the mere drift of the world is to lose the advantage of active co-operation on the part of the individual, and to disturb the relationship between morals and virtue. To rest upon the influence of diffused and growing knowledge is to ignore the fact that sentiment and feeling are among the great moving forces of human life. To believe that the cultivation of the heart, as it is said, or the proclamation of altruistic principles will regenerate the world, is to fall into the old error of imagining that the machine will work of itself as soon as we have put together its parts.

The substitutes offered for religion have been tried and found wanting; they have been found wanting because they do not embrace all humanity, because they do not touch the whole man, because they have no message to the weak, no response to the cry of him whose heart condemns him, and no answer to the soul that is athirst for the living God. And even were we to concede to these substitutes for religion all that they ask, we could not get rid of the fact that it is to the influence of religion that the great force of moral sentiment to-day is so largely due.[1] It would seem therefore fair to infer that it would be difficult and disastrous to attempt to get rid of religion altogether. To do so would be to ask man to stand once more at the foot of the ladder which all desire to climb, and to bid him look upward and to see the summit lost in the darkening of the clouds, but to see no longer the angels ascending and descending, to look in vain for the opened heavens and their heart-inspiring light. Far other is the future which, we believe, is in store for the sons and daughters of men. Religion will not perish, not only because religion is needed by men, but because the Divine One

[1] *Cf.* Lecky, "History of Rationalism."

will not leave men without the witness of Himself, and without some sweet ministry to their yearning spirits and their fainting hearts. The ladder which all true men long to climb—the ladder of noble endeavour, of stern self-control, of victory over the base and lower passions—will always be seen wherever men have caught, as the best thinkers of all time have caught, some glimpses of the true view of life's meaning and life's duty; but the guarantee of the realisation of their desires belongs only to those who believe that the world is governed by love and by wisdom, whose eyes are open to see not only the ladder, but also the hands from the unseen world which are stretched out to give help to the struggling sons of men. Moralism and Religion stand side by side at the foot of the ladder of life; but when they severally begin to climb, it is religion which will outstrip the tardy steps of Moralism, because religion moves forward with confidence as she points to the opening heavens; her eye alone can pierce the clouds and behold the light of the promised day; she sees the angels of God ascending and descending, and for her the hopes of humanity are assured in One to whom all power is given, Who is to her both Son of God and Son of man.

LECTURE VII.

RELIGION AND PERSONALITY.

No adequate substitute for religion being found, religion is a necessity in the future. In a perfect religion, religion and morals should be inseparable. The need, therefore, of a principle or basis on which religion and morals unite. This is to be found in the recognition of personality, *i.e.*, in the recognition that religion and morals are meaningless except they express relationships between beings who have wills and affections.

    I.—The recognition of Personality not an empty phrase. The power at work which aims at the education of man as a personal being.

        (i.) History shows the danger of forgetting that man is man.

        (ii.) Nature educates man to—
            (*a*) The consciousness of self.
            (*b*) The sacrifice of self.
            (*c*) A certain completeness of character.

        (iii.) Recent knowledge shows us stages of evolution in the same direction—(*a*) Physical, (*b*) Psychical, (*c*) Social.

    II.—The recognition of Personality affords a basis of reconciliation between religion and morals.

        (i.) The reconciliation afforded by the idea of personal beings—
            (*a*) The word Personality as applied to God.
            (*b*) Anthropomorphism inevitable to man.

        (ii). This recognition applies to (*a*) the source as well as to (*b*) the subject of religion.

        (iii.) To the varying standards of morals.

    III.—The religion of the future must be based on a Person, not on Creed, or Code.

        (i.) No necessary loss to Definiteness and to Conduct.

        (ii.) But an enormous gain to religion in Creed and Worship.

Conclusion.—Creed so based contrasted with the creed of science.

LECTURE VII.

RELIGION AND PERSONALITY.

"Hereafter ye shall see heaven open, and the angels of God ascending and descending upon the Son of Man."
—*St. John* i. 51.

THE position which we have reached is this. Religion is natural to man. Some religions have allied themselves to man's vices, but, on the whole, religion (not religionism) has supported man's moral nature. Viewing religion, then, as a moral power in the world, we may doubt the wisdom of dismissing it, since no adequate substitute has yet been found.

What is needed, then, is not to dismiss religion, but to secure complete harmony between morals and religion. We feel that ethics and religion ought never to be at variance. Religion without ethics seems little else than irreligious religion. Ethics without religion are rootless ethics. There ought to be no divorce between them. We seek, therefore, their meeting-point.

Between religion and morals we want the true synthesis. To reconcile the things which we feel ought to be at harmony with one another—to reconcile the interests of the many with the interests of the one, the pursuit of pleasure with the possession of virtue, science with religion, and faith with morals—have been frequent problems. But more than an intellectual synthesis is needed. We can live with a great many intellectual inconsistencies, but we cannot live with a moral or spiritual inconsistency. If we cannot reconcile to our mind's satisfaction determinism and freedom, faith and science, we can go on living a tolerably comfortable life, notwithstanding the intellectual discord; but discord between our moral and spiritual sentiments we cannot endure. Life involves beauty and culture. It involves also duty and the stern glories of virtue; and it involves, besides our relation with the unseen world, the harmony of our spirit with the unseen spirit; these factors of life must be brought into accord. The human spirit must be at one with the world, itself, and its God. It cannot rest till it has brought about the reconciliation of these elements. We feel that life ought to be beautiful and sweet; yet it is so sad. We feel that the beautiful ought to be always true, and that the true ought always to be beautiful. We feel that faith and right, goodness and success ought to be inseparable. We are doomed to disappointment, but though disappointed, we do not surrender our conviction of what ought to be.

When Philoctetes hears that Ulysses is alive, he says,—

> "I did not doubt it; evil never dies;
> The gods take care of that. If aught there be
> Fraudful and vile, 'tis safe. The good and just
> Perish unpitied by them."

But though he says this, he feels it ought not to be so, for when Ulysses pleads that he is but obeying the will of the gods, Philoctetes replies,—

> "Detested wretch!
> Mak'st thou the gods a cover for thy crime?
> Do they teach falsehoods?"

In the same spirit Neoptolemus is made to say,—

> "Can I offend the gods by doing good?"[1]

It is thus that everywhere men refuse to accept the discord between religion and morals. Refusing it, they seek the bond in which religion and morality are one.

This bond, I think, is to be found. Lines which diverge may also converge. Religion and morals

[1] Soph. "Philoc.," Act ii., Sc. 1; Act iv., Sc. 2; and Act v., Sc. 4.

seem to diverge, but by altering our position we may see the point of their intersection. When I hold a prism in my hand, I may scatter the ray of light and break it into broadening and various colours; but it is possible also to combine these scattered rays and to show that, various and divergent as they are, they may be reconciled in one pure beam of light. To apply this illustration, it is possible to take up a position in which religion and morals appear to contradict one another; it is possible also to find a point in which they are reconciled; that point, I believe, is found in Personality.

I.—Religion is a great force, but it requires a personality to exhibit that force. It is not in theories, nor in arguments, nor in controversies that its real power is manifested, but in the lives of men. Controversies are for the most part outside the tone and scope of religion, and serve often to demonstrate that "the wrath of man worketh not the righteousness of God."[1] In the same way, where does morality find expression, if it be not in a personal being? Where there is no personality, there can be no morality. Religion and morals converge in man. In moral and religious controversies it has been too often forgotten that neither religion nor morality have any meaning apart from the idea of personality.[2] It is

[1] St. James i. 20. [2] See Appendix, Note 36.

the remembrance of man as a personal being, with a character which can be perfected, which gives us the link.

We shall consider some points in support of this theory.

(i.) First, there are the facts of history. Is it not one of the truisms of history that the doctrinists have failed? When we ask the reason of their failure, we find that they have forgotten one great factor in life's problem—man. Men have vainly striven to drive the world by theories and by doctrines, religious, scientific and political. They have missed the mark by following bookish theories and ignoring man. The politician, no less than the theologian, has made this mistake. Alva had theories, and his failures were the failures of a theorist; for he forgot, as many others have forgotten, that he had to deal, not with mere inanimate matter, but with men and women who had will, intellects, feelings, personal power and consciences of their own. Alva failed in his plans because he forgot that man was man. England forgot this in her struggle with America. She was deaf to the voice of Edmund Burke when he reminded her that in this problem she had to deal with men; that not by "bonds, affidavits, cockets, and clearances" could she bind America to the mother country, but by a large and generous recognition of their common blood and common humanity. "You cannot falsify," he said, "the pedigree of this people. An Englishman is the unfittest person on earth to argue another Englishman into slavery."[1] Frederick the Great was wont to say: "If I wished to ruin a province I should commit it to the government of philosophers." He meant just this: that men with theories are of very little good, for they are liable to forget that they are governing men. Life is like a game of chess, which has its laws. But there is one piece upon the board conditioned differently from the rest. It is exempt from capture. Others may be taken; you may take knight, castle and bishop, but you cannot take the king. You may take and manipulate every other element in the world, because you know its materials and its laws, but man still remains man, and at unexpected moments he starts up and asserts himself. He is the little Oliver who disturbs the serene stupidity of the workhouse-politicians of the world. He is the piece on the board which refuses to be taken. History shows us that it is fatal to forget man as a personal being.

(ii.) The voice of nature proclaims the same, in the way in which she seems to be aiming at the formation of character. (a) For the first voice of

[1] Speech on "American Conciliation."

nature is ever saying to man, in one form or another: "Be yourself. Life may be 'labour and travail,' but yet be yourself." Her first utterance of this is in the primal law of self-preservation. The conflict for subsistence is the earliest experience of man. He must exert himself to live; he must find his food; it does not drop right into his hand. Necessity then becomes the mother of invention; the intellectual efforts of ingenuity and contrivance must henceforth be a law of his life. Physical necessity forces upon him manly effort; but, in being thus his stern guide and nurse, she teaches him what he is, and educates him in consciousness of self. But his selfhood is still further forced upon him. His days have bettered, his life is easier, he has leisure, and his energy is free to go into other channels. Nature, which taught self-preservation, tells him that to be himself he must express himself.[1] Under this guidance the man becomes the artist, the musician, the poet, the statesman. The artist seeks to express himself in form, the musician in song, the poet in verse, the statesman in law and authority. And this all teaches consciousness of self. For man finds it is only in the victory first over nature and then over his own powers, that it is possible for him to express himself. Self-

[1] See Appendix, Note 37.

expression is followed by self-possession. The feeling rises in a man's being, that even though he is able to express his thoughts in the way of art, or the way of poetry, or the way of government, he is not on that account complete master of himself. When things go wrong, and he becomes petulant and wrathful, he finds that he is not master of himself. We say, when a man loses his temper, that he forgets himself. It is only in the determination to do the thing from which he shrinks that man reaches his best. This victory over the flesh, or over the fear which the flesh engenders, is heroism. In the hero we admire, not courage, but the self-possession which we call presence of mind. It is this control of his faculties which enables him to rise superior to the fears which betray men of a weaker sort. And thus nature's first voice is: "Be yourself," for she teaches self-preservation, self-expression, and highest and best of all, self-possession. (*b*) But nature is not content to leave man here, she calls to him again, she says: "Sacrifice yourself." She has taught man the treasure of selfhood. She has taught him that he becomes great when he has himself well in hand, as we say. But the moment he finds himself in possession of this great treasure, he discovers that it is only put into his hand in order that it may be surrendered, for nature does not allow him long to possess himself without demanding that he shall sacrifice himself. This command to sacrifice self is first heard in the family. He must give time, labour, and thought for the sake of wife and children. His country calls him to sacrifice himself. Patriotism, which is but the love of the larger home, bids him go forth and lay down his life, if needs be, in his country's cause. Again, duty calls, and her cry of "Sacrifice yourself" finds an echo in man's conscience. There is a thing which duty bids a man do; it is better to die than to leave it undone. There is a thing to be resisted; it is better to die than to do it. Though it is noble to possess yourself, it is nobler still to do that homage to duty which prefers death to disgrace and would rather sacrifice self than ignobly preserve life. And if duty and conscience call to sacrifice, religion does so too. Faith cries: "Sacrifice yourself" to what you are convinced is true, and to the maintenance of that spiritual ideal which religion demands. Thus there grows up a feeling in man that all his acquirements are to be used for others; that the power to possess himself only confers the privilege and opportunity of self-sacrifice. (c) What is the result of these two voices of Nature, the one crying: "Be yourself;" and the other, "Sacrifice yourself"? I answer, it is character. Sometimes it is asked: Which is the higher, the good deed which is effortless, or the good deed which has cost effort? The answer is neither. The good deed without effort is the sign of a higher goodness; the good deed with effort of a higher virtue. For there is no virtue in the goodness which has involved no effort.

There are, indeed, three stages in the development of man's character. The first is effortless; the second has effort; the third effortless again. In the sphere of knowledge, for instance, a man begins with complete ignorance, and as long as he remains ignorant, there is no effort required of his mind. The stage which he next enters is the stage of learning, and here is the beginning of effort. The third stage is the stage of proficiency; that is to say, the stage in which he has knowledge, and the need of effort is at an end. The same is true in man's moral nature. At first his conscience is uninformed, and he follows unquestioningly his desires. There is no conscious need of the exercise of will or control in combating his passions. This is the animal stage. But there comes a time in which he begins to question the righteousness of his desires. A moral law says, "Thou shalt not." From that time forward he is impelled into a life of effort, if he is to be true to the moral instincts awakened within him. From this he can emerge into the third stage, in which, having become master of himself, his desires and passions are so well under control that there is no longer any need of effort to restrain them. He no longer struggles or cries out: "Oh, wretched man that I am!" He delights in the right, and in the doing of the right. He has passed the stage of mere morality; he has become a spiritual man, for the period of mere moralism is left behind. These stages are expressed by St. Paul: "I was alive without the law once," that is the animal stage; "but when the commandment came, sin revived," here is the stage of moral effort, "and I died." (Rom. vii. 24 & 9.) But this period passed and another stage came in which he cried, "Not I, but Christ liveth in me." (Gal. ii. 20.) That is, he passed from the effortless stage, through the stage of pain and effort, and on again to the stage of effortlessness. Apply this thought to the idea of sacrifice. Sacrifice is everywhere. It is not confined to human devotion. The law is written in nature. The harvests we reap result from the death of the seed, and the power of the earth is renewed by the life-toil of the earth-worms, as Darwin told us. The river only gathers the wealth and music of tributary streams to yield them up again, and to lose itself in the bosom of the ocean. The white cliffs of our own land and the coral islands of the distant seas owe their strength and beauty, nay, their very existence, to the labour and sacrifice of insect life. The lower civilisations which have passed away are sacrificed on the altar of the growing culture of mankind. But all these are sacrifices without that glory which belongs to sacrifice when self is a reality to consciousness. The sacrifice of the corn, which is all unconscious, or of the worm, which but follows the irresistible law of its being, has not a glory like the sacrifice of Winkelried. When Gareth stared at the spate he cried to the senseless cataract, "Thou dost His will, the Maker's, and not knowest." But the eager obedience of the spate had no glory like the glory of Gareth's own sacrifice when wearing "the sooty yoke of kitchen-vassalage." The stream which sacrifices itself in tumbling over the rocks has no sense of effort, but you and I— and here is the dignity and glory of sacrifice—are conscious that it is a sacrifice. It requires effort. The dead sacrifices of nature do not compare with the living sacrifices of human consciousness. The act of the little child who rushes into the street where the bullets are raining thick and fast, does not compare with the act of the fireman, who, taking his life in his hand, climbs the crumbling and tottering walls and faces a flaming death to save the lives of others; or that of the soldier who charges against overwhelming odds ; or that of the doctor who puts his lips to the patient's wounded throat and draws the poisoned breath. These, and men such as these, know exactly the measure of their danger, the terrible reality of the risks they run are vividly before them, and it is this knowledge which makes them heroes. Our Lord gave a touching emphasis to this thought, and a transcendent example of this heroism. Speaking of His own life He said, "No man taketh it from Me. I have power to lay it down" (St. John x. 18); that is, the sacrifice which I make is a sacrifice which it is within my power to make or not to make, but which is willingly and consciously made.

It would seem, then, that nature is emphasising selfhood, character, and personality. She leads man up to a conscious possession of himself, and when he reaches this point the altar is before him, and he learns to sacrifice himself. Here is the education of his character. Here is a law which has been working up to the perfecting of the personality and the development of character in the conscious possession of our will, and in the obligation of sacrifice. Of course, it may be argued that this consciousness of self-possession in man is only imaginary; that his freedom is only a sense of freedom, that actually, all is determined beforehand, and that where determinism rules, freedom is absurd. This may be an argument, but this is not the place to argue it. But even were it so, and the freedom of man an illusion, the consciousness of that freedom would be enough for the education of man's character. The child who is learning to walk runs an imaginary risk; the mother is at hand and she will not let it fall; but though the risk is imaginary the education is real, for the child does acquire that physical self-mastery which is needful for walking. In the same way, man may be surrounded by laws which look strangely like the laws of necessity, but the education of his character may be going forward. The sense of freedom is within him, and is sufficiently strong to form the basis of the development of his character. He becomes persuaded that he is a free agent, and this is sufficient for the education of his character.

(iii.) The voice of nature is thus impressing upon man the sense of his personality as a being who can possess himself, and who ought to sacrifice himself. (a) The voice of science has a word upon this subject. It may be objected that we are falling into the wholly exploded heresy which taught that man is the centre of the universe. Man was made, by that heresy, the victim of pleasing delusions and imagined himself an important personage. Like Christopher Sly, he was intoxicated by flattery, deceived by his dreams, and imagined himself a king, the favourite of heaven to whom all things ministered. Like the raw son of the patriarch he believed that sun, moon and stars, and the fruits of the ground bowed down and did him obeisance. But all that is changed now. The stern hand of truth, in the form of science, has shown him his insignificance. Facts have been too strong for fancy. The Copernican theory has dethroned man in space. The discoveries of geology have dethroned him in time; and, unkindest cut of all, the Darwinian theory has dethroned him from that unique position which he believed himself to have occupied in the earth, and has traced his origin to a lowly ancestor. He is no longer a special creation enthroned in time and space. He thought that earth was the centre of all things, and heaven's dome the roof of his palace, but he is only a dweller in one of the minor mansions of the universe. He believed himself the privileged possessor of a brand-new world which was specially completed for him, but behold there were æons and races before him, and he is only one in a succession of tenants of a very old planet. He believed himself to be created by a special act of the Creator, that deep revolving thoughts on the Creator's part led to his birth; but behold he is only a link in the vast far-

x

reaching chain of life holding kinship with the lowest forms of existence. Man's pride has been humbled, he has been rudely awakened from his dream. He is king no longer. But even if these words of science be true, man is not necessarily dethroned. Everything depends on the view we take of God, and the view we take of man. If we believe in some special localization of God, then we may believe that man on the earth was nearer or further from God, as the case might be; but if our thought of God is of that one Spirit who pervades all things, in whom we live and move and have our being, then no astronomical theory can remove men further from God. Do we believe that God inhabits a metropolis, so to speak, and that the influence of His power grows faint and indistinct at the distant parts of the universe? Hazlitt said, "In Jacob's day there was a ladder between heaven and earth, but now the heavens have gone further off, and become astronomical." But this is only true in the minds of those who have misunderstood the nature of God. There is no dethronement of man by any theory of astronomy, for he is neither less nor more man than he was before, he is still the work of God's hands, and the creature of His love. The true greatness of man is not lessened by these theories. Our view of man is that his greatness is not determined by place, time, or antecedent history. Geography does not make a man great. A man standing on the top of the Himalayas is not a greater man than the man standing on the plain. Position is nothing; true greatness is in character. A man's greatness depends upon the moral energy which he displays. The stage is nothing, the part he plays is little, but the way in which he plays his part is everything. His greatness is in his character, and there is no need to suppose that any theories which have altered our ideas of man's physical relationship to time, space, or animal life, can rob him of the heritage of being a moral creature.

(*b*) But the voice of science, through some of its interpreters, shows that there is in nature a marvellous care for the development and growth of man towards moral perfection. The increase of our knowledge seems to intensify the glory of man, and to indicate that man's moral perfection is, in some sort, the end of nature's work. One eminent writer has taken the pains to show this very clearly. Evolution is to him a natural term, and an admitted fact. But he holds that the evolution, which is first physical, is afterwards psychical, and finally moral. The physical evolution we understand; but, according to him, there came " a wonderful moment . . . at which psychical changes began to be of more use than physical changes to the brute ancestor of Man."[1] A new chapter was, as it were, opened in the history of the universe. When "the process of zoological change had come to an end, a process of psychological change was to take its place. Henceforth along this supreme line of generation there was to be no further evolution of new species through physical variation, but through the accumulation of psychical variations one particular species was to be indefinitely perfected and raised to a totally different plane from that on which all life had hitherto existed." And in relation to this, he notes this fact: the increase of size in the cerebrum and the lengthening of the period of infancy. And he sums up the case by saying: "Whereas in its rude beginnings the psychical life was but an appendage to the body, in fully-developed Humanity the body is but the vehicle for the soul." But this leads to the evolution which is moral. The rudimentary moral sentiments are, it is thought by some, observable in the higher members of the mammalian orders; and, however this may be, it will be admitted that "the primordial unit of human society is the family, and it was by the establishment of definite and permanent family relationships that the step was

[1] Fiske, "Destiny of Man," p. 28.

taken which raised man socially above the level of gregarious apehood." And this was attained by the prolongation of infancy, knitting together more closely the feelings of family life, and causing a realization of the general welfare to supersede selfish feelings, and thus the way was opened for the development of ethical feelings by showing that conduct must be judged by principle and not by individual caprice. The result of all this is that by a perpetual reaction "a creature different in kind from all other creatures has been evolved." The creature thus evolved has become dominant over the earth, in a sense in which none of its predecessors ever became dominant, and "henceforth the work of evolution, as far as our planet is concerned, is chiefly devoted to the perfecting of this last and most wonderful product of creative energy."[1]

(c) The further perfecting of man is carried on by means of social influences. For the same writer shows how the history of war has passed through changes, clearly manifesting a movement in a higher direction. War, in the first instance, had for its aim mere conquest without incorporation; in its next stage it was conquest with incorporation, and the privileges of citizenship were in a measure extended to the

[1] Fiske, "Destiny of Man," pp. 28, 30, 65, 67, 70. See Ap., Note 38.

conquered, and these stages prepared the way for the idea of Federation. Thus the perfection of man, individually and socially, has been carried on, and the genesis of the high spiritual qualities in man is the goal of Nature's creative work. If Nature is thus still making man the object of her care, man is not so far dethroned. It does not matter for our purpose whether the view be correct scientifically, or not; but it does illustrate this—that men who think and look into the world, and ask concerning its history and its meaning, are beginning to agree in this—that the evolution of the world is not a meaningless thing, but is suggestive of a purpose. So that the men, whose standpoint is not that of religion, are yet the men, who are telling us that nature works for an end and expresses ideas. Fouillée, no friend of religion, asks: "Is there, then, in history a pre-established design?" This he dismisses as the mere hypothesis of the metaphysician. But he declares that there is certainly a *self-accomplishing* design which must be recognised, if sociology is not for ever to remain a barren speculation, instead of being a practical study.[1] The metaphysician has a perfect right

[1] "Y a-t-il dans l'histoire un *dessein préétabli ?* Pure hypothèse de métaphysique; mais il y a assurément ' *un dessein qui se fait*,' qui s'établit lui-même et c'est la une vérité scientifique

to say that there are directing forces working towards an ideal in nature, and that the ideal is, when stripped from all religious and mythical creeds, Justice, Morality, Liberty, Fraternity.[1] What is this but saying, that if you look into the face of Nature, and ask what Nature is doing, you discover that she has somehow or another been exercising a kind of parental interest, and has been watching over the development of man. Man, mark you, not as a physical being, but man as a moral being; man as possessed of high moral and spiritual qualities; or in other words, Nature has emphasised this thought of his personality. Renan also says: "The business of all living things is to make God perfect, to contribute to that grand ultimate resultant which will establish universal unity. Hitherto this work has been accomplished in the dark by the secret instinct of all living creatures; some future day Reason will take the task in hand, and after having organised humanity, will organise God."[2]

However much these views may shock us, they are at least expressions of the thought that we are not living in the midst of chaos, but that the influences around us are directed towards the

sans laquelle la sociologie demeurerait une spéculation stérile au lieu de devenir une étude pratique."—"La Science Sociale," p. 386. [1] *Ibid.* p. 385.
[2] "Theophrastes," *Westr. Review*, vol. l., N.S., July, 1876, p. 119.

working out of an idea; and that idea, the moral and spiritual amelioration of man. Man, though dethroned, has become the centre of the problem. We are moving towards the goal of which Professor Huxley speaks: "The goal for the schoolmen, as for us, is the settlement of the question how far the universe is the manifestation of a rational order."[1] I almost think I can see beneath these expressions a trembling towards the recognition of that great living force behind the universe whom we call God. If all things are tending towards the development and perfection of moral and personal character in man, we may be at least forgiven for calling this a rational order. But whether this be so or no, our conclusion at this point is this: There is an enormous and varied force working out the education of man, developing his sense of freedom, responsibility and nobility. Life's facts, life's progress, duty's call, and religion's aspirations, all are working for man and promoting his development as a personal being, whose highest perfection is character.

II.—(i.) The recognition of personality affords a basis of reconciliation between religion and morals. This recognition must apply to the subject as

[1] "Scientific and Pseudo-Scientific Realism." *Nineteenth Century*, Feb., 1887.

well as to the source of religion; to man, and to God the object of man's worship. (a) An objection is felt on the part of many to the use of the word personality in connection with the unseen Power of the universe. Personality, they say, is an expression tainted with anthropomorphism,[1] and further, it implies limitations. With regard to the first of these objections, it may be remarked that it is impossible to escape altogether from anthropomorphism; as long as men are men they will speak in the language of men, and no phrase or conception expressed by the mouth of man can wholly escape the accusation of anthropomorphism. No doubt there are exaggerated descriptions of God. No doubt many speak and think of the Great Power which lies behind the whole world as though in that power there were the weaknesses, the passions, the caprices, and the limitations of humanity. But the exaggeration or the misuse of a term is only a caution in the eyes of sensible men; it cannot destroy the truth that even in the language to which we take exception there is an effort to describe some real thing. (b) The second objection to the use of the word personality is that it implies those limitations which belong to personal beings as we know them on earth. This, I am ready to admit,

[1] See Note 39 in Appendix.

is a more serious objection. In answer, we can only say that we are not tied to the word if any one will invent a better. I am quite prepared to admit that the word personality is inadequate to express all that we mean, and may imply much that we do not mean, but I think that it is a word which expresses an honest attempt to say something which we do mean, and for which we have as yet no better word. It does not express all that we want; I am quite content to believe with Mr. Herbert Spencer "that the choice is not between personality and something lower than personality, but between personality and something higher;"[1] and if you will, I am ready to call that Great Power the personality which is above personality, only I cannot call that power "it." Every word we use is weak and unfit. In speaking of that Great Power we say "He;" but "He" is an inadequate word, for it implies limitation of sex. "They" is misleading, because it suggests the possibility of divergence of will. But if "He" and "They" are inadequate or misleading words, "It" is still more so, for we cannot think of the power which is behind all things, and upon whom humanity must depend, as being a mere abstraction, or a neutral and will-less thing. Réville says, " Abstract infinities, infinite time, infinite space, are empty notions, silent to the

[1] "Retrogressive Religion." *Nineteenth Century*, July 1884.

religious soul."[1] And if we speak of the Great Unseen One as being not personal, as being such as we may describe by the word "It" rather than "He," the same silence and deadness is felt; for the soul of man can hardly worship, reverence, love, or rely upon that which he is forbidden to regard as possessing the sympathy and life which we believe to be the heritage of those only who are personal beings.

Further, the life and order of the universe seem to rebuke us if we speak of the Guiding Power behind all as "It." We have seen the beauty of the world, the influence of laws which are fitted to compass the education of man. We have seen that great progressive order moving forward with dexterous footsteps, changing its methods to meet the growing intelligence and will and affection of those beings who seem to be nature's chiefest charge. We have seen the advance of religion, pointing humanity, from age to age, forward and onward to higher ideals and larger life. All these things, we say, are due to the influence of one mighty force, that unseen Power, that will within the world, which seems recognised in one form or another, by the clearest and profoundest thinkers; and seeing all this, we cannot speak of that power

[1] "Proleg.," p. 23.

and that will as being less than personal, as being "It" rather than "He." Hence I cannot but believe that the true account of life is that it is an education of beings who can think, will and love, by a Being who can will and love; and, till some better phrase is found, I shall call this the education of persons by a person, whose personality is as much higher than theirs, as the consciousness of a human being is higher than the consciousness of a plant, and in comparison with whose love our love is but the faintest shadow of a shade.

(ii.) Recognising then personality alike in the source and in the subject of religion, it is needful to point out that in this recognition we have the means of reconciling religion and morality. (*a*) First, with regard to their source. If the great Power behind all things may be regarded by men as a Being having personality, then religion and morality have union in the source from which they both spring; they are not at variance, they are but different aspects of the same power. Morality is the expression of God's will; religion is the expression of our trust in that will. If the sentiment of duty involves the feeling that God is trusting us, we may add religion is our trusting God.[1] The sense of duty and the emotions of religion are

[1] *Cf.* Martineau, "Hours of Thought," vol. i., S. 22. See Appendix, Note 40.

but different moods of the consciousness of the relationship between personal beings, and One whose personality is higher than theirs. As light, and heat, and energy are but variations of one force, so truth spoken by prophets, noble and generous feelings springing up in the hearts of men, strong and energetic resolutions for good, determined endeavours of philanthropic enthusiasm, spring from one source whose inspiration has never failed the sons of men. The force which expresses itself in moral feeling, in deep emotion, or in lofty aspiration bears witness to One from whom all good things do come.

As in the ancient story the Shekinah light moved before the hosts of Israel, now luminous, now cloudy, now in advance of them, and now behind them, now guiding them in their forward march, now sheltering them from the pursuit of the enemy; so has Divine power in human history, working in nature, welling up in consciousness, witnessing in conscience, inspiring in faith, guiding, elevating, restraining and impelling, marched ever with the forward march of all mankind. Religion and morals become but expressions of what God would have us feel, and what God would have us be. In essence they are one, and only the moralist or the religionist divorces them. From of old they were one; morality is the expression of rectitude in conduct, and rectitude in conduct is only conduct in harmony with the order of God; religion is the turning of the soul to God as the source of its life. They are one, and what God has joined together man must not put asunder. Thus moral life and religious life owe their being to the one fountain of righteousness and peace.

(*b*) Secondly, with regard to their subject. Here too the reconciliation of religion and morality may be seen in the recognition of man as a personal being. Morality deals with the relation of man towards those around him; religion deals besides with what man is towards One above him; and both relate to man as a personal being who can will and think and love.

(iii.) Further, the recognition of personality reconciles the difficulty which has been often felt regarding the varying standard of morals. It has often been said that morality is an indeterminate science, for what is moral in one age is deemed immoral in another. There is no fixity it is said in the standard of morals. The objection that there is no fixed code of morals, and that what is right in one age is wrong in another, is an objection which can only arise from the disregard of man as a being who is to be educated through the ages.

We are perfectly aware and ready to admit

that the saint of one age would perhaps hardly be tolerated in another; that the morals of David, and the conduct of Samson, would not be the level of morals and conduct required of every ordinary Christian in the present day. If the aim of life be morals, the objection is a valid one.[1] If the aim of life, however, be character, the objection is null and void. It is character which God seeks to improve in a world which is being educated, and it is perfectly possible that morals may be high when character is low, and that character may be high when morals are low. The morality of an age is just the standard of morals which prevails at that particular time, but character is the energy, the moral energy in an individual man which is striving to rise to the highest level possible in his day. There may be as much credit to a man in achieving, in an age of low morality, what we to-day would deem a low moral standard, as there is in a man attaining a very high moral standard in an age when the level of morals was high. We measure a man's powers of climbing, not by the position which he happens to occupy upon the mountain side, but by the difference between the position from which he started, and the position to which he has attained. An illustration may make this

[1] See Appendix, Note 41.

clear. The merit of a clock is that it shall keep time; that is to say, that when once it is set it shall work with regularity and precision. The hour indicated on the face is in one sense of no moment. If all the clocks of the world were brought together to one place, the varieties of the time indicated would be numberless, and any man who objected that there was no fixed standard of time because all the clocks contradicted one another would only betray his ignorance of the duty of clocks. The variety to which he objected would be the witness of the fidelity of the clocks. The merit of the clocks from Dublin, or Greenwich, or Calcutta, would not be that they agreed with one another, but that they faithfully recorded the position of the sun with regard to their respective homes. There is virtue in their diversity, in so far as it indicates fidelity to their meridian. In the same way the measure of men's conduct is not to be judged by the meridian of our age, but by the meridian of the age in which they lived. Their merit is fidelity, regularity, precision, in regard to those things which were of the moral order of their day. Just as Macaulay said "that poems might be better when poets were worse;" the rude inspiration of one age may be a nobler thing than the smooth versification of a later time. Men's lives may be measured as poems in proportion as they express the moral force and energy of their day.

Thus, it is the moral energy put forth in response to the bidding of duty or the call of faith, which constitutes the measure of men's actions. When we realize this, we can view without perplexity the varying standards which tempt us to believe that there is no fixity in morals. There is no fixity in one sense, because there is progress; but there is fixity in another sense, because there is always a point from which we can measure the progress of the past. It is a cheap and easy thing to deride men whose advantages were less than our own, and to treat the great characters of the past without reference to the stage upon which they played, or to the circumstances of the drama in which they were engaged. A larger wisdom and a kindlier charity is shown by those who measure men's achievements as we measure the efforts of children, not so much by what they do, as by what they seek to do, or, in other words, not by the cold standard of a rigid code, but by the truer measurements of those who remember that the world is growing under the educating hand of God.

III.—From these considerations we may forecast somewhat the religion of the future.

It has been asked, on what will the religion of

the future be based? Will it be founded on new intellectual conceptions, or will it be the promulgation of some lofty and stately morality, or will some new prophet arise who will lead the world forward to its promised land? Will it be founded on a creed, or a code, or a Person?

Our answer, I think, must be: not on a creed, nor on a code, but on a Person. Not on a creed, unless we desire to have a cold religionism instead of a living, moving religion. Not on a code, unless we are prepared to hand over the race-progress to the chill ministry of a bloodless moralism. But on a Person, for in a Person alone is the conception of religion real and the thought of morality a living thing. (i.) The strictest theologian and the most anxious moralist need not fear that either doctrine or conduct will suffer at the hands of a faith which is founded on a Personal Being. It is only in a Person that a creed can be truly preserved. Sundered from a person the creed becomes a series of interesting speculations, or a voiceless assemblage of lifeless dogmas. It is only in a Person that morality can be vitalized. Morality without a Person becomes at best a cold convention or an inherited necessity. But with a Person, faith and morals alike live and are kept alive. We can have a creed without a Person

VII.] *Religion and Personality.* 275

and a code without a Person; but when we have the Person we possess both a creed and a code. The creed is what we believe of him; his character becomes itself a code of morals. It is in the thought of One, of whom we may say, "*He is*," that we find the life of faith and the life of morals.

But however this may be, it is well to observe that much of the force of the world's history lies here.[1] In persons centre all the deepest and most abiding interest of this world's mingled story of sorrow and joy. The drama may be old or new, but the strong and undying interest is in the characters who walk the stage. From persons radiate the powers which have made history. Thought is great; but thought is powerless till it is wedded with the man who gives it expression. Action, action, action, has been the cry; but what is action in its noblest sense if it be not the expression of personalized thought? In great movements, the time of action follows the time of theorizing; but where were either without the men who preached and lived the truth? All great religions have centred round a person; and no religion has ever achieved any real greatness or established position which has been without a person as its author, or the hero of its early days. The need of this personal element is, perhaps,

[1] See Appendix, Note 42.

nowhere more significantly expressed than in the attempt to supply the lack of a being to be worshipped in the *Grand Être* of the religion of humanity. It is everywhere felt that religion loses its significance, when there is no personal being with whom it can bring its worshippers into relationship.

(ii.) And as religion cannot do without this personal being, so his presence elevates, enlivens and widens religious thought and worship. The creed, as we have said, becomes ethicized. There is need of this. There has been enough philosophizing of creeds; they have been treated as though they were a series of propositions demanding the assent of the mind, and to which the assent of the mind was sufficient. The eager and shallow dogmatist who worshipped not God, but clung vehemently and immorally to his creed, demanded intellectual assent. Heedless of the need of intellectual honesty, or of the ethical significance of the creed, he saw no alternative between the declaration of assent to a theological proposition and the eternal damnation of a human soul. He made it possible for men to say, and to say it with a measure of truth, that orthodoxy was the sin against the Holy Ghost. His creed became a fetish, instead of "Believe in God, believe in the Lord Jesus Christ;" he held aloft his creed, and cried, "Believe *It.*" "*It*" was substituted for "*Him*," and the whole plane of religion was lowered. No era of the Church's history, perhaps, is wholly free from this fatal mistake; no party in the Church is without need of guarding against it. When men say of anything—creed, book, ordinance,—"*it* can save us," then the downward road towards fetishism has begun. Men, devout and pious in their way, write religious books about the Bible, or the Creed or the Sacraments, and they scatter their pages with profane capital letters when they speak of what *It* can do for men. This is perilously near rank and degraded fetishism! It is certainly heresy. There is no power in the Creed to help man, except in so far as the Creed reveals to man a Person who can help. There is no power in the Bible to help man, except in so far as it reveals Him who has never left the world without His present aid. There is no power in the Sacrament to help man, except in so far as He is made known to us in the breaking of that bread. It is Himself, not the dogma about Him; the Word, not the words; the true Bread, not the outward sign; His presence, not His memory, that must be sought, if living power is to be ours. To forget this is to degrade the Bible to the level of a charm, the Creed to the level of cabalistic words, and the Sacraments to the level of magical rights. These—Creed, Bible, Sacraments,—exist as witnesses of One who is Himself the life and power of all. He is greater than these; He is greater than any *It.* Men need to check themselves, and to ask whether they have sunk back to lower and pagan conceptions of spiritual things, and whether they are seeking the living among the dead; whether, in the access of their furious partizan zeal, they have not lost faith in the living personal God, for whom the soul of man cries out, who is behind the Bible, behind the services of the Church, behind the Sacraments, behind all the operations of the universe, and who is the energizing power behind every movement for good. The realization that the end of all worship is the benediction of persons in the recognition of a Person, will produce a wider toleration of varieties of form. If the end of religion be the perfection of man's whole nature, the development of man's character in the formation of a true resemblance to God, then we must see that the essential aim may be secured in an almost measureless variety of means. There are differences of administrations as well as diversities of gifts; there are methods which help the rude and ignorant, which would be valueless for the instructed; there are creeds which help the cultured, but which would be powerless to evoke a responsive Amen from the unlearned. Had the true aim been more clearly recognised, a nobler toleration of variety would have been seen, and the Church might have been saved from the practice—the fountain-head of Schism as far as I can see—dear to narrow souls and feeble brains, of declaring the things which they have found helpful to be essential to the Christian life of all. The schismatic is the child of the fanatic who insists that the custom which has aided the weak should be adopted by the strong, or who would keep the wise and educated, who have need of strong meat, feeding on the children's milk. No modern practice is more calculated to promote division in the Church, than the pernicious habit of those sectarian minds, who persistently call every novel custom or mediæval revival by the name of Catholic usage, when the usage in question is only temporary, local, partial, and not by any means observed always, by all, in all places. Self-opinionated men or ignorant men are naturally intolerant of variation, and believe only in that to which they have been accustomed. Thoughtful and kindly men understand the variety of method which is directed by unity of purpose. The Pharisee saw inconsistency between the habits of John the Baptist and those of our Lord, and failed to recognise the value of either or of both. He failed because he was a Pharisee. It was only a Satyr who charged the man with inconsistency for blowing hot and cold. Neither the Pharisee nor the Satyr have wholly disappeared from the world. But he who is neither Pharisee nor Satyr, but just a man, who realizes that the function of religion is to lift humanity higher, and bring men of differing habits, feelings, and thoughts to the One true God, will not only tolerate but will try to meet with joyous sympathy, the varying modes in which the One Spirit of God works in the Church of God.

With the realisation that religion expresses the relationship of persons to a Person will come clearer views. Doctrines will be seen to be based on that relationship, and will be interpreted accordingly. Men will awake out of their dreams of petty dogmatism into the recognition of eternal facts. They will remember that they and all men are in the hands of One eternal, man-educating, man-redeeming God. They will see that the paramount aim of all must be to help forward men and mankind towards likeness to God; that salvation is indeed salvation from sin; that damnation is just want of harmony between the soul and the God who made it, between the

VII.] *Religion and Personality.* 281

spirit and the life of the spirit. The highest gladness is reached by man when his will is lovingly merged in the holy and righteous and loving will of God; when without effort the spirit responds joyously and naturally to the promptings of the Holy Spirit of all life; when the "I" is "not I" but the "I" which has most truly found itself in the life of another; when the "I" is "not I," but the Christ within (Gal. ii. 20), yet not within only, but both without and within, making harmony between man and his environment, between desire and duty, between the self and the higher than self. For such a man, all things work together for good.

Such are some of the advantages which arise when religion is based on Personality, rather than on a creed or a code.

On a person, then, the religion of the future will be based; on one who will supply both the ideal and the power of the ideal.

The defect of the scientific creed is that it supplies no ideal. There are excellent precepts, there are strong reasonings, there are stern enforcements, but there is no ideal. Its power of looking forward is bounded by its power of looking backward, and its backward glance is limited by the range of knowledge. But the spirit which claims an ideal refuses such limitations; it refuses to believe that an arbitrary combination of virtues can make up an ideal; it asks for an ideal which is free from the too obvious touch of the labouring tool, it asks for an ideal which exhibits that self-evidencing touch of genius and inspiration, a royal unity of conception.

But the religion of the future must not only supply an ideal, but also a power; a power, that is to say, which shall enable men to rise towards the ideal presented to their gaze. In that religion, we must have not merely the high, pure, beautiful life, the code of moral and spiritual activity, but the living, breathing, inspiring embodiment of that ideal. From this alone can radiate that quickening power, which can rouse and kindle the desire and the endeavour of men. And where shall we meet with this power? The doctrine of the new religion must satisfy these requirements, must teach men that the force, which they need in order to attain this ideal, is near to them and available for their assistance.

Humanity needs not only a leader, but an inspirer; not only the guide who will go before the people, but the life which will link itself with them, which will bind up the broken in heart, give strength to the faint and medicine to heal the sicknesses of humanity. The recognition of this need is at the root of those dreams of an

Incarnation which we find scattered throughout the religions of the world. Apotheosis which is a kind of inverted incarnation, and idolatry which is its caricature, alike postulate the idea of personality. No religion has given in stronger, more touching, or more dependable form the manifestation of this idea of an Incarnation than Christianity. She is distinguished in this, that she has not only presented to the world an ideal which is unsurpassed, but that, moreover, she has proclaimed to the world the presence of a power which will enable men to grow towards the realization of that ideal. She says not only, "Rise and follow this ideal, for it is worthy," but she says that "the ideal life may be formed in the hearts and characters of men."

But, it will be said, this is the thing for individuals, and do you not know that philosophy requires that man should not be regarded merely as an individual, but as belonging to an organism which is humanity? It is true, but the Christianity which has a sweet message for the individual has also its grand message for the race. She proclaims that the Incarnation was the Incarnation of One, who should be not only the type and the power of every individual life, but also the power of the organic life of humanity. The Incarnation, according to the Christian faith, was not the conversion of the Godhead into flesh, but the taking of the manhood into God. Thus it is witnessed that humanity lies wholly within the grasp of God. In Christ, it is brought into contact with Him who thus has overshadowed it, and has breathed into it the power of the regenerated life. Thus there is opened to humanity the possibility of realising for the race that golden dream of a social and political paradise, which has been attempted by unpractical dreamers, striven for by large-hearted philanthropists, cried out for by the weary and the toiling, but whose realization can never come through the efforts of man, but through the power of God. The ideal city, like the ideal man, descends out of Heaven from God. What then do we see? The religion of the future; and the religion of the future based upon personality, upon personality in man, and upon that personality in God which is above all personality. I see at last the heavens open, and the angels of God are ascending and descending, but the ladder of the patriarch is gone, and that which binds heaven to earth, and round which angelic light is hovering, is a form like to the form of the Son of Man.

LECTURE VIII.

THE RELIGION OF THE FUTURE.

The survival of Religion being probable, the question arises whether any existing Faith can fulfil the conditions needful for survival.

I.—The conditions needful.
 (i.) Religion must—
  1. Satisfy men's wish for unity.
  2. Give guarantee of Permanence.
 (ii.) Religion must supply the three elements— Dependence, Fellowship, Progress.
 (iii.) Religion must possess a Power of Inspiration.

II.—The application of these conditions to existing Religions.
 (i.) How far existing Faiths possess needful conceptions.
  1. Non-Christian Systems— Islâm, Buddhism, Positivism.
  2. Christianity.
   (a) The three elements—Dependence, Fellowship and Progress. (b) The test of unity and permanence. (c) Some further features.
 (ii.) The power of Inspiration.
  1. This both in subject and object of Religion.
  2. The relation of this inspiring power to—
   (a) Law of Environment. (b) Law of Organism. (c) Law of Sacrifice. (d) Law of Indirectness.
  3. This power pervades Christianity.

Conclusion.—Changes of form may be expected, but Christianity in its essential elements abides.

LECTURE VIII.

THE RELIGION OF THE FUTURE.

"Hereafter ye shall see heaven open, and the Angels of God ascending and descending upon the Son of Man."—*St. John* i. 51.

WILL there be a religion in the future? This was the question with which we began. We have tried to reach an answer; and the answer has been that from our knowledge of man's nature, and from the evident permanence of that nature, it is at least unlikely that religion will perish. In this view we are supported by those who have studied the question from different standpoints. For instance, M. Renan says, "Religion is the organisation of self-devotion. Let no one therefore hope to dispense with religion and religious associations."[1] Professor Max Müller, to whose labours in this field we owe so much, says : "I maintain that religion, so far from being impossible, is inevitable, if only we are left in possession of our senses."[2] Mr. Herbert Spencer,

[1] "Hibbert Lect.," p. 30. [2] "Origin of Religion," p. 32.

who has shown a deep interest in the future prospects of religion, reminds us that the element which gives rise to religious feeling is one which is not likely to disappear from human life or thought: "This consciousness of an incomprehensible Power, called Omnipresent from inability to assign its limits, is just that consciousness on which religion dwells."[1]

We may believe then, that religion will survive; but we are naturally led to further questions. Will religion in the future be one or many? Is the germ of it extant? If so, can we find this germ in any known religion?

I.—We shall endeavour to answer the first two questions, in the belief, that we may thus discover some tests by which to arrive at an answer to the last question.

Will religion in the future be one or many?

We have seen that there is reason to believe that religion will survive. It seems to me that there are grounds for believing that in the future there will be one religion for all mankind.

(i.) 1. First, there is the acknowledged craving for synthesis, which will not be set aside. Man asks for it, and remains restless till he finds either it or something which he persuades himself is a

[1] Quoted by J. B. Crozier, "Religion of the Future," p. 104.

substitute for it. The love of systems, the striving to reduce everything to a law, the persuasion that there is somewhere an eternal order, illustrate this intellectual necessity. The impatience of creeds shown by some is a pain to others; but it is one of the paradoxes of human nature, that those most eager to maintain certain forms of religious belief, and those most impatient of them, may be seeking the same thing. The same instinctive feeling lies at the root of the obstinate conservatism of the one, and of the destructive criticism of the other. Both are eager for unity of thought and feeling among men; both are earnestly desirous that the principles which will express and maintain this unity should be reached and manifested. Both are aware of the fact, that forms are but the expressions of things greater than all form. One, however, sees in the special form of his choice the expression of those principles which he feels are needful, and which cannot otherwise be so fully expressed. The other man is impatient of the forms which, as he believes, half conceal the eternal principles which they seek to express.

Much of the perplexity which surrounds our thoughts to-day arises from the conviction of the inadequacy of forms to express "the thing itself.'

All modes of expression are imperfect; even the intellectual Puritan must learn to put up with much that is imperfect; to tolerate the child-language because it is spoken by children; and in doing so, he may, perhaps, even feel that he too would be content to use the faulty speech of childhood, if only he could have the child-heart given back to him. The desire to reach the underlying principles of life and thought; the belief that forms are but efforts to express the thing itself; the longing to pass behind the forms, and grasp the root from which they derive their life; these are ways in which a craving for the divine synthesis shows itself. The faith of men turns to religion in the belief that it is her function to reveal this synthesis, or at least to supply some unifying power to life if not to thought.

(a) The recognition of the unity of the race points the same way. Men are grasping at everything which gives promise of unity. The nations of the world are dreaming of the brotherhood of man. In various quarters significant attempts to give reality to this dream may be noted. The worship of Humanity is a religion with some. Commerce, science and navigation draw closer the bonds of the world. The study of history and of the laws which govern life, exhibits the solidarity of the human race. Again, the progress of the race is an advance from lower to higher; such progress makes more easy the recognition of the brotherhood of men. It is in the baser things that men are divided. In regions where interest and ambition, greed and self-glory have sway, men find themselves at feud. In the higher regions of faith, hope, kindliness, the discord ceases. There was a stormy day in France when an angry crowd were ready to sacrifice a woman as the victim of their wrath; in a moment of inspiration, a friend gave a child into the terrified and threatened woman's arms, and she passed through the crowd in safety. The touch of Nature stilled the storm of passion. It did more. It transfigured the feelings of the people, by the influence of a tenderness which rebuked their rage, and cried, "Ye are brethren." It lifted them into these higher regions in which manhood is one. Armed with a like strength, bearing in her arms the symbol of our common nature, religion may yet appear, allaying men's baser passions and bowing their hearts as the heart of one man. The acceptance of one faith, as embodying the eternal principles of religion, ceases to be impossible when men have recognised the common blood, and common ties, and common interests of all mankind.

It would seem therefore not over sanguine to believe that the Religion of the Future will recognise and embody this growing desire for union. Religion will hardly survive if it is the source of division instead of the power of concord. When we ask whether religion in the future will be one or many, we feel justified in saying, "it will be one." It may include varieties of thought and feeling; but it must supply a power of union to mankind. It must realise, in some way, the hope and prediction of the Prophet, that in a future day, men would recognise one Lord and His name as One.

We turn to our next question. Is the religion of the future extant? Is its germ to be found among us to-day? Or are we to look for a religion built on new lines, the outcome of new conditions?

We look into the faces of the religions and prophets which the world has seen and worshipped, and we ask, "Art thou he that should come or do we look for another?" As we ask the question, we feel that it is possible to-day, as it was of old, that the prophet and faith of the future are in our midst. It is not given to every man to discern the prophecy of power written on familiar faces. It is not every one who sees the dove descending on the Christ. There may stand among us one whom we know not, but who yet will baptise future generations with fire. It is possible that the religion which is to rule in the future may be among us to-day.

2. Is it too much to say that it is more than possible, that it is next to certain that it must be so? Religion, if it is to survive, must have a pedigree which defies the analysis of time. There is a sense in which, if she is to be without end of days, she must be without beginning of life also. We sometimes, indeed, confuse the beginning of things with their first manifestation; but we are living too late in the world's history to be excused if we make this confusion. The laws of gravity and the laws of motion, as we call them, were at work thousands of years before Newton and Kepler proclaimed them. They embody principles which stretch beyond the reach of known time; they defy change and they know no death. Like the trees which the Heavenly Father has planted, they cannot be rooted up.

Her basis must be eternal. She must draw her light from Him who is before all time, if she is to embody principles which are for all time. She must reveal herself as belonging to every age. She must be the bond between the humanity which has passed away, and that humanity which is, and that which is to come. Humanity indeed, may paint religion in different colours and in different forms in different ages; but the essential principles of a religion must be those of all time, or it is not a religion for man. It cannot, therefore, owe its life to the ingenuity or wisdom of any man; it cannot be invented, though it may be discovered. It cannot be made, but like the best things it must grow. If this be so, the essential elements of the future religion must be in existence now. Whatever manifestation of them may take place in the future, whatever changes of form may be seen, we may be sure that the seed and living principle of the religion of the future will be no new thing, but old as the eternal hills.

We are now in a better position to deal with the further question. Will any of the religions familiar to us supply the germ of the future faith? Is the cradle of the religion of the future to be sought in the home of any existing creed? What religion among us is great enough, and holy enough, to be the mother of the religion of the ages to come?

(ii.) We have seen that men look to religion to supply unifying power, and that it must be for all time, and not the mere creation of to-day or yesterday. It must be one and eternal. It must also minister to the never-failing demand of man for Dependence, Fellowship, and Progress. Its conceptions must, therefore, be of an order to meet these conditions ; but even more is needed.

(iii.) Religions, like men, are great in proportion as they combine great ideas with great personality. Greatness of thought wedded to greatness of soul seldom fails to win its way to ascendancy. For, while one defines the range of life, without the other, life would lack inspiration. Like the sun, such characters rise upon the world gifted with powers to illumine men's thoughts and kindle men's hearts. Cold illumination is not enough ; the fire must be burning upon the altar. Religion must inspire as well as instruct.

Thus the question whether any existing religions will supply the seed of the religion of the future seems to depend upon two other questions, viz., Do they possess fitting conceptions ? Have they the power of inspiration ?

II. (i.) The ideas or conceptions of religions may be taken first.

1. In regard to non-Christian systems we have seen that there are three elements needful and demanded by man—Dependence, Fellowship, Progress. We have already applied this threefold test to various religions. We have seen that Islamism meets the demand of Dependence, fails to satisfy naturally the instinct of Fellowship, and can scarcely be reckoned upon as affording

any efficient stimulus towards Progress. In Buddhism we have found an attempt to meet the desire for Fellowship; but Buddhism supplies nothing upon which man can rest, none upon whom he can Depend; and it offers no countenance to Progress, seeing that it turns away from life as evil. We have interrogated Positivism, and we have found that in it the three elements are apparently provided for. There is all nature for man to Depend on; all humanity for man to hold Fellowship with; and scientific order as the guarantee of Progress. But it may be questioned whether the satisfaction promised is not illusory. Man is promised Dependence, but the object offered for his trust is nothing higher than himself. Instead of the relation between the weak and one who is strong and good, we are put off with the relation between ourselves as individual men and humanity taken in the abstract. Instead of an equation, we are offered an identity. The satisfaction offered is only the idealized form of that which asks the satisfaction. Man has gone too far on the road of life to be satisfied with such an offer as this. As Mr. Herbert Spencer says, " The religious sentiment can never again (unless by retrogression) take a Finite Knowable, like Humanity, for its object of contemplation."[1]

[1] " The Classification of the Sciences." p. 41.

The conceptions or ideas, therefore, of these religions stand in relation to the threefold test we have applied as follows : Islamism and Buddhism must be reckoned as deficient and incapable of meeting fully or adequately the demands of mankind; Positivism, on the other hand, shows itself alive to this triple need of human nature, but the satisfaction she offers is more theoretical than real.

We have now to ask, whether these religions meet the requirements which the religion of the future must fulfil, by possessing unifying force and that characteristic which raises them above any special time, and is the pledge of perpetuity.

We commence with Islamism. Has it unifying force? Has it power to meet the hopes and desires of men for a religion which shall embrace every race, complexion and character? The answer must be that Islamism is essentially rigid and frigid. Islamism is great, but great as an iceberg is great; its tendency is to stiffen and harden. Whenever, under more genial influences, it melts to meet the needs of humanity, it ceases to be Islamism. It was destined—such is the view of those who have studied it— to stereotype itself once for all and assume unalterable shape. " Almost as old as Islam itself, and destined to last as long, there stood and there stand immoveable the Koran and the tradition."[1]

> " So while the world rolls on from change to change,
> And realms of thought expand,
> The letter stands without expanse or range,
> Stiff as a dead man's hand."

It can hardly supply the unifying force requisite in a great religion of humanity.

It cannot claim perpetuity. There are indeed elements in it which never die, but these are common to other creeds. In its special characteristics it is limited; it is of an epoch; "it is a side branch of Christianity, or, better still, as we should now say, of Judaism: a selection, as it were, from Law and Gospel, made by an Arab and for Arabs."[1]

Buddhism can hardly exhibit unifying power in the world, seeing that, as we have shown, it turns away from all life. It is true that sorrow, disappointment, the readiness to pronounce the verdict that life itself is an evil, is a universal feeling. But a religion which offers to man, as the foundation principle of union, the vanity and hopelessness of life, is superfluous; we are already united in sorrow; we need no religion to tell us this; we need a religion which will unite

[1] Kuenen, "Hibbert Lectures," p. 54. See Note 43, in Appendix.

us with our suffering brothers in the bonds of hope. But here Buddhism fails, and, in failing, pronounces sentence of sterility in the future upon itself. There is no golden age before the Buddhist's eye. There is no "belief in the ultimate triumph" of God over all, no "confident trust in the realization of a moral ideal. This is what Buddhism does not possess and cannot give."[1]

Positivism, in a measure, meets the demands of mankind for Dependence, Fellowship and Progress as elements in a universal religion. Can it fulfil the conditions of possessing unifying force and independence of time? In so far as it makes the service of humanity an aim of its followers, it possesses a capacity for drawing men together. But a fatal difficulty, in its path to ultimate success, is its avowed limitation to the things of the present life and the existing visible world; it denies to itself any grasp upon the great eternity of things; it is of time, and belongs to time; the temple of humanity which it rears is vast in structure, and noble in its proportions, but it has no Holy of Holies, no shrine where the soul of man can enter into the presence of the Eternal. It is, at best, "the worship of man by man." "He (Comte) succeeded in founding a true

[1] Kuenen, "Hibbert Lectures," p. 291.

mysticism on this narrow base."[1] But we feel that the base is too narrow for the temple of universal worship. The foundations of the temple which will endure must not alone be built upon the holy hills; it must have foundations which are not of time. Man cannot find the temple in any city made with hands. It can only be found in the city which hath the foundations and whose builder and maker is God.

2. We have applied certain tests to certain religions. It is our duty to apply the same to Christianity.

(a) We have already tested it in relation to the three elements—Dependence, Fellowship, Progress; and we have seen that it possesses power and fitness to meet these requirements of mankind. It tells us of One on whom we may depend, with whom we may hold fellowship, and in whose strength we may fulfil our life and help forward the progress of the world.

(b) Can it stand the twofold test? Does it come to us with the promise of perpetuity and the prestige of unifying power?

Perpetuity. We must revert to the caution on which we insisted in a previous Lecture. We are interrogating Christianity; we are separating it in our thoughts from Christianism. There are

[1] Réville, "Prolegomena," p. 19.

many in the Christian Church who believe in Christianism more than they do in Christianity. Probably they do not know the difference, having perhaps never thought upon the subject. But many Christian people would feel no hesitation in saying that they believed in a religion founded by Christ, and called Christianity because it was founded by Christ. But this is Christianism, not Christianity. To treat the religion of Christ in this way is to sin against the spirit of the religion which we pretend to honour. There is no word in the New Testament to sanction such a thought. Our Lord and His apostles set up a far nobler and larger conception. Jesus Christ did not come to found a religion, except in a secondary sense. He is not the founder of Christianity; He is its foundation. And even thus we do not express all the truth, unless we see in Him the foundation of all the higher faiths of men. He came to make manifest eternal facts; the manifestation of these facts was a new revelation, but it was not a revelation of things which were new in themselves. The proclamation of these eternal facts was the foundation of a new covenant, but did not set up any new religion without root in the past.

There was in the life of Christ a manifestation of glory; but it was a glory which He had with the Father before the world was, a glory which men might fail to recognize, but which was recognized in heaven and by those who were heavenly-minded. Only pure hearts could see God; and only loving and pure spirits could see that the glory of life consisted in purity, sacrifice, and love. There was the manifestation of a mystery, but it was a mystery which existed beforehand; it was unrevealed, but existing, a mystery which in these ages was not made known to the sons of men.

The events of our Lord's life took place in time; but in the eye of the Christian Apostle these too were not of time. The Redeemer, who hung upon the Cross on Calvary, was "the Lamb slain from the foundation of the world." (Rev. xiii. 8.) No new principles came into existence with what we call Christianity; even those which seemed to be new were eternal. Jesus Christ did not invent a religion, He revealed the laws of the eternal kingdom of God; laws older and more abiding than the laws by which rivers run and planets move. Christianity was the manifestation of eternal principles; it was the making known of the kingdom of God. Against any conceptions of it, which tended to give it a time-born foundation, St. Paul contended. When they cried at Corinth,

"I am of Paul, of Apollos, of Cephas," he rebuked the partizans, not only as partizans, but as those who would limit Christianity, making it a Paulinism or a Petrinism; he would not suffer them to say "I am of Christ," lest Christianity should degenerate into a Christianism. To say so was to alter the conception of the faith, and to view it as a novel religion founded by Christ. He said with tender earnestness, "Ye are Christ's;" he recognized the love which had redeemed them; but the love, which he saw there, was no love which had its birth in time—it was eternal. He carried them to the source of life and love. "Ye are Christ's, and Christ is God's." (1 Cor. iii. 23.)

But has Christianity unifying force? Is not Christianity exclusive? In one sense, Christianity is intolerant. She refuses to be classed among other religions. She declares that she is not one religion among many of equal or varying respectability and authority; she claims to be everything or nothing. But the principle which lies at the root of this intolerance is, when rightly understood, the principle which makes Christianity magnanimous, tender, and tolerant. She refuses to be classed with other religions, for she refuses to enter into rivalry with them. She does not claim in their sense to be a religion; she views the contests of rival systems, with the calm self-possession of one who dwells in a region wholly different from theirs, and above the reach of storms. She is not a religion competing with others for man's attention; she seeks not her own glory; she asks men to observe the laws of the kingdom in which they dwell; and to believe in that kingdom which, being the Kingdom of God, is eternal and above the small systems of men. She claims to bring into fuller view the light which was before all the wisdom and opinions of men, which dwelt among them often unseen, sometimes half apprehended. She reveals the eternal order which was before the consciousness of men, and before the existence of systems and the creeds of churches. Christianity truly understood is the manifestation of eternal facts—He who is its light was the light of this world in all ages, shining more and more unto the perfect day.

It is needful to realize this claim. When grasped firmly, it saves timid Christian people from needless fears and causeless doubts. Many, for instance, are anxious on what they call the claim of Christianity to originality. It is the survival of a foolish controversy which has existed too long, and chiefly from a want of understanding Christianity. There was a time in which Christian apologists refused to see good in any other religious system. When any good element was pointed out in a non-Christian system, they were eager to prove that it was derived by some side stream from the Christian or Jewish Scriptures. For a time the Christian apologist had matters his own way. Now the argument is plied on the other side. There are men eager to prove that every characteristic feature of Christianity has been derived from some other system. It owes its virtue and teaching to the Therapeutæ. It is an offspring of transplanted Buddhism. It is needless to enumerate further. There are those who would deny to it every vestige of originality.[1]

Extremists are seldom right, because extremists are mostly men who have a theory to maintain, and who are apt to overlook some obvious principle. The apologist who sought to strip all good from every system but Christianity, and the antagonist who denies every good to Christianity, are alike in their misapprehension. They incline to the belief that originality is a test of truth. Originality is a cant word, and is, in its current sense, a very poor ambition for men or systems. There is only one originality worth striving for, and that is truth. All truth is original in a large sense. It is original because it is of the eternal origin and order of things. In this way, all real originality in men is but a brightness shining in

[1] See Appendix, Note 44.

them from the eternal light. Christianity therefore may well be heedless of the ambition of being called original. She is original, because she manifests facts and truths original in the order of the kingdom of God. But she has no sympathy with the schoolroom squabbles of men and systems who wrangle like boys over the question, "Who said it first?"

Christianity is the manifestation of facts, laws, and principles which are eternal—not first created when Christ appeared, but then brought into clearer and fuller manifestation. Christianity does not deny the brightness and splendour of those beams of light which in all ages shone amongst men.[1] She points to them in proof of the eternal basis of the kingdom of God. She throws new meaning into truths which men had already perceived. She draws together the scattered beams which men saw, but did not wholly comprehend; and uniting them, she is able to diffuse throughout the world a purer light. She takes freely the loaves which are handed to her by wise and the good; and the holy bread multiplies in her hands, stretched out to feed the famine of the world. She collects the scattered fragments of marble; she reconstructs the broken statue and its beauty becomes a joy to men. She does

[1] See Appendix, Note 45.

more, she touches the dead image and it lives. Thus, she comes not to destroy, but to save. She does not seek to make a new system, but to open men's eyes to the kingdom which was always there. In this way she proclaims the One Life which is the life of all—the One Light which is the light of all—the One God who is the Father of all.

(c) The value of this light diffused by Christianity will become more evident, as we examine some of the characteristic ideas which she gives to the world, and notice how these meet and satisfy men's thoughts and dreams.

Take for instance the idea of God.

There are obvious difficulties in the way of presenting the thought of God to men. If He be God, He must be the Universal Sovereign ; but also if He is to be God truly to men, men must be sure of His friendship. Men's thoughts have on these matters run into extremes. In their wish to preserve the idea of God's sovereignty, they have sacrificed His nearness to man. To make Him great, they have banished Him from man. This has been the tendency of Deism. To bring Him near, they have identified Him with the work of His own hands, and, in their effort to realise His nearness, they have lost Him as God. This has been the tendency of Pantheism.

To steer a middle course between these extremes is needful. Christianity, like every other system of faith, has to meet this difficulty; and she does so by presenting the idea of God as that of the Father. This idea of the Fatherhood of God is regarded by Professor Max Müller as specially characteristic of Christianity.[1] And it meets the difficulty. There is no danger that by this thought God will be thrust far away from men. The Heavenly Father knows what things they have need of. There is no fear that the thought of God will be lost in the works of His hands. He, who is the Father of men, gives the rain and the fruitful seasons, clothes the flowers in their beauty and watches the bird in her flight. He who is Father is also God of all. "One is our Father, which is in heaven." (St. Matt. xxiii. 9.)

Or examine the same idea in the light of the needs of men. The search which man made for God has been described as the search for the principle of fatherhood. "Men wanted a Father in heaven, who should take count of their efforts and assure them of a recompense."[2] The process of their search has been stated by Professor Max Müller; he says that they have passed through three stages, the first in which they were tempted

[1] "Biographical Essays," p. 120.
[2] Renan, "Hib. Lect.," p. 42.

to say " God is *not* a Father," the second in which they said with hope, " God is *like* a Father," and the third the stage of a happy assurance when they said God *is* a Father.[1]

The craving of man, therefore, was for the recognition of God as his Father. Religious conceptions have not always fully grasped the fatherly idea of God; men ran to extremes. Augustine and Calvin, no less than Mahommed, were inclined to push God far away. Looking upon Him as the Supreme Ruler, the Absolute Sovereign of the universe, they were tempted to dwell upon His arbitrary power till the thought of His fatherly care dropped into the background; losing the wholesome doctrine of Fatherhood, men lapsed away from all that was highest and best in religious life. "Without it," says Dr. Fairbairn, "the religions of the West had perished amid license and apathy, while the more fervid spirits of the East took refuge in the thought of annihilation."[2]

Nor is the importance of the idea of Fatherhood less evident when we come to modern times. The notion of God, as an absolute and irresponsible ruler, is needlessly at variance with the spirit of modern scientific thought. We are reminded of this by Mr. Fiske, who says : " It "

[1] " Origin of Religion," p. 228.
[2] " Studies in the Philosophy of Religion," p. 56.

—that is, the Deistic conception of God—" is chiefly responsible for that complicated misunderstanding which, by a lamentable confusion of thought, is commonly called the conflict between religion and science." And again he says : "It is all the more instructive to note how closely Athanasius approaches the confines of modern scientific thought, simply through his fundamental conception of God as the indwelling life of the universe." [1] It would seem then that, when the ideas of God sink below the true Christian level, the misunderstandings and conflicts between knowledge and faith increase; but, when the higher Christian idea of God prevails, conflict disappears. Knowledge and faith become then united as children of the same family, and as joint ministers to the needs, the thoughts, and the hopes of humanity. In the recognition of God as the Eternal Father, we avoid the dangers which arise from naked Deism; we are saved from falling into the confusions of Pantheism; we satisfy both the scientific spirit and the religious spirit alike. In other words, the conception of God which is offered by Christianity is that which avoids the pitfalls into which the religionist of the past has fallen.

Again, the conception of man presented by

[1] " The Idea of God," pp. 96, 86.

Christianity is equally helpful. If God is the Father of man, man is the child of God, and a child who is therefore under the educating hand and care of wisdom and love. Life here is the carrying forward of man's education, the gradual ripening under the trials, temptations, and sorrows of life, of his moral and spiritual character. The Sermon on the Mount shows that this was Christ's view of life. He held up before us the true aim and end of life; it was not wealth, it was not success, it was simply character, and the perfection of character meant resemblance to Him who is our Father. From the beginning to the end, His sweet and divine words are the pleadings of One who wishes men to realize how greatly God cares for them, how ceaseless is His love, how earnest is His desire that they should ripen like the corn under the changing seasons of life, into that perfection which can make glad the heart of God, as when the father sees the features and the form of perfect manhood growing in the life of his son. Nor was this all. Before men's eyes this aim was made still more clear, by the simple and noble ideal and example set before them. To grow like to God men must realize what God was like; they could guess at His power and acknowledge His wisdom, but how could they form a true conception of His character? The ideal and pattern took human form, and lived and breathed in the life of Christ. The ideal was not that of the acquisition of power, the achievement of success, or the display of dazzling wisdom; it was the manifestation of a perfect character; the ideal was moral and spiritual.

It has indeed been objected, that the Christian ideal gives undue prominence to the more feminine virtues; that it makes more of charity than of justice, more of purity than of courage, more of humility than of decision. But it is forgotten that there is comparatively little need to emphasise the more masculine virtues. The teaching of Christ will be found on examination to take for granted the value of those masculine virtues. The man who has to make money by trading must be a man of force, of courage, of alertness. The man who would build his tower must possess decision, prudence, and a certain heedlessness of the derision of his fellow men. It can never be said that to bear the Cross needs the exercise of the softer virtues only. But there is a reason why it was needful to give prominence to the more feminine virtues. Masculine energy resembles talent which sees what has to be done, and exerts itself in a regardless, perhaps unscrupulous, way to attain it. The feminine virtues are more analagous to genius, which catches, in quietness and in retirement, inspirations which seldom reach the more stormy soul. It has often been the gentle and timid spirit which has risen to acts of heroism and self-devotion impossible to one who possessed merely the masculine virtues. And the reason is simple: such a soul, like genius, lies more open to inspiration. As woman's enthusiasm in her more exalted moments puts to shame the more prudent courage of man, so the possession of what are called feminine virtues has often been a source of higher and more conspicuous heroism than could have been achieved by force or firmness or courage. But let this pass. Christianity did not depreciate the manly virtues when she insisted on the need of sweetness and purity. In Christ an ideal was set up which is practically accepted. It has been pointed out, by a writer of deep insight and careful thought, that the ideal figure which has survived all the conflicts and anxieties of centuries is the ideal set up by Christ.[1] Men recognised that that ideal met all their needs; the active virtues and the passive virtues were alike included in it. It has survived, and, if it has survived, science must admit that it was the fittest ideal.

It satisfied them because it witnessed against all

[1] Matheson, "Can the Old Faith live with the New?" ch. xiv., p. 384, et seq.

forms of weakness and sin, and men will be satisfied with no faith which does not set itself against the moral evil, not only in the world, but in themselves. But the idea of redemption and the idea of fatherly care brought hope to all, and with it the inspiration of endeavour; for though the ideal was high and beyond his dreams, it was no impossible ideal to him who was the child of God. God had stretched forth His hand and endowed him in Christ with the opportunity of reaching the best and noblest ideal. The revelation of Sonship was the revelation of a Divine education. There was now within reach that high character and holy image, which, without Divine help, was an impossibility and a despair.

Once more, the conception of the kingdom of God presented by Christianity is in accord with the widest and truest views of life. There has been a vain and foolish struggle between the religionist and the secularist. Both have missed the mark, because both have lost sight of the fulness of life in the division which they sanctioned between the sacred and secular. Christianity recognised no such division; nothing was secular in a kingdom which was wholly God's. The kingdom proclaimed by Christ was a kingdom which was everywhere and all-embracing. All life, and all life's powers were embraced within its scope.

A modern writer, after saying that the conception of the kingdom of God was a chief factor in the genesis of Christianity, shows that in this idea "it joins in every legitimate effort of individuals or of the peoples who profess it;" "strikes right into the course of their development, and gives it the true direction, the genuine inspiration, the higher consecration."[1] It is easy to see what flows from this. The Divine hand is in everything. The Divine Spirit is everywhere. The gifts of God are sacred gifts, though they may be employed in what we call secular life. No gift comes but behind it comes also the grace—if men will but receive it—to use their gift aright. No duty is put before men, but that the ever-present help of God is near to enable them to rise to the doing of it. The infirmities which spring from sin, the weaknesses which are hereditary, the despairs which are born of the experience of life, all are free of the help which heaven is even more eager to give than humanity is to receive. Hope may visit every human heart and every human home, since the sense of Divine power and Divine sympathy in every department of life brings to humanity the conviction, that the progress of the world which is desired by men is dear also to the heart of God.

Thus in the conception of God presented by

[1] Kuenen, "Hib. Lect." p. 291.   [2] Appendix, Note 46.

Christianity, in her conception also of man's position, and in the idea which she puts forward concerning the kingdom of God, she gives to the world what the world has wanted, and she avoids those extreme views which, embraced with eagerness, end by provoking the sense of helplessness. To mankind she declares that all things are tending towards a golden age; to the individual she says, God is educating you that you may grow like Himself. And all this is true, because God is neither the arbitrary monarch which was conceived of by Mahomet, nor the impersonal All which the Orientalist imagined, but One who in the brightness of His perfection, and in the tenderness of His love, is the Father of all.

(ii.) But a religion must be tested by the force of its inspirations as well as by the fitness of its conceptions.

We have seen how the principles of Christianity meet the needs which are recognised by men's thoughts. But behind the sanctuary of holy thoughts there is a Holy of Holies. Behind the thoughts to which religion gives expression, there is its spirit. Its secret strength lies there. The author of the "Patience of Hope" reminded us that there were books which, though not ostensibly religious, were really religious, and more fully so than many a formal treatise on faith. A theological work may be irreligious; a literary or scientific work may be eminently religious. This is a way of stating the well-known truth that the spirit is more than the letter, "the life more than meat, and the body than raiment." (St. Luke xii. 23.) It is possible, then, that a religion may present conceptions eminently fitted to satisfy men's thoughts, and yet fail to inspire them with the ardour of goodness. Its form may be good, but the spirit which animates it may be a spirit far from religious. It becomes then a question of interest, what will be the spirit of the religion of the future? I think there can be but one answer: the religion of the future will be animated by Love. There are good grounds for this assertion. Differing schools of thought recognise this need, and seek to promote the spirit of love. Men proclaim Altruism, "the service of man," "the brotherhood of the race," and in doing so express their belief that only in love can the true spirit of the religion of the future be found. But the preaching of a doctrine is not the inspiration of a life; and in the proclamation of Altruism, or "the service of man," or the "brotherhood of humanity," we only possess intellectual conceptions of religion, and these are inadequate. A moment's reflection will show that these are, at the best, only affirmations of the duty of life. They are like excellent and well-planned machinery; the construction is perfect, but the power of movement is still wanting. You preach to men the duty of love and service and brotherhood, but who will create in man the spirit which responds to your appeal, and which triumphs over egotism and selfishness? Man needs not only theories but inspirations. The religion of the future must not only tell a man what he ought to do, it must also bring with it the inspiring force which will create in him the desire to do it. Hence the need of the religion of the future is an inspiring love.

1. But seeing that love only can create love, love must be found in the Object of worship as well as in the heart of the worshipper. In other words, the religion of the future must be based upon a Person rather than an idea. In the recognition of this truth will be found the synthesis of religion and morals. Knowledge becomes virtue and virtue becomes knowledge[1] in the relationship between God and man; to know God is to be like Him, and to be like God is to know Him, and this can only be when religion is a bond between living beings and the Living One, whose breath is their life, from whom they came and to whom they go. We may take it for granted,

[1] See Appendix, Note 47.

then, on every account, that the religion of the future must be a religion inspired by love.

2. It will be well to point out the wide bearing of this conclusion. Go back in thought to the four laws of which we spoke in our first lecture: "as we think, we are;" "as we are, we see;" "sacrifice is the root of progress;" "indirectness is the law of sacrifice." Now what do these amount to? The first is equivalent to saying that there is no religion without a creed, that is, without ideas. The second is equivalent to saying there is no religion without character, that is, without moral fitness and affinity in man. The third is equivalent to saying there is no perfection of character without sacrifice; and the fourth is equivalent to saying there is no sacrifice without fire. Now if these four laws be true, it seems clear that they can only be provided for by a religion of love. The reasons are these :—

(a) Love alone can give the interpretation of life aright. Our first law was, "as we think, we are;" that is, a religion must present men with ideas. These ideas should supply a key to life's perplexity and difficulty. Life is capable of opposing interpretations. The pessimist can see in it abundant reasons for his pessimism: everything is dark; hope is dim; failure is frequent, all is vanity, men are more vicious than virtuous. So into gloom the pessimist would lead us. But it is possible to interpret life in an opposite way. The optimist bids us look at the eternal upspringing of hope; he asks us to behold the flowers, and to sit in the sunshine, and to see how life to most creatures is but joy. Life is like a game of chess: the pessimist sees only the victory of the black pieces, and the optimist only that of the white. But neither of them quite sees the real value of the game, which is not in the victory of white over black, or black over white; the victory is nothing, the game is the thing; the colour of the men is nothing, but the intellectual practice is everything. Whether the player is victor or vanquished he may gain good, his powers of observation, reflection and self-control have been exercised. This inward good is the real gain from the game. It is thus that love would teach us about life. "As we think, we are." If we think that life is to be interpreted by its pleasing successes, then we shall become self-complacent, as the optimist; or, if we think that it is to be interpreted by its disastrous failures, we shall become cynical, as the pessimist. But if we think of love as behind all that we see, if faith has taught us that education is the end of life, and that inward good wrought in man is more than man's worldly success or worldly failure, that the game and the practice of the game is the thing which the Divine Love has in view, then the interpretation of life becomes a happier and a truer one. Life is discipline, education; there is an unseen good greater than vulgar and shallow worldliness can perceive. Seeing this, we learn that by our onesidedness and selfishness we may be wronging Him, who orders all things by a wisdom and a love larger than our knowledge.

We may understand this by reflecting on our own experience. How often have we done our best, sincerely endeavoured to do what was right and just towards man, and yet have only been met by the accusation of base motives. We have grown indignant. We pour out words of scorn against the base world, which cannot believe in good intentions because it is base itself. May it not be that we, too, have misinterpreted God? God is unknowable, we say. It is true that there are depths in Him which we cannot fathom, heights which we cannot climb; to our poor failing intellects God may be unknowable, but the reproach, which will visit us in the other world, will not be that we have deemed God unknowable, but that we have so often misinterpreted Him. In misunderstanding Him and disbelieving in the goodness of His government, we not only do Him wrong; but in wronging Him we wrong also

B B

ourselves. "As we think, we are." As are our thoughts of God, and as are our interpretations of life, so are we ourselves. Disbelief in goodness becomes pain, and afterwards degradation; like Timon, vexed at our failure, often the result of our own stupidity, we refuse to believe in the faithfulness and good of our dearest friend. Like Hamlet, having met with disappointment in the object we deemed pure and good, we leap to the conclusion that there is no purity and goodness anywhere. Like Othmar, we have lived with good, but we have rejected it and disbelieved in its purity, its loyalty and its truth, and we wake up like Othmar at last to find that our obstinate disbelief in goodness is visited with its penalty; the good angel of our life perishes from our side, and we are left poorer and sadder by the loss. It is wise to think that we may have been wrong with regard to God; we may have been wrong in our interpretation of life. If the end which is set before us be the education of our characters, then we shall not think it strange that we are called on to struggle, permitted to fall, given the experiences of success, and exposed to the vicissitudes and the seasonal trials of life,

> " Esteeming sorrow, whose employ
> Is to develop, not destroy,
> Far better than a barren joy."

For it is thus that a Divine Love deals with us, that in the end we may become possessed of that wealth which the world cannot take away, the spiritual wealth of a perfected and developed character. Notwithstanding then our feebleness and our misrepresentations, after all God may be Love. It is certain that only the religion which proclaims the love behind all life will meet and satisfy men in the future.

(*b*) But again, love alone gives the standpoint for the interpretation of life. Our second law is, "as we are, we see;" that is to say, each man's character is as a view-point, from which he beholds the world; what is wanted is the true view-point. To behold the sweep and beauty of the landscape aright we must take the elevated ground; to understand the action and conduct of men we must stand where they stand. The criticism which is levelled against public men is often unfair, because it is criticism made by those who occupy a different standpoint, and cannot see things as they do.

> " Who would the poet understand,
> Must go with him to the poet's land."

The cheap critic of the kitchen or of the attic may be mistaken in his estimate of a great man. The French saying, "To know all is to pardon all," expresses this truth; if we could only stand where we could fairly survey all the conditions, inheritances, temptations, difficulties, and complications of a man's life, we should understand and be tender to his errors. "Put yourself in his place," we often say, as if we felt that only when we stand where the derided or the criticised man stands can we possibly perceive the meaning of his actions, measure the amount of his failure, or understand the greatness of his success.

But how shall we do this in the case of God? We cannot stand where God stands, or view the universe with His eye, or measure its march with His wisdom. The agnostic tells us it is impossible to know God; we must let such knowledge alone for ever. It is true that we cannot understand all His ways. His thoughts are very deep. But it is not true that we cannot understand Him. What He does we may not know now; we must wait for the hereafter; but what He is we may know. There is one choice spot to which we can climb, and climbing there we can stand at His side, and see the world with eyes anointed of God. There is one temple into which we may enter and surely meet with Him, and meeting with Him we shall hear the music of the universe, not understanding it all, but marking the keynote to which every melody is set. That choice spot is the eminence of Love. That temple is the Temple of Love. The keynote of all the music of all the world is assuredly Love. But only on that eminence and only in that Temple is God understood. As the eye is needed to behold beauty and the ear to catch melody, so Love is needed that we may know God. He who loves stands where God stands, and may see the world with the eyes of God. God is Love. "He that dwelleth in love, dwelleth in God, and God in him." (1 St. John iv. 16.) If we could climb to this point, if our hearts could be filled with deep and measureless love, how much that now perplexes and saddens us would be clearer! Where love dwells there is a double gain. Love has a power of vision; love is the friend and not the servant that knoweth not what his Lord doeth. (St. John xv. 15.) But love is blind also. She too confesses her sweet and patient agnosticism; she is content to wait, for her Lord has said, "What I do, thou knowest not now, but thou shalt know hereafter." (St. John xiii. 7.) She has the source and the solace of her patience, seeing that, even when she cannot understand, she loves. And as she loves, she stands on that hill whence indeed she may not descry all God's wondrous works, but where God Himself may be seen and known. Love is the instrument of that knowledge. God is not to be discovered by analysis, nor understood by argument. He will not be found by exploration of the universe, by mere investigation of the dry facts of life. "I have searched the heavens for years," said one, "and I have not found God." No sane man expected that he would. We do not test friendship by the stethescope, nor God by telescope or microscope. We do not know man by dissection, we know him by something higher and nobler than physical analysis. We may examine his brain, his sinews, his bones, his arteries, but we shall not find in them the touch of his genius, the breadth of his wisdom, or the force of his love. We must live with him, and then, though from a scientific standpoint we cannot fully trace the movements of his inward life, we shall know him. The key to life's deepest things is not so far away as the intellectual pride and untamed ambitions of men believe. It is not in Heaven for some Prometheus' hand to pluck it down; it is not in the dark places explorable only by profound wisdom: it is near; the key is in the hand of daily kindnesses and in the heart of daily love. The simple may hold it when the sage has forgotten it, or flung it away. Love knows love. Man may know God, as the child who knows little of his father's thoughts, but who yet knows his father and stretches out his tiny hands for greeting or embrace. But alas for us! how many of us, spoiled by life, forget the sweet child-nature and shut ourselves up in dark despair, when the key, the golden key, is still within our bosom as long as our hearts can beat with love of what is good.

The recollection of this may enable us to perceive that there is a truth, which underlies the teaching (hateful to so many), that unbelief is a sin.

Inability to recognise intellectually the truth of certain theological dogmas is not a sin. But there is a sense in which unbelief may be a sin. "As we are, we see." The reason that we do not see may arise from moral as well as from intellectual causes. If we have lost the power of love, and cannot therefore see the love which lies around us, then the fault is in ourselves, and such fault surely is a sin. It is not simply intellectual defect which causes the child to leap to the conclusion that he will no longer trust his father, because his father does some things which are hard to understand. Is it too much to say that some of the hard things said about God betray want of heart no less than want of head? For example, God's apparent inconsistencies are made much of by the literalist who insists on what he calls consistency; he cannot understand the flexibility and variations of method which are so characteristic of love. Shallow and idle chatterers, narrow-headed and stony-hearted, are ready enough to cry out that God's ways are not equal; but love understands that mutability of method may proceed from immutability of love. The captain may still be making for the port when he tacks to meet the varying gale. Love may now pipe to us and may now mourn, but love, understanding love's unchanging earnestness as manifested in the changing experiences of life, is able to see what is unseen by the heart which cannot love.

(c) Our third law is—sacrifice is essential to progress. Sometimes indeed we are angered at what we call the apparent needlessness and heedlessness of the sacrifice required in life. But suppose that sacrifice on our part is the opportunity God gives us of promoting good. Suppose that He means us to understand that in this way we shall best make known the highest good, then we may be content that life should be full of sacrifice. The men of Thermopylæ, who laid down their lives for their country's good, did not understand indeed all that their sacrifice achieved. We, who look back upon it, know that when they stood and died there that day, the voice of the Divine wisdom and love was saying to them, " This is the sacrifice I ask on behalf of freedom, your death will minister to the world, and you will illuminate the ages with the light of liberty." It is the same in the case of suffering which is inherited. The man is born blind; it is a hard case, no fault of his can be urged, but how does Christ interpret it? Through this infirmity of his the works of God were to be known. (St. John ix.) If pain and weakness become the means of higher revelations to men, who will not be content to suffer? Human life becomes exalted as man recognizes that not out of caprice, but for the sake of making man through pain the instrument of good to others, does suffering enter into his lot. If the blow, which causes the string to quiver as in pain, brings forth music to make men glad, the thrill of anguish is abundantly repaid. Did we know what power lies in weakness, we should, like the Apostle, glory in our infirmities. Men who start in life deprived of the powers needful for temporal success are, like those who play a game of chess, deprived of their best piece. It is little matter. The game is the thing. The difficulty of playing the game with enfeebled forces is greater, but the very difficulty which they encounter is the sign that a larger trust is reposed on their skill. The need of greater thought, and more adroit management, brings its reward of more fully exercised judgment. Increased skill is a better reward than victory. The pains and sacrifices of life have a recompense, and the man who seems to lose his life may be the man who most fully finds it.

(d) Fourthly, there is no real sacrifice without Love. If the fire of love is not there, the sacrifice is not acceptable. Great sacrifices need the consecration of inspired motives.[1] Such inspirations destroy self-consciousness. Sacrifice offered with the full consciousness that it is sacrifice, and accompanied by the sense of merit in making it, is not perfect sacrifice. Energy of will, it must be remembered, is not the same thing as perfection of character. Sacrifice indeed tends to the perfecting and energizing of our will, but energy is nothing without inspiration. Self-consciousness spoils sacrifice, even though the self-oblation be consummated with commanding energy. The perfection of the fruit is not its size but its flavour. Perfection of character is not found in the greatness of the sacrifice, but in its beauty. Perfection of character is only reached when the sacrifice, made for the sake of good, is not so much felt to be meritorious as to be simply natural.

Very moral men may be very conceited men; chivalrous men may be proud, being conscious how

[1] See Note 48, Appendix.

chivalrous they are ; and the altruist may probably be the greatest egotist. For perfection we need to sweep away the conceit of egotism and the pride of men; as long as these remain, human character is defective. Love alone can sweep these away. Love, like fire, burns ; unworthy feelings perish at her presence. This is that fire from heaven which consumes the sacrifice—making the sacrifice the more real, and yet the less visibly a sacrifice. Love's offering is ever the whole burnt offering. Her sacrifice is full, perfect and complete, free from pride and self-consciousness. The mother does not pride herself on her devotion when she dashes into the flames to save her child. The true hero does not know that he is a hero. Christ Himself laid down His life freely, without the consciousness of His own heroism, but as One who felt that the sacrifice that He made in life and in death was necessary and natural to Him. It was His meat and drink to do His Father's will. Love, love to His Father, love to the world, was the law of His being and the motive force of His life.

3. For the perfection of character the crown of love is wanted. Sacrifice is essential to character ; love can give us the true standpoint for the interpretation of life ; and love recognised behind the world makes us content with life. The religion of the future must be a religion of love. Where then is

such a religion to be found? If men are to look anywhere among the existing faiths of the world for the religion of the future, they will nowhere find a religion of love better realised than in the faith which Christ taught. Doubtless there is much in popular Christianity which would be more fitly called Christianism than true Christianity; the clay clings to the pure ore, the tares mingle with the wheat; these will disappear in the future. The great cathedral has been hemmed in by ungainly structures. Round transept and choir crowd huts and shanties which hinder our view of the stateliness of its walls or the majesty of its proportions; but these cannot count as original blemishes, the glory of the fabric is distinct from these. These are additions, which time and the growing sense of order, fitness and beauty will remove. Criticism, whose rude touch sometimes makes us fear for the future, will aid in this work, and will restore to the building its pristine glory. The accretions of time will vanish; the everlasting elements will remain. Before these, the additions which time and human weakness have made, are as nothing. Nothing can rob Christianity of the glory which she possesses of giving to men the very things which history shows that man has needed.[1] She gives them those right and

[1] See Appendix, Note 49.

high views of life which foster in men the power of right feeling. She tells men that God is Love, and men, learning this, gather fresh courage for the duties of life. Knowing that they are loved, they learn to love; and learning to love, they learn to know God. Knowing that love alone can know God, in learning to know Him they begin to grow like Him. The love is no dream; for Christianity speaks of the power of an incarnate love, which makes it easier for men to know God. She, in common with other creeds, points to the necessity of sacrifice, but she shows it to us as the highest manifestation of love. The Cross wins for men the education of life. But further and above this, she so inspires men that sacrifice is no longer felt to be sacrifice. In all the trials, conflicts and struggles of life, men, in whose hearts God's love is shed abroad, are more than conquerors. In that love they vanquish, and from that love they cannot be sundered.

The many things which have been built up upon the Christian basis, but which are not of the essence of Christianity, will disappear; the wood, the hay, the stubble, the materials out of which men have fashioned their own fancies and their own interpretations of faith will be burnt up, but "the foundation of the Lord remaineth sure," and this foundation will not fail, "nor shall the gates of hell prevail against it."[1] There will no doubt at all times be difficulties in human life. In the present and in the future, varying characters of men will be found; we shall still have the agnostic, like Thomas, who says, "Lord, we know not whither Thou goest, and how can we know the way?"[2] We shall still have the men of philosophy, like Philip, who will say, "Show us the Father and it sufficeth us;"[3] or the materialist, like Jude, who will say, "How is it that Thou wilt manifest thyself unto us and not unto the world?"[4] But the Teacher of mankind is patient and loving, and He will educate all. He will invigorate the weak, and illumine the blind. Great and noble men may still stand aside doubting. Achilles may "ponder in his tent," many may still stumble at the thoughts which Christianity presents, but it will be found to be a living power, promoting the spirit of Altruism, and preaching the service of man. Slowly its force will be felt. In various ways its worth and power will be recognised. And thus, almost without perceiving the road by which they came, men will be led to a knowledge of God. It is not by hard thinking that we are filled with the joys

[1] 1 Cor. iii. 11—13; Matt. xvi. 18; 2 Tim. ii. 19.
[2] John xiv. 5.   [3] John xiv. 8.   [4] John xiv. 22.

and the beauties of nature, it is by loving them and dwelling with them. Let us put away anxious thought; we cannot interpret nature when the mind is filled with harassing cares. Let us walk down life's leafy lane; the lark is singing, and there is still joy in the world. Let us try the same method with religion. Let us lay down our eagerness, and forget our disputations for awhile; and we too may reach a joy which springs from the presence of God. His song is still in our life; His smile is upon us, we may find Him and put our hand in His, and know that He is love indeed. Heaven may yet break into new glory above our heads; life may be filled with new meaning; duties may become delights; obstacles and hindrances, doubts and despairs, may become steps of the Heaven-mounting ladder. Even the dark things of life may be as ministering angels to help us upward. But who shall see that vision, and be assured of that hope! He sees it whose heart is purified by love, and who knows that love is incarnate in the world. For him all things work for good. Out of darkness comes light; the wind and the storm fulfil the biddings of love; he sees in all life's fiercest trials a form like the form of the Son of God; for him evermore the heaven is open, and the angels are ascending and descending in sweet and ceaseless ministry on Him who binds earth to Heaven and man to man—who is Lord of Life and Lord of Love, Son of God and Son of man.

NOTES TO LECTURES.

LECTURE I.

NOTE 1, pp. 11, 13, 16.—MAN AS A RELIGIOUS BEING.

"THE result of my investigations is exactly the opposite of that to which Sir John Lubbock and M. Saint-Hilaire have arrived. Obliged, in my course of instruction, to review all human races, I have sought atheism in the lowest as well as in the highest. I have nowhere met with it, except in individuals or in more or less limited schools, such as those which existed in Europe in the last century, or which may still be seen at the present day." So writes M. De Quatrefages (" *The Human Species,*" p. 482), who enumerates three causes of mistake respecting the religious condition of savage tribes :—

1. Arising from contempt of barbarian peoples : a traveller asks a few questions; he speaks the language badly; understands answers imperfectly.

2. Arising from the hidden character of the religion : he would not understand the customs and superstitions, or perceive the religious character of them.

3. Arising from the missionary; who assumes the most extravagant notions of the degradation of those to whom he goes, and is inclined to undervalue their faith or to ignore it.—*Ibid.*, pp. 473, 474.

He also gives examples of cases in which no religion was said to be found, yet afterwards the most full religious notions were discovered.

" Wallis, after a month's intimacy with the Tahitians, declared that they possessed no form of worship, whilst it entered, so to speak, into their most trivial actions." —*Ibid.*, p. 474.

Other similar cases may be referred to. In the journal of the Anthropological Society for February, 1878, Mr. C. H. E. Carmichael draws our attention to a mission established by Benedictine monks in Western Australia. These monks took great pains to ascertain the religious sentiments of the natives, and for a long time they were unable to discover even the faintest traces of anything that could be called religion. After three years of missionary life, Monsignor Salvado declared that the natives did not worship any deity, whether true or false. Yet he states that they believe in an Omnipotent Being, creator of heaven and earth, a tall, powerful, and wise man, whose method of creation was by breathing. They believe, too, in an author of evil, of whirlwind, storm and death. Yet the Bishop adds, "Never did I observe any act of external worship, nor did any indication suggest to me that they practised any internal worship."

Similarly Dr. Codrington speaks at a missionary

meeting held in St. John's College Hall Oxford:—
"Some people imagined that the heathens had no idea
of good and bad, and that they had no conscience. He
knew for a fact that these Melanesians had words
expressive of moral goodness. They had a very clear
notion of the separate existence of the soul and body.
. . . They had this idea, that there was a power in
nature surrounding them on every side, not in one
particular place, but everywhere. . . . He could bear
testimony to this truth, that wherever one might go
amongst whatever people, there was sure to be found
some religious truth."

Prof. Tylor describes the case of non-religious tribes
as "in some degree similar to that of the tribes asserted
to exist without language, or without the use of fire;
nothing in the nature of things seems to forbid the possibility of such existence, but, as a matter of fact, the
tribes are not found."—(*Primitive Culture*, vol. i., p. 418.)
Prof. Oscar Peschel is even more emphatic. *Cf.* "*The
Races of Men*," p. 261, quoted by Mr. Newman Smyth,
"*The Religious Feeling*."

A paper was recently (Jan. 16, 1888) read at the
Victoria Institute on this subject. The writer of the
paper, Dr. Fraser, of New South Wales, from his own
experience gave interesting evidence calculated to
dispel the popular mistake that the aborigines of
Australia have no belief in a Deity. Much of the controversy on this subject has arisen—like so many other
controversies—from the want of defining the sense of
the words employed. If religion is to be limited only
to the possession of a certain level of theistic conceptions, many races may be shown to have none; but
where the object is to ascertain how far man is a

religious animal, we must be content with much less than this: religion then means any customs, tendencies, conceptions however crude, which show a faith in any thing or person outside things sensible. "The mere savage," says Prof. Max Müller, "may not even have a name for religion; still, when the Papua squats before his *karwar*, clasping his hands over his forehead, and asking himself whether what he is going to do is right or wrong, that is to him religion." ("*Origin of Religion*," p. 13.) Mr. Fiske hits a point of importance when he says, "Travellers have now and then reported the existence of races of men quite destitute of religion, or of what the observer has learned to recognise as religion; but no one has ever discovered a race of men devoid of a belief in ghosts." ("*The Idea of God*," p. 66.) It is just in the cases where the conceptions of a tribe or race are very low that the greatest care is needed. There may be nothing which the traveller would call religion, but there may be much which the natives feel and treat as religion. The belief in ghosts is evidence of the belief in things outside things sensible, and is not improbably allied in the native mind with much that is to it religious. Prof. Max Müller's words are clear as to the universality of religion at certain stages of civilization:—

"Wherever there is human life, there is religion, and wherever there is religion, the question whence it came cannot be long suppressed. When children once begin to ask questions, they ask the why and the wherefore of everything, religion not excepted; nay, I believe that the first problems of what we call philosophy were suggested by religion.—"*Origin of Religion,*" p. 7.

Taking Réville's definition of religion (quoted in Lecture II., p. 55), we may safely recognize the religious instincts of men in the lowest forms and under the most grotesque conceptions. As we note the maternal instinct in the fondness of the little girl for her doll, we may note the religious instinct in the blunders and failures which yet betoken the gropings of man's mind and the longings of man's heart after the unseen. We may be among those

> "Who believe that in all ages
> Every human heart is human,
> That in even savage bosoms
> There are longings, yearnings, strivings,
> For the good they comprehend not;
> That the feeble hands and helpless,
> Groping blindly in the darkness,
> Touch God's right hand in that darkness
> And are lifted up and strengthened."
> *Longfellow*, "*Hiawatha.*"

On this subject it is important to remember that feeling precedes reflection, and sentiment precedes argument. Dr. Matheson, one of the most careful and entirely truthful as well as deeply spiritual teachers whom God has given us, reminds us of this in the opening of his latest work: "The religious sentiment is the earliest and the latest fruit of the religious spirit; it begins before the birth of dogma, and it survives after dogma has passed away. Men feel before they have learned to see. As in the individual life the first impressions of the mind are those of simple pleasure and pain, so in the life of the religious spirit the earliest impressions

of the recipient are those of feeling and sentiment."—
"*Psalmist and Scientist*," p. 1; cf. Schopenhauer, "*The World as Will and Idea*," vol. i., pp. 309, 310.

NOTE 2, p. 23.—THE DOCTRINAIRE.

The doctrinaire demands that we shall reduce our faith to intelligible form. He is brisk, and intensely logical, though often within somewhat narrow range. He is useful in showing how very unsatisfactory are the nebulous-minded folk who prefer vagueness, not because they are large-minded, but because they are loose thinkers. He is useful, as the man who insists on classification is useful. He is probably right in saying that the progress of knowledge depends upon our determination to reduce it to formal expression and correct classification. The value of this is recognised. Kuenen insists on its importance in the study of religions. "As the chronicle must yield to history, so must the bare enumeration of phenomena yield to classification. If this is true in general, it is true likewise in its special application to one of the youngest in the rank of sciences—the science of religion."—*Introduction to "Hibbert Lectures*," p. 4.

Emerson says that "in all unbalanced minds classification is idolized, passes for the end, and not for a speedily exhaustible means." (*Essay on "Self-Reliance.*") We may admit the truth in this without losing sight of the importance of classification. We may admit, too, that in reducing faith to form and creed, we have not reached the end of religion, but only manifested a means of its working, without losing sight of the importance of intelligible statements of faith as a means of educating men in the knowledge of faith.

and of reaching the heart through the understanding. We may say that to understand a theological proposition does not necessarily make a man better; but we may also ask whether a man who can give no intelligible account of his faith is therefore a better man than his neighbour, who has, or thinks he has, some definite ideas on the subject. But whatever we may say on the matter, the tendency of man to reduce his belief and his knowledge into form is irresistible. It is part of that desire for expression which seems universal.

We may note also that art and science must have their leading principles, which serve the same place as creeds in religion. Without such foundations, the lecturer on science and art would be able to teach nothing. Mr. Ruskin reminds us that art must have a grammar which must be mastered before a man may take liberties with the language.—*See Lamp of Obedience in " The Seven Lamps."*

NOTE 3, p. 27.—LAW I.

The authority of Mr. Herbert Spencer may be cited against this law. He says, "Ideas do not govern and overthrow the world: the world is governed or overthrown by feelings, to which ideas serve only as guides. The social mechanism does not rest finally upon opinions; but almost wholly upon character." ("*Classification of the Sciences*," p. 37.) But Mr. Spencer admits that ideas do count for something in the advance of the world. They serve as "guides to feeling;" and, further, "advanced ideas when once established, act upon society and aid its further advance."—*Ibid.*, p. 38.

The perception of this law must have been present in

Quinet's mind when he wrote his " Génie de Religions," a leading object of which was to show "how entirely each of the civilizations was the offspring of a religious dogma."

With this seems to agree what Mr. Ruskin has written in the "*Art of England.*"

"A beautiful thing may exist but for a moment, as a reality;—it exists for ever as a testimony. To the law and to the witness of it the nations must appeal '*in seculae seculorum;*' and in very deed and very truth, a thing of beauty is a *law* for ever. That is the true meaning of classic art and classic literature ;—not the license of pleasure, but the law of goodness ; and if, of the two words, καλὸς κ'ἀγαθός, one can be left unspoken, as implied by the other, it is the first, not the last. It is written that the Creator of all things beheld them—not in that they were beautiful, but in that they were good. This law of beauty may be one, for aught we know, fulfilling itself more perfectly as the years roll on; but at least it is one from which no jot shall pass. "The beauty of Greece depended on the laws of Lycurgus ; the beauty of Rome on those of Numa ; our own, on the laws of Christ."—"*Art of England,*" pp. 105, 106.

With this we may compare Goethe's saying, "No evil can touch him who looks on human beauty; he feels himself at one with himself and with the world."

The following seem to illustrate this law :—

"The key to every man is his thought."
Emerson, "*Essay on Circles.*"

" All characters
Must shrink or widen as our wine skins do,
For more or less that we can pour in them."
"*The Spanish Gypsy*."

With this we may compare Schopenhauer ("*The World as Will and Idea*")—writing of the object of art: "Imitators, mannerists, *imitatores, servum pecus*, start, in art, from the concept; they observe what pleases and effects us in true works of art; understand it clearly, fix it in a concept, and thus abstractly and then imitate it, openly or disguisedly, with dexterity and intentionally. They suck their nourishment, like parasite plants, from the works of others, and like polypi, they become the colour of their food." The influence of the artistic standards, which in less gifted men becomes servile imitation, is a real influence in the case of men of genius: " for he is indeed educated and cultured by his predecessors and their works; but he is really fructified only by life and the world directly, through the impression of what he perceives; therefore the highest culture never interferes with his originality."—p. 304.

Again: " Greek sculpture devotes itself to the perception, and therefore it is *æsthetical;* Indian sculpture devotes itself to the conception, and therefore it is merely *symbolical.*"—*Ibid.*, p. 304.

In the same spirit writes Lord Byron :—

"I live not in myself, but I become
Portion of that around me, and to me
High mountains are a feeling."

NOTE 4, p. 33.—LAW II.

Illustrations of this law will occur to the reader's mind. They are numerous. The following, drawn at random from the less obvious sources, will illustrate the widespread recognition of this law:—

"Chacun ne comprend que ce qu'il retrouve en soi."
Amiel, "Journal," vol. i. p. 63.

"Ein Jeder sieht was er im Herzen trägt."
Goethe, " Faust."

It is curious to read Amiel's criticism on Goethe and his school:—

"Le malaise de notre époque n'existe pas pour Goethe et son école. Cela s'explique: il n'y a pas de dissonances pour les sourds."—"*Journal,*" vol. ii., p. 121.

Similarly Charles Dickens: "Men who look on nature and their fellow-men, and cry that all is dark and gloomy, are in the right; but the sombre colours are reflections from their own jaundiced eyes and hearts. The real hues are delicate, and need a clearer vision."—"*Oliver Twist.*"

Mr. Herbert Spencer says: "Practically, the popular character and the social state determine what ideas shall be current; instead of the current ideas determining the social state and the character."—"*Classification of the Sciences,*" p. 38.

The same principle underlies Lord Beaconsfield's saying that "A man's fate is his own temper." It is included in the often quoted, "Like can only be known by like." Ruskin reminds us that when we read we gather food for our own dispositions. He says that those who are naturally proud and envious will learn from Thackeray to despise humanity; those who are naturally gentle, to pity it; those who are naturally shallow, to laugh at it. ("*Sesame and Lilies.*") Mr. Howells, in the same strain, speaking on Spiritualism, says, " I wonder that I was never struck before by that element of derision in it. The Calvinist gets Calvinism ; the Unitarian gets Unitarianism; each carries away from communion with spirits the things that he brought." ("*Undiscovered Country.*") In "Festus" we have the hint that the conflict between faith and reason arises from a forgetfulness of this principle—

" The golden side of Heaven's great shield is faith ;
The silver, reason. I see this, you that ;
The junction is invisible to both."

P. J. Bailey.

So writes Emerson : "Not in nature, but in man, is all the beauty and worth he sees. The world is very empty, and is indebted to this gilding, exalting soul for all its pride. ' Earth fills her lap with splendours ' not her own."—"*Spiritual Laws.*"

Mr. Lowell gives quaint expression to the same law. "Truth is said to lie at the bottom of a well, for the very reason, perhaps, that whoever looks down in search of her sees his own image at the bottom, and is persuaded, not only that he has seen the goddess, but that she is far better-looking than he had imagined."— *Address at Birmingham*, 1884.

" We see matter, because only love can see love, and where there is not love is matter. Christ Himself would have been but matter to a crocodile."—*Hinton*, "*Philosophy and Religion.*"

"Empedocles said: Like can only be known by like: only nature can understand itself: only nature can fathom itself: but only spirit can also understand spirit." — *Schopenhauer*, "*World as Will*," vol. i., p. 288.

Sir F. Leighton, in his address to students at the Royal Academy (December, 1881), spoke on the relation between character and work. He said:—"The man is stamped on his work, and his moral growth or lessening faithfully reflected in the sum of his labours. I believe this to be a cardinal truth, the disregard of which may bear fatal fruits in an artist's life. . . . The more closely you consider this subject, the more clearly will you feel, for instance, the mischief to us as artists which must infallibly attend a tolerant indulgence within ourselves of certain moral weaknesses and failings to which nature is too often prone. Of these failings some are palpably ignoble and in the long run debasing; others are not, on the surface, so evidently mischievous. Amongst such as are palpably ignoble, I will instance the greed for gain. I believe no evil to be more insidious, none more unerring in its operation than this sordid appetite. Its poisonous taint creeps into the moral system; numbs by degrees all finer sense; dulls all higher vision; is fatal to all lofty effort. No worse snare lies across our path. Another such deadening taint is the vulgar thirst for noisy success, the hankering of vanity for immediate satisfaction; of this the outcome is a deliberate sacrifice of the abiding appreciation of the intelligent for the transitory and noisy clamour of the unintelligent and shallow, with the fatally-sure result of a paralysis of the sense of self-respect, a lowering of standard, and, in the end, an important disinclination for every sustained and serious effort. Other failings there are of which, as I said, the bearing is not so immediately evident, but of which the dangers are scarcely less. As one instance of these, I will quote the indulgence in a narrow, unsympathizing spirit, a spirit ever awake to carp and cavil, feeding its self-complacency on the disparagement of others. This spirit stunts and shrivels those who yield to it, and by blinding them more and more to the work and Beauty that are in the work which is not their own, deprives them of the priceless stimulus of a noble emulation. . . . Whatever of dignity, whatever of strength we have within us will dignify and will make strong the labours of our hands; whatever littleness degrades our spirit will lessen them and drag them down. *Whatever noble fire is in our hearts will burn also in our work; whatever purity is ours will chasten and exalt it; for as we are, so our work is, and what we sow in our lives, that, beyond a doubt, we shall reap for good or for ill in the strengthening or defacing of whatever gifts have fallen to our lot.*"

"The malicious are perforce the very worst judges of human nature, for only charity sees far into another's heart. Malice, moreover, invariably implies a defect of intellect."—*Geo. Gissing*, "*Thyrza*," vol. ii., p. 134.

With this compare Renan's saying that, "The moral value of the man is in proportion to his faculty of admiration."—"*Marcus Aurelius*," p. 8.

There are thousands of illustrations of the same principle; many of them will occur to the reader. There is one with which we may fitly conclude this Note, as it comes from a little poem which, notwithstanding one strange mistake, is one of the brightest and best little pieces among many that are bright and good in Mr. Lowell's last volume:—

"All round about our feet shall shine,
A light like that the wise men saw,
If we our loving wills incline
To that sweet Life which is the law."
"*Heartsease and Rue.*"
(*Christmas Carol for the Sunday School Children.*)

NOTE 5, p. 35.—LAW III.

To illustrate this principle within reasonable limits is impossible. It is a principle as universal as it is obvious. The dimmest and crudest ideas of sacrifice are shadows of it. There are few enlightened men who will doubt it. The higher life in man is only possible to those who live by it. "It is only with Renunciation that life, properly speaking, can be said to begin." (*Carlyle*, "*Sartor Resartus.*") "In a valiant suffering for others, not in a slothful making others suffer for us, did nobleness ever lie." ("*Past and Present.*") "There is but one sole virtue in the world—the eternal sacrifice of self."—*George Sand.*

"May I reach
That purest heaven; be to other souls
The cup of strength in some great agony.
. . . . . .
So shall I join the choir invisible,
Whose music is the gladness of the world."
George Eliot.

"You talk of self as the motive to exertion; I tell you it is the abnegation of self which has wrought out all that is noble, all that is good, all that is useful. nearly all that is ornamental in the world."—*Whyte Melville,* "*Bones and I.*"

"A man was born, not for prosperity, but to suffer for the benefit of others, like the noble rock-maple, which, all round our villages, bleeds for the service of man."—*Emerson,* "*The Method of Nature.*"

Indeed this principle belongs everywhere to our world. Darwin, in his book on earth-worms, shows us that the worms under our feet are God's ministers to us in more than we think. Prof. Taylor writes about "Altruism in Plants." The poet sang, "*Sic vos non vobis.*" The Apostle says the same: "No man liveth to himself: no man dieth to himself." Lamartine sang of the perfume wafted forth at death: "La fleur tombe en livrant ses parfums au zéphyre" (*L'Automne*), as Talfourd did of the

"wild myrtles, which preserve
Their hoard of perfumes for the dying hour
When rudeness crushes them."
"*Ion.*"

The legend of the Pelican, of the Dying Swan, and the fancy of the Greeks (referred to by Professor Westcott in "Christus Consummator,") that the clay of which man was made was moistened not with water but with tears, among other similar legends, show the drift of men's thoughts; they felt that pain or sacrifice was the root of life.

"And when God formed in the hollow of His hand
This ball of Earth among His other balls,
And set it in His shining firmament,
Between the greater and the lesser lights,
He chose it for the Star of Suffering,"
"*The Disciples.*"

NOTE 6, p. 41.—LAW IV.

This law is, as far as I can see, most frequently forgotten. Men are impatient, they like direct methods. It is hard to tell a man that the moment he has seen the ideal is the moment in which he must look away from it, lest he should imagine that it can be reached at a single bound, or by some short cut. Yet experience soon teaches us that there is an enormous difference between the realization of what ought to be done and the power of doing it. Blunt understanding or blind theory says, "There is the thing to be done— do it." The imperative mood, however, is not omnipotent. The psychologist can correct the false expectations of the theorist or philosopher. He has been studying the instrument, and can tell something about its powers and its needs. The student of history is inclined to say, "The facts are obvious; the lessons of history all too plain; men can never fall into the same mistakes again, when once they know what the past can teach." But men do fall into the same mistakes again, and history does repeat itself; men learn nothing and forget nothing. They are the same passion-led creatures which they ever were. Professor Seeley hit the right mark when he said that if people do not follow or care about history, he would never dream of attempting to make history interesting. Of course not; no amount of tinkering up facts to suit a garish taste would produce that real love of history which creates of itself true taste. Men must be inspired by the love of the thing before they can do the thing. Admiration is not enough; inspiration is required. Christianity is right when it teaches men to pray that they may *love* the thing which God commands. Love is not only the inspirer of ardent desires, but it is the destruction of that hideous self-consciousness which accompanies the man who pursues what is noble because he feels that there is nobility in pursuing it. One chief characteristic of Christianity lies, as I think, in the recognition of this law or principle, "To be good" is the aim which the moralist puts before men. "To be like God" is the aim which Christianity puts before men, and in doing so, she adds the force of a persuasive and inspiring love. She achieves her aim indirectly, by dwelling upon the love which the Holy One had for the unholy. Mr. Cotter Morison, in his book, "The Service of Man," would never have assailed the Christian doctrines of Grace and Forgiveness had he understood this law of indirectness. Two of the best modern novels illustrate this law. "The Son of Vulcan," by Mr. Walter Besant, and "John Herring," by Mr. Baring Gould. In both these books the rescue of outcast characters is effected by their becoming aware of the fact that some one better and holier than themselves cares for them. When Jesus Christ said, "Thy sins be forgiven thee," He did not put a premium on wrong, He bestowed a fresh incentive to right. It is possible that men may be effortless towards right, because they have been the victims of harsh judgments as well as of hard circumstances. We need to remember that men do not start equal in the race of life. The most demoralized are often just those who have had little chance of high morality, and who have smarted under the Pharisaic opinion that there is no use trying to rescue them. Such will not be helped much by the modern Pharisees who tell them that they are past hoping for, and that there is no power to whom they can be prayed for. Such will be helped into righteousness through love. This is only another way of stating that they may be justified by faith. The consciousness that they are loved evokes trust, and the awakening of trust shows them the possibilities of a purer life; they are taught to see their potential self; they are told that love sees that nobler and better self; they grasp hope and life in thus seeing themselves as love sees them. They are conscious of salvation then; they are justified by faith, as St. Paul would say.

The law of indirectness enters into the very heart of Christian doctrine. It has been noticed by various thinkers who have not had a directly theological object in view. The following may stand as specimens.

"O Aristotle! if you had had the advantage of being 'the freshest modern,' instead of the greatest ancient, would you not have mingled your praise of metaphorical speech as a sign of high intelligence, with a lamentation that intelligence so rarely shows itself in speech without metaphor—that we can so seldom declare what a thing is, except by saying it is something else?"—*George Eliot,* "*Mill on the Floss.*"

"Those movements of which the uninterrupted performance is essential to the maintenance of Life" (such as the beating of the heart and act of respiration) "are *primarily* automatic."—*Dr. W. B. Carpenter*, " *Mental Physiology*," p. 16.

Mr. Ruskin says the earth is an entail, not a possession. Self-denial must be exercised for the sake of posterity, practising economy for them, and planting forests we shall not enjoy.—" *Seven Lamps (Memory)*."

"Nature has happily ordained it as one of the great laws on which she has founded our moral happiness, that the performance of love and kindness to others should be a genuine and never-failing source of pleasure to our own hearts. It is thus strictly, as well as poetically true, 'that, seeking other's good, we find our own.' The exercise of the profession is, when followed out in its proper spirit, a continued realization of active beneficence."—*Sir Jas. Simpson*, " *Address to Students.*"

" In our great hall there stood a vacant chair.
. . . .
And Merlin call'd it ' The Siege perilous,'
Perilous for good and ill; ' for there,' he said,
' No man could sit, but he should lose himself.'
And once by misadventure, Merlin sat
In his own chair, and so was lost; but he,
Galahad, when he heard of Merlin's doom,
Cried, ' If I lose myself I save myself!' "
Tennyson, " *The Holy Grail*," p. 43.

" To aim at thine own happiness is an end idolatrous and evil.
In earth, yea, in heaven, if thou seek it fro itself, seeking thou shalt not find.

Happiness is a roadside flower, growing on the highway of usefulness:
Plucked, it shall wither in thy hand; passed by, it is fragrance to thy spirit.
Love not thine own soul, regard not thine own weal."
Tupper, " *Of Discretion.*"

"Patience and abnegation of self, and devotion to others,
This was the lesson a life of trial and sorrow had taught her.
So was her love diffused, but like to some odorous spices,
Suffered no waste nor loss, tho' filling the air with aroma." *Longfellow,* " *Evangeline,*" part II., canto v.

Speaking of Spinoza, Goethe says, "His all-reconciling peace contrasted with my all-agitating endeavour; his intellectual method was the opposite counterpart of my poetic way of feeling and expressing myself; and even the inflexible regularity of his logical procedure, which might be considered ill-adapted to moral subjects, made me his most passionate scholar and his devoted adherent. Mind and heart, understanding and sense were drawn together with an inevitable elective affinity, and this at the same time produced an intimate union between individuals of the most different type."—*Quoted by Prof. Caird,* " *Contemp. Review,*" *Dec.,* 1886, p. 794.

"What we seek
Is but our other self, other and higher."
L. Morris, " *Narcissus, Epic of Hades.*"

"We must not forget another characteristic of poetry by which it is separated at once from science and philosophy—viz., its spontaneous and even unconscious character. After all, the effort of the poet is to provide a free channel for a power that works in him like a natural force. Wordsworth's criticism of Goethe's poetry, that it was not inevitable enough (a criticism which is singularly wide of the mark in regard to the best of Goethe's work), is an apt expression of this truth. Creative imagination is a power which is neither lawless, nor yet, strictly speaking, under law; it is a power which, as Kant said, *makes laws*."—*Prof. Caird,* " *Contemp. Review,*" *Dec.,* 1886, p. 790.

"Poets are the unacknowledged legislators of the world."—*Beaconsfield,* " *Venetia.*"

" There is not an Angel added to the host of Heaven but does its blessed work on earth in those that loved it here."—*Dickens,* " *Old Curiosity Shop.*"

We may close with a word from a philosopher. It carries with it the germ of much which Christianity has made clear. Zeno, when asked what a friend was, replied, "Another I."

LECTURE II.

Note 7, p. 59.

In places where ethical conceptions are low, and are little related to religion, religion is found to be largely a mere dependence on a power which can help and protect. Examples will occur to the reader, but it is important to notice that religion, when criticised as being mere selfishness, is conceived of in this very limited sense. No doubt the criticism would be true were religion a mere instinct of dependence, but it is hardly scientific to criticise the crude and undeveloped form, or make the part stand for the whole..—Cf. *opinions of Wundt and Gruppe, given in Introduction*, p. xlvii.

NOTE 8, p. 64.

The Khonds are a small aboriginal Indian race, near the top of the Bay of Bengal, 250 miles or so from Calcutta, who worship the earth-goddess with human sacrifices, which the English Government has had great difficulty in suppressing. The victims, called *mérias*, are mostly children, bought of traders, and luxuriously kept, sometimes for years, till wanted for sacrifice. The Khonds practise infanticide of females, holding that the principle of evil is incarnate in the female sex. An account of this will be found in Larousse, "*Dict. des XIX. Siècle.*"

Writing of the Algonquin and Mingwe Redskins, De Quatrefages tells us that their great Spirit, the Michabou of the Algonquins—the Agrescoue of the Iroquois—is the father of all existing things. He himself, or by his messengers, watches over children, and directs the events of the world. To him the Redskin prays: the following is an example of prayer or song of the savages, on departing for war, preserved by Heckewelder:

"Oh, poor me—who am just about to depart to fight the enemy—and know not if I shall return —to enjoy the embraces of my children and wife.

"Oh, poor creature—who cannot order his own life— who has no power over his own body—but who tries to do his duty— for the happiness of his nation.

"Oh, thou great Spirit above—take pity upon my children—and upon my wife—keep them from sorrowing on my account—grant that I may succeed in my enterprize—that I may kill my enemy—and bring back trophies of war.

"Give me strength and courage to fight my enemy—grant that I may return and see my children again—see my wife and relations—have pity upon me and preserve my life—and I will offer to thee a sacrifice."—*De Quatrefages*, "*The Human Species*," p. 492.

NOTE 9, p. 65.

The recognition of the moral link between the seen and the unseen is an acknowledgment of the principle of Fellowship.

A priest told Byron that, when a child, he had eaten something deposited in sacred images. Surprised and reprimanded by his father, he excused himself by saying that he had found out by various experiments that these gods of wood neither saw nor heard. The old priest then said to him in a severe tone: "My son, the wood, it is true, neither sees nor hears; but the spirit which is above sees and hears all, and punishes wicked actions."—*De Quatrefages*, "*The Human Species*," p. 491.

We are reminded here of Quinet's remark, "The first great step was made when the human head was substituted for that of an animal in the statues of the gods."—"*Génie des Religions*," ch. vi., sec. 2;

And of Mr. Browning's Lines in "Sordello:"

"One character
Denotes them through the progress and the stir,—
A need to blend with each external charm,

Bury themselves, the whole heart wide and warm,—
In something not themselves; they would belong to
What they worship——"

On this, the element of fellowship, compare Dr.
Döllinger's words:—

"His (Socrates) position, that the Deity only was wise,
and that human wisdom was little or nothing worth, in
comparison with divine, might have carried him a long
way further; much depends, too, on the sense he attached to another expression reported by Xenophon
that the human soul partook of the divine.

". . . . . If he had really worked out the thought
of the 'soul's partaking in the divine,' the influence
of it upon his other views must necessarily have been
considerable.

". . . , . He instructed his disciples to ask nothing
by prayer of the gods, except only the good generally, as they, the gods, best knew themselves what
was good for man; also that it was not the most
costly sacrifices they preferred, but those that came from
religious hearts."—" *The Gentile and the Jew,*" p. 276-7.

The Ascetic tendency is a witness of the element
of fellowship in religion.

" This theory, which is developed at length by the
Stoic [the theory that the more prodigies are believed,
the more they are announced] in the first book of the
De Divinatione of Cicero, grew out of the pantheistic notion that the human soul is a part of the
Deity, and therefore by nature a participator in the
Divine attribute of prescience. The soul, however,
was crushed by the weight of the body; and there

were two ways of evoking its prescience—the ascetic way, which attenuates the body, and the magical way, which stimulates the soul. Apollonius declared that his power of prophecy was not due to magic, but solely to his abstinence from animal food."—*Philost.* "*Ap. of Tyana,*" viii., 5; *Note in Lecky's* "*Hist. of European Morals,*" vol. i., p. 368.

NOTE 10, p. 67.

"Cannibalism, in ordinary life, was no longer practised. The city of Mexico underwent all the horrors of famine during the siege conducted by Fernando Cortes. When the Spaniards finally entered the city, they found the streets strewn with corpses, which is a sufficient proof that human flesh was not eaten, even in dire extremities. And, nevertheless, the Aztecs not only pushed human sacrifices to a frantic extreme, but they were *ritual cannibals*, that is to say, there were certain occasions on which they ate the flesh of the human victims whom they had immolated."—*Réville,* "*Hibbert Lectures,*" p. 89.

NOTE 11, p. 69.

"Perhaps that quasi-messianic expectation of the return of Quetzalcoatl, to be accompanied by a complete renewal of things, may have given an additional point of attachment to this belief in the caducity of the whole existing order. What is certain is that this sentiment itself was very widely spread. It served as a consolation to the peoples who were crushed beneath the cruel yoke of the Aztecs."—*Ibid.*, p. 115. Cf. *Article in the* "*Gentleman's Magazine,*" Sept., 1888, *on the* "*Messiah of Mexico.*"

With this account of the god of the Mexicans may be compared what Prof. Rhys tells us of the Celtic god Woden. After alluding to the change, which at some time came over Gaulish paganism, whereby the Gaulish Mercury or culture-god, became practically the head and chief of the Gaulish Pantheon, he proceeds to show that the Teutonic counterpart was Woden, and that both families of nations, the Gauls and the Norsemen, proceeded on the same lines, in that they made the culture hero paramount over the old gods. "It is gratifying to come upon such traces of progress in the theology of our early ancestors, whether Celts or Teutons; and still more so to think that in the practice of their heathen religion it meant the establishment, probably, of a milder worship, making in some small degree, for humanity and greater regard for human life."—*Prof. Rhys*, "*Hibbert Lectures*," 1886, pp. 231 and 232.

NOTE 12, p. 71.

To this Nemesis, self-judgment, (often inaccurately rendered as revenge) Menelaus appeals when exciting the Greeks to defend the body of Patroclus from insult ("*Iliad*," xvii., 254, ἀλλά τις αὐτὸς ἴτω νεμεσιζέσθω δ'ἐνὶ θυμῷ). But the whole matter is best learned from an address of Telemachos to the Suitors, where he says, (*a*) "Rouse within you of yourselves a nemesis (or moral sense); and (*b*) an αἰδώς (a sense of honour, or regard to opinion of your fellow-citizens); and (*c*) fear the wrath of the Gods" ("*Odyss*," ii., 64—67). These three principles were the three great pillars of morality. . . . . "This αἰδώς is a sentiment which has ultimate reference to the standard of opinion; but it does not require that opinion to be in present and immediate action. It is self-judgment, according to the standard supplied by the ideas of others; as nemesis is self-judgment by the inward law."—*W. E. Gladstone, "Juv. Mundi,"* p. 383, 384.

LECTURE III.

NOTE 13, p. 78.

There is considerable difficulty in ascertaining the exact number of the adherents of various religions throughout the world. The estimated population of the world varies from twelve to fourteen hundred millions. M. Hubner sets it at 1,392½ millions. Of these, from 150,000,000 to 200,000,000 may at the utmost be claimed for Mohammedanism. M. Hubner's estimate is 80 millions. The numbers ranged under the complex term of Buddhism have been placed at from 400,000,000 to 500,000,000, while Christianity claims from 300,000,000 to 400,000,000.—*Cf. Rhys Davids, "Buddhism,"* p. 6 (S.P.C.K.); *W. Scawen Blunt's article in " Fortnightly Review,"* 1881, vol. ii. p. 208 ; also an article on *" Missions " in " Quarterly Review,"* July, 1886. *De Quatrefages, " Human Species,"* p. 485.

NOTE 14, p. 82.

"Mohammed was a man of middle height, but of commanding presence ; rather thin, but with broad shoulders and a wide chest ; a massive head, a frank, oval face with a clear complexion, restless black eyes, long heavy eyelashes, a prominent acquiline nose, white teeth, and a full thick beard are the principle features of the verbal portraits historians have drawn of him.

"He was a man of highly nervous organisation, thoughtful, restless, inclined to melancholy, and possessing an extreme sensibility, being unable to endure the slightest unpleasant odour or the least physical pain. . . . From youth upwards he had suffered from a nervous disorder which tradition calls epilepsy, but the symptoms of which more closely resemble certain hysterical phenomena well known and diagnosed in the present time, and which are almost always accompanied with hallucinations, abnormal exercise of the mental functions, and not unfrequently with a certain amount of deception, both voluntary and otherwise."—*Prof. Palmer, Introduction to vol. vi. of " Sacred Books of the East"* (Qur'ân) p. xix.

The following may illustrate some of the positions adopted in the Lectures:—

"For three days they lay concealed, their enemies once coming so near that Abu Bekr, trembling, said, 'We are but two.' 'Nay,' said Mohammed, 'we are three; for God is with us.'"—*Ibid.*, p. xxxiii.

"Mohammed, in one point at least, used his supreme authority as prophet to make provision for the flesh" (*Prof. Wellhausen, Article on " Mohammedanism," Encyc. Brit.*, 9th ed.). This refers to the affairs of his harem. One of these marriages, it is well known, "gave great scandal to the faithful, namely, that with the wife of his adopted son, Zâid, whom her husband divorced and offered to surrender to Mohammed on finding that the latter admired her. This also required a revelation to sanction it."—*Prof. Palmer, Introduction to vol. vi. of " Sacred Books of the East."* p. xxix.

"It is a fact that the politician in him outgrew the prophet more and more, and that in many cases where he assigned spiritual motives he merely did so to give a fair appearance to acts that emanated from secular regards." — *Wellhausen,* "*Mohammedanism,*" "*Encyc. Brit.,*" 9th Ed.

"It is less easy to free him from the reproach of perfidy and cruel vindictiveness. The surprise of Nakhla in the month Rajab (ordered by him, though he afterwards repudiated it), the numerous assassinations which he instigated, the execution of the 600 Jews at the close of the war of the Fosse, burden the Prophet heavily, and sufficiently explain the widespread antipathy in which he is held."—*Ibid.*

"Mohammed, though deeply grieved at losing, as he feared, his uncle's protection and goodwill, exclaimed in reply, 'By Allâh! if they placed the sun on my right hand and the moon on my left, to persuade me, yet while God bids me, I will not renounce my purpose!' and bursting into tears turned to leave the place."—*Prof. Palmer, Introduction to vol. vi. of "Sacred Books of the East,"* p. xxv.

"I demand no reward of you for my preaching unto you; I expect my reward from no other than the Lord of all creatures."—*Sale's "Koran,"* ch. 26 (The Poets), vol. ii. p. 207.

Compare also Sir William Muir's "*Life of Mohammed,*" *passim,* and Article on "*Islam*" by E. Deutsch, in "*Quarterly Review,*" vol. cxxvii., reprinted in "*Essays and Remains.*"

NOTE 15, p. 86.

Súfism—" the mysticism of Islâm "—among Moslems was believed to have been founded by a woman,

Rabi'a by name, who lived in the first century of the Hijra.

"Her doctrine was simply the theory of Divine Love. She taught that God must be loved above all things, because He alone is worthy of love; and that every thing here below must be sacrificed in the hope of one day attaining to union with God." (*Prof. S. Guyard*, "*Encyc. Brit.*") One feels a sense of high fitness on reading that this woman was buried at Jerusalem.

It has been thought that this movement, which carries the hope of reformation for Islâm, may supply the bridge by which the Moslem may yet pass to a higher faith.

"It is to the progress of Sûfism, which is constantly spreading amongst the people of Persia, that we must look for that preparation of the Mohammedan mind, which in due time may lead to the overthrow of Islâm for a purer creed."—"*Persian Literature,*" by *E. B. Cowell*, "*Oxford Essays,*" 1859.

In some cases Sûfism led to Pantheism. "In the reign of Moktadir, a Persian Sûfí, named Halláj, who taught publicly that every man is God, was tortured and put to death."—*Prof. Stanislas Guyard*, "*Encyc. Brit.*," "*Mohammedanism,*" 9th Ed.

"The Khárijites are the most interesting feature of the then phase of Islam (time of Alí, Caliph). In the name of religion they raised their protest against allowing the whole great spiritual movement to issue in a secular and political result, in the establishment within the conquered territories of an Arabian kingdom, a kingdom which diametrically contradicted the theocratic ideal. . . . The Khárijites protested, not merely against the dynastic principle and the rule of the Omayyads, but also against orthodoxy; they disputed the doctrine of predestination and the proposition that a great sinner could yet be a good Moslem, because they did not understand how to divorce religion from practice. To some degree they call to mind the Montanists, but their opposition was much more energetic in its expression."—*Prof. Wellhausen,* Article on "*Mohammedanism,*" *Encyc. Brit.* 9th Ed.

NOTE 16, p. 93.

See *Oldenberg,* "*Buddha;*" *Prof. Rhys David's* "*Hibbert Lectures*" and "*Buddhism*" (*S.P.C.K.*); *Bigandet,* "*Legend of Gaudama.*" Trübner's Oriental Series, 3rd Ed., 1880.

"Now at the end of the night, Kunda, the worker in metals, made ready in his dwelling-place sweet rice and cakes, and a quantity of dried boar's flesh. And he announced the hour to the Blessed One, saying, 'The hour, Lord, has come, and the meal is ready.' And the Blessed One robed himself early in the morning, and taking his bowl, went with the brethren to the dwelling-place of Kunda, the worker in metals. When he had come thither he seated himself on the seat prepared for him. And when he was seated he addressed Kunda, the worker in metals, and said: 'As to the dried boar's flesh you have made ready, serve me with it, Kunda; and as to the other food, the sweet rice and cakes, serve the brethren with it.' 'Even so, Lord!' said Kunda, the worker in metals, in assent, to the Blessed One. And the dried boar's flesh he had made ready he served to the Blessed One; whilst the other food, the sweet rice and cakes, he served to the members of the order. Now the Blessed One addressed Kunda, the worker in metals, and said: 'Whatever dried boar's flesh, Kunda, is left over to thee, that bury in a hole. I see no one, Kunda, on earth nor in Mâra's heaven, nor in Brahma's heaven, no one among Samanas and Brâhmanas, among gods and men, by whom, when he has eaten it, that food can be assimilated, save by the Tathâgata.' 'Even so, Lord!' said Kunda, the worker in metals, in assent, to the Blessed One. And whatever dried boar's flesh remained over, that he buried in a hole. . . . Now when the Blessed One had eaten the food prepared by Kunda, the worker in metal, there fell upon him a dire sickness, the disease of dysentery, and sharp pain came upon him, even unto death. But the Blessed One, mindful and self-possessed, bore it without complaint." —"*Sacred Books of the East,*" vol. xi., p. 71; "*Mahâ-Parinibbâna-Sutta,*" ch. iv., sect. 17—21.

NOTE 17, p. 93.

"The best of ways is the eightfold; the best of truths the four words; the best of virtues passionlessness; the best of men he who has eyes to see."—"*Dhammapada,*" v. 273.

"There is no fire like passion; there is no losing throw like hatred; there is no pain like this body; there is no happiness higher than rest."—*Ibid.*, v. 202.

"One's own self conquered is better than all other people; not even a god, a Gandharva, not Mâra with Brahman could change into defeat the victory of a man who has vanquished himself, and always lives under restraint."—*Ibid.*, vv. 104, 5.

"Self is the lord of self, who else could be the lord? With self well subdued, a man finds a lord such as few can find."—*Ibid.*, v. 160.

"Even in heavenly pleasures he finds no satisfaction, the disciple who is fully awakened delights only in the destruction of all desires."—*Ibid.*, v. 187.

"He is not a friend who always eagerly suspects a breach and looks out for faults; but he with whom he dwells as a son at the breast (of his mother), he is indeed a friend that cannot be severed (from him) by others."

"He who hopes for fruit, cultivates the energy that produces joy and the pleasure that brings praise (while) carrying the human yoke."—"*Sutta-Nipata Kúlavagga* 3. *Hirisutta,*" vv. 3, 4.

"As a mother at the risk of her life watches over her own child, her only child, so also let every one cultivate a boundless (friendly) mind towards all beings."

"And let him cultivate goodwill towards all the world, a boundless (friendly) mind, above and below and across, unobstructed, without hatred, without enmity."—"*Uragavagga,* 8 *Mettasutta,*" vv. 7, 8.

"As I am so are these, as these are so am I, identifying himself with others, let him not kill nor cause (anyone) to kill."—"*Mahávagga,* 11, *Nálakasutta,*" v. 27, "Sacred Books of the East," vol. x.

NOTE 18, p. 108.

Personal religion, or the realization of communion with the Divine, was lacking. "Devoutness is a defect; it implies a dangerous exaltation in the popular mind. Calm, order, regularity—this is what is wanted. Anything beyond this is excess (*superstitio*). Cato absolutely forbids that slaves should be allowed to entertain any sentiment of piety—'Know,' he says, 'that the master sacrifices for the whole household.'"—*Renan,* "*Hibbert Lectures,*" p. 13.

"The utter powerlessness of the Roman people in matters of religion was expressed by this sacramental phrase: 'The plebeians have lost the right of their auspices.'"—*Edgar Quinet,* "*Génie des Religions,*" ch. vii., sec. 1.

LECTURE IV.

NOTE 19, p. 132.

The absolutism in Islâm Theology can hardly be more strongly expressed than in the following:—

"Dieu a implanté le bien et le mal dans la nature humaine, ainsi qu'il l'a dit lui-même dans le Coran : 'la perversité et la vertu arrivent a l'áme humaine par l'inspiration de Dieu.'"—"*Ibn Khaldoun,*" i., 268.

"The central idea of this religion," writes Archbishop Trench, "in its noblest aspect is just the surrendering of oneself to God as the absolute Power." In the same strain Wellhausen puts God and His mastery as the strength of the Moslem system; and thus the view which Bishop Butler expressed is seen to be true, when he said, "Submission is the whole religion of Mohammed."—Cf. "*Mohammed and Mohammedanism,*" *by Bosworth Smith,* p. 161, 2nd ed.

"Who will be averse to the religion of Abraham but he whose mind is infatuated? . . . When his

(Abraham's) Lord said unto him, Resign thyself unto Me; he answered, I have resigned myself unto the Lord of all creatures. And Abraham bequeathed this religion to his children," &c.—"*Al Koran*," ch. ii., Sale's Ed., 1812, vol. i. pp. 24, 25. Cf. "*Mohammed and Mohammedanism*," *by R. Bosworth Smith*, p. 161, 2nd ed.

NOTE 20, p. 135.

Sale calls attention to one verse in the Koran, which he thinks, perhaps, indicates that the Mohammedans were no strangers to Quietism. He speaks, however, doubtfully. The words on which he lays stress are these: "O thou soul that art at rest!" He thinks that these may indicate the deep soul-quiet so dear to the mystic; but he admits that they may have a more superficial meaning, and may be understood of the soul secure of salvation and free from fear. The words afford a very slender foundation on which to build any superstructure of Quietism. It is ill hanging doctrines on the frayed thread of a doubtful text. The Quietism which appeared in the history of Islâm, sprang from other sources than the Koran. It had a much securer foundation in the heart of mankind than in the language of the Prophet, from whom, according to Wellhausen, "contemplative piety received only the praise of words." —*See Encyc. Brit.*: "*Mohammed*." 9th Ed.

NOTE 21, p. 139.

"The influences it met with on this (Persian) soil, and out of which peculiar religious tendencies were developed, were foreign—Indo-Germanic; and these tendencies besides have always been regarded by Moslem orthodoxy as aberrations and heresies, and were therefore soon, with a greater or less degree of decision, expelled from Islam."—*Pfleiderer*, "*Phil. of Rel.*," vol. iii. p. 180. Cf. also vol. iv. 98—100.

NOTE 22, p. 141.

"The tendency to deify Scripture only reached satisfaction in the dogma that the Koran, just as it is written, its very letters and breathings, was 'uncreated,' and had an eternal and independent existence as God's own word, having no part in the conditions and the imperfection of all created things."—*Pfleiderer*, "*Phil. of Rel.*," vol. iv., p. 63.

With this we may compare:

"Dans le Coran, un grand nombre de versets témoignent que ce livre fut communiqué au Prophète sous la forme d'une lecture (*Coran*) faite à haute voir et dont chaque sourate était un miracle (de style qui surpassait le pouvoir des hommes."—*Ibn Khaldoun*, "*Proleg.*," vol. i., p. 195.

An orthodox and authoritative Moslem treatise (used as a text-book in all Turkish schools and colleges), entitled " Risála-i-Berkevi," says: "The Koran is the word of God, and is eternal and uncreated."—See *Sell's* "*Faith of Islam*," p. 118.

NOTE 23, p. 142.

"Mohammed cursed the painter or drawer of men and animals (*Mishkát*, bk. xii., ch. i., pt. 1) and consequently they are held to be unlawful."—*Hughes*, "*Dictionary of Islam*," *Pictures*, p. 458.

"The making of carved, graven, or sculptured figures is understood to be forbidden in the Qur'án . . . .

Consequently sculpture is not allowed according to Muslim law."—*Ibid.*, *Sculpture,* p. 566.

Ibn Khaldoun (see Canon MacColl's account of him in the *Contemp. Review*, Ap., 1888) gives a dissertation on the arts generally (*Proleg.*, French ed., vol. ii., pp. 357—406), but says nothing about painting and sculpture, because they are forbidden by the sacred law. And even of the arts which are allowed, he observes, "La pratique des arts est en général très-limitée dans le pays dont les Arabes sont originaires et dans les contrées dont ils se sont emparés depuis la promulgation de l'islamisme."—*Proleg.*, vol. ii., p. 365.

Mohammed had no love for the poets:—"They rove as bereft of their senses in every valley," he said. But he had a shrewd appreciation of the advantage which he and his cause might derive from the employment of satire:—"Ply them with satires," he once said to Caab Ebn Malec; "for, by him in whose hand my soul is, they wound more deeply than arrows."—*Sale's* "*Koran,*" vol. ii., p. 211, and note.

NOTE 24, p. 144.

"Mohammedanism is the only form in which the knowledge of the true God has ever made way with the native races of Africa; and the form of Christianity which it supplanted in the North—that of the Donatists and of the Nitrian monks; of Cyril, strangely called a saint; and of the infamous George of Cappadocia, still more strangely transformed into St. George of England—was infinitely inferior to Mohammedanism itself."—*Bosworth Smith,* "*Mohammed and Mohammedanism,*" p. 285, 2nd Ed.

With this we must compare what is said by Prof. Pfleiderer:

"We must, however, observe that Islam cannot be called a universal religion in quite the same sense as Christianity and Buddhism. Its founder certainly contemplated the universal spread of his religion; but he certainly lacked the true universal human spirit. Though the founder of a religion he never ceased to be an Arab, and he impressed on his religious community forms of thought and life, which however well they answered the genius of the Arabs, were to the members of all other peoples nothing but a heavy yoke, and a fetter which prevented all sound and living development. Even the customary spread of Islam by force of arms shows that the religion now before us is not a religion of humanity, which overcomes the limits of race by the inner influence of spiritual universality."
—"*The Philosophy of Religion*," vol. iii., p. 180.

NOTE 25, p. 150.

"Not by (any philosophical) opinion, not by tradition, not by knowledge—O Mâgandiya, so said Bhagavat,—not by virtue and (holy) works can any one say that purity exists; nor by absence of (philosophical) opinion, by absence of tradition, by absence of knowledge, by absence of virtue and (holy) works either; having abandoned these without adopting (anything else), let him, calm and independent, not desire existence."—"*Mâgandiyasutta*," v. 5.

"The Brâhmana, for whom (the notions) 'equal' and 'unequal' do not exist, would he say, 'This is true?' Or with whom should he dispute, saying,

'This is false?' With whom should he enter into dispute?"—*Ibid.*, v. 9.

"There are not many different truths in the world, no eternal ones except consciousness: but having reasoned on the (philosophical) views they proclaim a double Dhamma, truth and falsehood."—"*Kúlaviyúhasutta,*" v. 9.

"A dogmatist is no leader to purity, being guided by prejudiced views, saying that good consists in what he is given to, and saying that purity is there, he saw the thing so."

"A Bráhmana does not enter time, (or) the number (of living beings), (he is) no follower of (philosophical) views, nor a friend of knowledge; and having penetrated the opinions that have arisen amongst people, he is indifferent to learning, while others acquire it."

"The Muni, having done away with ties here in the world, is no partisan in the disputes that have arisen; appeased amongst the unappeased he is indifferent, not embracing learning, while others acquire it."

"Having abandoned his former passions, not contracting new ones, not wandering according to his wishes, being no dogmatist, he is delivered from the (philosophical) views, being wise, and he does not cling to the world, neither does he blame himself."—"*Sutta-Nipata Maháviyúhasutta,*" vv. 16, 17, 18, and 19; "*Sacred Books of the East,*" vol. x., p. 173.

"The wandering monk, Vacchagotta, spake to the Exalted One, saying, 'How does the matter stand, venerable Gotama, is there the ego?' When he said this, the Exalted One was silent. 'How then, venerable Gotama, is there not the ego?' And still the Exalted One maintained silence. But the venerable Ananda, when the wandering monk Vacchagotta, had gone to a distance, soon said to the Exalted One, 'wherefore, sire, has the Exalted One not given an answer to the questions put by the wandering monk Vacchagotta?' 'If I, Ananda, had answered 'the ego is,' then that, Ananda, would have confirmed the the doctrine of the Samanas and Brahmanas who believe in permanence. If I had answered, 'the ego is not,' then that would have confirmed the doctrine of the Samanas and Brahmanas who believe in annihilation.' "—*Oldenberg*, "*Buddha*," p. 272.

"The truth is, that a strong conviction with the resultant zeal to propagate it is hardly consistent with the quietism commended by the Buddha." "Buddhism raises the rejection of every affirmation to the rank of a principle."—*Kuenen*, "*Hibbert Lectures*," pp. 283,4.

"But he who is dependent undergoes censure amongst the Dhammas; with what (name) and how should one name him who is independent? For by him there is nothing grasped or rejected, he has in this world shaken off every (philosophical) view."— "*Sutta-Nipata, Dutthatthakasutta*," v. 8; "*Sacred Books of the East*," vol. x., p. 150.

"The belief in self or soul is regarded so distinctly as a heresy that two well-known words in Buddhist terminology have been coined on purpose to stigmatise it."—*Rhys Davids*, "*Buddhism*," p. 95.

"In the *Times* of Oct. 14, 1886, you will find recorded a remarkable conversation between a Lāma priest and a Christian traveller, in the course of which the Lāma says that 'Christians describe their religion as the best of all religions; whereas among the nine rules of conduct for the Buddhist there is one that directs him never either to think or to say that his own religion is the best, considering that sincere men of other religions are deeply attached to them.'"—*Monier Williams*, "*The Holy Bible and the Sacred Books of the East,*" p. 12.

NOTE 26, p. 152.

"He who maintains a wife, and is at the head of a household; and that other who lives righteously, possessing nothing, these are not equals. The head of the house lives unrestrained, and brings about the destruction of men; but the wise and restrained is a protection to all living beings."—"*Muni Sutta,*" 15, given by Rhys Davids, "*Buddhism,*" p. 156.

"His thought is quiet, quiet are his word and deed, when he has obtained freedom by true knowledge, when he has thus become a quiet man."

"The man who is free from credulity, but knows the uncreated, who has cut all ties, removed all temptations, renounced all desires, he is the greatest of men." "*Dhammapada Sutta,*" vv. 96, 97; "*Sacred Books of the East,*" vol. x., p. 28.

NOTE 27, p. 166.

"Surely the lesson that the new covenant conveys by its substitution of baptism for circumcision, is, that the time for asceticism has passed away, that we may no longer think to please God by self-inflicted sufferings— a 'voluntary humiliation,' which is 'will worship,' and not the religion of Christ—but that we are to live, as Christ did, in the world, eating and drinking such things as are set before us, not abstaining from wine, not holding marriage in disesteem, not flying human society or its harmless pleasures and amusements, not macerating the flesh by austerities, but still taking care that we deal not with these things as the worldly and fleshly deal, but in every case purify what the ascetic cuts off and casts away, and only use it after such purification."

Canon G. Rawlinson, "*Contrasts of Christianity with Heathen and Jewish Systems,*" p. 105.

LECTURE V.

NOTE 28, p. 175.

It would not be difficult to illustrate the two levels of religion. It has been said by Professor Max Müller that "religions often deteriorate." The tendency to reduce religion to this "Fetish" level is only too common. The note of superstition is frequently sounded at the same moment that lofty thoughts find utterance. An example of this is given in the following, which is all the more striking as it shares Zoroaster's thirst for righteousness.

"2. The reciter is represented as standing in the appropriate place as a priest, with hands stretched towards Ahura, or His Fire, and praying for the possession of spiritual graces from an unselfish motive, and in order that he might appease the grief of the Kine's soul (explained elsewhere as representing the herds of the holy Iranian people, their only means of honourable livelihood) for whose relief Zarathustra had just been appointed.

"3. He approaches Ahura Mazda, spiritually inspired by the Good Mind as he declares, and asking for attainments and boons for both the bodily and spiritual lives, derived from Righteousness, whereby that personified Righteousness might establish the elect in a beatified state.

"6. With a piety as fervent as it is profound, and speaking with great earnestness, he asks Righteousness, as a person, when he shall see him, becoming fully acquainted with the Good Mind of God, the way which leads to Him, and above all with Obedience. But although he addresses these lofty abstractions as persons, it is utterly out of the question to suppose that he did not speak in the deepest meaning of the words as expressing states of mind and qualities of character: O Thou Divine, Righteous order! (thus he seems to have meant)—O Thou Divine, Righteous order! when shall I see Thee as if present in my own soul and in those of the people whom Ahura has committed to my charge?.... One cannot well exaggerate the religious depth or subjectivity. Then, with a bathos which shows how then as ever superstition could hold its own side by side with the truest piety, he exclaims (if the third line was really so composed by him, as it has come down to us) 'By such a prayer as a Mâthra spell we can with the greatest vigour repel the unclean beasts and creatures which defile our sanctity, or endanger our lives.'

"9. He prays for . . . . . . all the duration of the Good Mind, using the expression in its concrete sense as heaven; for heaven to him consisted in an inward state. . . . . (It is the mind which chiefly enjoys or suffers)."

Introduction to Yasna, xxviii., " *Sacred Books of the East*," vol. xxxi. (" *The Zend-Avesta* ") p. 14.

"The exaggeration of dependence leads often to Fatalism. Its effect is to degrade. "This horrid doctrine of fatalism is the barrier which obstructs the way to the improvement of the Hindoo on every side,—which shuts his heart against every better impression; it makes him like a block. Both the poor and rich regard their sins as the necessary consequence of actions performed in a former state of existence; hence the greatest criminal never considers himself guilty; his conscience is seared, and repentance is unknown to him."—*Weitbrecht*, "*Missions in Bengal*," p. 256.

NOTE 29, p. 180.

"Irish Druidism absorbed a certain amount of Christianity; and it would be a problem of considerable difficulty to fix on the point where it ceased to be druidism, and from which onwards it could be said to be Christianity in any restricted sense of that term."— *Prof. Rhys*, "*Hibbert Lectures*," 1886, p. 224.

Mr. Borlase tells us that a canon in King Edgar's reign forbade well-worshippings and necromancies and divinations and stone worshippings. The Council of Tours forbade stone-worship by name. "Yet the Pagan element has survived through it all. 'Pisqy stones' are still haunted by their fairies; pins are still dropped into wells; and in West Penwith strips of crape are still hung upon the plants in the window when a death has occurred in the house, for fear the evil influence might resent the neglect, and strike other living things dead also."—"*The Age of the Saints*," p. 52, by *William Copeland Borlase* (Truro, 1878). A curious instance of the survival of old and foreign customs is to be found in the practice (still extant in some parts of Cornwall) of hanging a piece of "*Passover*" cake in the house as a protection against fire.

NOTE 30, p. 188.

Parallel to the passage from M. Renan is the following from M. De Quatrefages, respecting the Tahitians:—
"Trusting in his religious observances, in the prayers of his priests, and in the indulgence of his gods, the Tahitian thought himself at liberty to do almost anything." ("*The Human Species,*" p. 488.) He remarks, so did the Christians of the Middle Ages, everywhere indeed, there is the tendency to get rid of the moral force or claims in religion. Mr. Weitbrecht, for many years Missionary in Bengal, was of opinion that there was a distinctly demoralizing influence in Brahminism, and that no system was better calculated to destroy every disposition towards that which is true, lovely, and of good report, and so entirely to eradicate every moral feeling.—"*Missions in Bengal,*" p. 72.

NOTE 31, p. 190.

". . . . The island of Cozumel was reputed a holy place, and contained many considerable temples, to which the Indians went on pilgrimage from several parts of the continent to sacrifice to their gods, and their idolatry moved the religious zeal of Cortes to bring them to a knowledge of 'the true faith.' The account which Bernal Diaz has given of this attempt on his part is very characteristic. 'One morning we perceived that the place where these horrible images stood was crowded with Indians and their wives. They burnt a species of resin, which very much resembled our incense, and, as such a sight was so novel to us, we paid particular attention to all that went forward. Upon this, an old man, who had a wide cloak, and was a priest, mounted on the very top of the temple, and began preaching something to the Indians. We were all very curious to know what the purport of the sermon was, and Cortes desired Melchorijo to interpret it to him. Finding that all he had been saying tended to ungodliness, Cortes ordered the caziques, with the principal men amongst them and the priests, into his presence, giving them to understand as well as he could, by means of our interpreter, that if they were desirous of becoming our brethren they must give up sacrificing to their idols, which were no gods, but evil beings, by which they were led into error and their souls sent to hell. He then presented them with the image of the Virgin Mary and a cross, which he desired them to put up instead. These would procure a blessing to them at all times, make their seeds grow, and preserve their souls from eternal perdition. This, and many other things respecting our holy religion, Cortes explained to them in a very excellent manner.'"— "*History of Yucatan,*" by C. St. J. Fancourt, p. 30.

Mr. Borlase, in his "*Age of the Saints,*" calls attention to similar methods employed nearer home. "It was by engrafting the new faith on to the Pagan superstitions as they found them that they finally succeeded in winning over the nation. The great Pagan festivals of Beltine and Samhain became our May Day and All Hallow-Een."—p. 27.

NOTE 32, p. 194.

"First of all, their tone, like that of all morality except the Christian, is negative; whereas Christianity is wholly positive: and this is really the difference between the finite and infinite. What a difference, for example, between saying with Hillel or Confucius, 'Do not unto another what thou wouldest not have another do unto thee,' and saying, 'Whatsoever ye would that men should do to you, even so do ye unto them;' between saying, 'Do no harm even to enemies,' as Plato said, and saying, 'Love your enemies;' between 'It is better to suffer wrong than to do wrong,' though that was a noble paradox of Socrates, and 'Bless them that curse you, do good to them that hate you and persecute you.'"—*Campbell*," *The Christian Ideal*," p. 207.

LECTURE VI.

NOTE 33, p. 210.

"If in every mind the springs of action had strength in exact proportion to their worth, and in their application were directed by correct judgment of their effects, the best forms of conduct, and nothing else, would spontaneously arise. They would arise, however, not by reason of their goodness, but by reason of their force, with no more virtue in them than in the growing of the clover or the incubation of the bird. 'Nothing takes place morally,' says Rothe, 'except what takes place *through one's own self-determination;* and this it is that converts it from a mere taking-place into an action.'"—*Martineau*, " *Study of Religion*," vol. ii., p. 109.

"We never judge our *spontaneities*, but only our *volitions*."—*Martineau,* "*Types of Ethical Theory,*" vol. ii., p. 32.

Cf. Plato's treatise, "*Meno*," in which he labours to show that virtue must be divinely bestowed and cannot be taught.—*Lewes,* "*Biog. Hist. Phil.,*" p. 261.

NOTE 34, p. 216.

"Since, then, in the two most important phenomena which the progress of society presents, the moral laws have been steadily and invariably subordinate to the intellectual laws, there arises a strong presumption that in inferior matters the same process has been followed. To prove this in its full extent, and thus raise the presumption to an absolute certainty, would be to write not an Introduction to History, but the History itself. The reader must, therefore, be satisfied for the present with what, I am conscious, is merely an approach towards demonstration; and the complete demonstration must necessarily be reserved for the future volumes of this work: in which I pledge myself to show that the progress Europe has made from barbarism to civilization is entirely due to its intellectual activity; that the leading countries have now, for some centuries, advanced sufficiently far to shake off the influence of those physical agencies by which in an earlier state their career might have been troubled; and that although the moral agencies are still powerful, and still cause occasional disturbances, they are but aberrations which, if we compare long periods of time, balance each other, and thus in the total amount entirely disappear. So that, in a great and comprehensive view, the changes in every civilized people are, in their aggregate, dependent solely on three things; first, on the amount of knowledge possessed by their ablest men; secondly, on the direction which that knowledge takes, that is to say, the sort of subject to which it refers; thirdly, and above all, on the extent to which that knowledge is diffused, and the freedom with which it pervades all classes of society."—*Buckle*, "*History of Civilization,*" vol i., p. 224.

Knowledge "can never bring about that the will shall will something actually different from what it has hitherto willed; this remains unchangeable, for the will is simply this willing itself, which would have to be abolished." The modifications of conduct through knowledge may extend so far that a man may seek to attain his unalterable end, "at one time in the real world, at another time in a world of imagination, adapting the means to each. . . . But its effort itself has not therefore changed, still less the will itself."—*Schopenhauer*, "*The World as Will and Idea,*" p. 380.

"He (man) learns to develop his powers in one direction, curtail them in another, in order to secure for himself the maximum of benefit and the minimum of injury, hoping thereby to establish his own position in the scale of human beings. Is action directed to this end and guided by this view of self to be called moral? Many moralists (including the whole of the hedonistic body) assert that it is: in the development of my thesis I may perhaps be allowed to assert, for the present dogmatically, that it is not. It is only when a second result of the action of reason asserts itself that a man can properly be termed a moral being."
—*Courtney*, "*Constructive Ethics,*" p. 60.

"It is not to be expected, and it is not maintained, that men in all ages should have agreed about the application of their moral principles. All that is contended for is that these principles are themselves the same."

"In every age virtue has consisted in the cultivation of the same feelings, though the standards of excellence attained have been different."—*Lecky*, "*History of European Morals*," vol. i., pp. 102, 109.

NOTE 35, p. 221.

The conscience is not something apart from the man, but it is the witness of something which is greater than the man. Conscience may be the conventional name given to man's consciousness of right and wrong, but it is more than this, for it implies that passing of judgment upon self, which brings shame, or the feeling of self-consciousness. Conscience is not merely consciousness of right and wrong, it is self-consciousness in regard to it. It is not necessary to assume an organ or a special faculty; it is enough that man judges in a special way concerning matters of right and wrong. He weighs them in the balance of the sanctuary, not in that of the market-place. The mode of action may not imply any special faculty. There is a danger of speaking as though conscience were apart from the man himself. The same mistake in theology which speaks of *grace* as though it were something apart from God, occurs in ethics when conscience is spoken of as a thing apart from man.

But notwithstanding this, conscience bears witness to that which is above man, to a law, if it may be so called, higher than that of interest, or pleasure, or public opinion. This law sets a restraint upon man's actions, it may be called an interference with his liberty, and yet it is a law which, being obeyed (and man is free to obey or to disobey it), leads to a nobler liberty, setting a man free from all bondage to desire, or fear of public opinion. This is the case even when conscience is but poorly informed.

Conscience is not to be viewed as a well-filled library, possessing a well-learned librarian, who can answer any question, and furnish any authority. Conscience is the name given to that consciousness of ourselves, and of our own actions which implies the perception of some ideal, and the power of self-judgment in relation to it. The ideal may be low, the process by which this class of consciousness was aroused may be gradual; but, when once it is aroused, it is different in its judgments from other consciousness. It may have grown up through the influence of social feelings and public opinion; but its greatness lies in this, that it judges often in spite of, and always independently of, public opinion. We may be confused in our estimate of ourselves, but we can recognise the difference between our actions when motived only by fear of public opinion, and by our own sense of right.

Man can refuse to quit the
"Curule seat,
To please a people's veering will."

This does not imply wide knowledge or acquaintance with facts. Indeed, the conscientious man, who goes against public opinion, may be quite wrong, and yet it would be immoral of him to run counter to the inward voice. This it is impossible for him to ignore without losing self-respect, and the sense of harmony between himself and such law or principle higher than self, and higher than the world's opinion.

When such a state of consciousness is reached in man, by whatever stages of development it may have been preceded, he is standing on a different platform than previously.

He is as one who has climbed through deep and darkly-foliaged woods up the steep side of a mountain, and has at last emerged upon a lofty spur, from which he can see the beauty and character of the country he has been traversing. He has reached a spot, and he begins to know where he is. His view point is altered. Or, to change the illustration, he judges things by a different standard. At an earlier stage he judged by quantity, he now measures by quality. Then he reckoned values by size —now he reckons by weight. Conscience is the balance of the soul. It is not responsible for what is put in the scale; it weighs whatever is given to it. It is a principle of judging, not between the greater and the less, but between the higher and the lower.

Prof. Max Müller, then, is right in cautioning us against viewing conscience as a thing apart from man. Whether we call it a faculty or not, depends upon our mode of using the word. It does not seem to me that those who urge the authoritative power of conscience mean to affirm that it is a power apart from man, but only that it is the witness of some law or power higher than man: it witnesses to man's origin, it prophesies of his destiny, but it is always in man's voice that the oracle speaks.

After mentioning Mr. Stephen's objection to

the theory which "sets up the conscience as a separate and permanently fixed faculty, 'an ultimate factor,' privileged against analytical scrutiny," . . . as "inconsistent with the conception and with the evidence of evolution," Dr. Martineau says that this objection "depends entirely upon an arbitrary interpretation put upon the word 'conscience,' and disappears when that interpretation is renounced. True, it *does* imply a function in our nature so far 'separate' as to leave with us an idea which else we should not have. Whenever you come upon an idea which baffles analysis, I suppose you can say no less than that it is ' an ultimate factor;' and till you can analyse it and resolve it into something else, so it must remain. But, in affirming this, you do not say, either, that the idea was always present in all the possible animal progenitors of the existing race, in the first mollusc as in the last Christian; or, that it is an idea incapable of growth and ramification, of blossoming and fruit-bearing. I cannot indeed point out the moment in the chronology of species or in the history of our own, when the idea of Right entered the consciousness; but the evolutionary expositor is here just as much at fault, and, as we have seen, cannot pretend to have no lacunæ in his story. And as for conscience, supposing it a primitive datum, being thereby precluded from development, I can only appeal to the friendly alliance in which they have worked together in the foregoing exposition: the germ being in the first felt difference of claim between two competing instincts."—" *Types of Ethical Theory,*" vol. ii., p. 377.

"At the root of all morals lies an intellectual judgment which is clearly distinct from liking or disliking, from pleasure or from pain."—*Lecky, " Hist. of European Morals,"* vol. i., p. 67.

"The fact is that evolution, taken by itself, as a scientific dogma, does not necessarily imply amelioration, as so many thinkers seem to suppose, but only advance. And a moral theory which is based on evolution does not derive from it the explanation of a moral ideal, unless there be added to the dogma an ontological principle, which can be construed as conscious intelligence."—*Courtney, " Constructive Ethics,"* p. 316.

"Confining ourselves rigorously to the region of facts, and carefully avoiding the territory of philosophy and theology, we may state, without hesitation, that there is no human society or even association in which the idea of *good* and *evil* is not represented by certain acts regarded by the members of that society or association as morally *good* or morally *bad*. Even among robbers and pirates theft is regarded as a misdeed, sometimes as a crime, and severely punished, while treachery is branded with infamy; the facts noticed by Wallace among the Kurubars and Santals shew how the consciousness of moral good and truth is anterior to *experience*, and independent of questions of *utility*."—*De Quatrefages, " The Human Species,"* p. 459.

LECTURE VII.

NOTE 36, p. 246.

This applies to the reality of the object of worship as well as to man.

"We would not *need* religious faith if its objects *were* not. For if man has made belief in those objects because he needs it, he did not create the circumstance that he needs belief in them for his continuance and welfare, and is therefore obliged by that necessity to make it. The production of this faith by man must therefore be based on the same real nature of things which produced man with his needs. It would be to impute an absurdity to the nature of things, and it would be contrary to experience, so far as we can speak of experience in such a matter, to say that nature had constituted man in such a way that he could only prosper while cherishing a belief in a thing that is not."—*Fechner, quoted by Pfleiderer, " The Philosophy of Religion,"* vol. ii., p. 296.

"Morality requires the supposition, not only of an Absolute, in contrast to ourselves, who are relative and individual, but an Absolute and Self-conscious Spirit. Without such a supposition the moral law lacks validity, the moral ideal has nothing whereby to explain its aspiration, and, more than this, the amelioration of the world and of humanity is an impossible conception."—*Courtney, " Constructive Ethics,"* p. 317.

NOTE 37, p. 249.

"L'univers entier n'est il point lui-même une vaste société en voie de formation, une vaste union de conscienses qui s'élabore, un concours de volontés qui se cherchent et peu à peu se trouvent?"—*Fouillée*, "*La Science Sociale*," Introduction, p. vii.

"Qu'y a-t-il en effet de vrai dans la philosophie métaphysique de l'histoire? C'est cette pensée que la société humaine a un certain *idéal*, qu'elle prend pour *fin*, et dont la poursuite plus on moins consciente doit donner un sens à son histoire."—*Fouillée*, "*La Science Sociale*," Introduction, p. vii., p. 385.

"In every phenomenon the trace, intimation, and plan of the higher phenomenon that lies next to it in point of development shows itself, but also because all these forms belong to the world as *idea*, it is indeed conceivable that even in the most universal forms of the idea, in that peculiar framework of the phenomenal world space and time, it may be possible to discern and establish the fundamental type, intimation and plan of what fills the forms."—*Schopenhauer*, "*The World as Will and Idea*," p. 187.

"There is nothing in nature that does not manifest its internal form externally; for the internal continually labours to manifest itself. . . . Everything has its language by which to reveal itself. . . . And this is the language of nature when everything speaks out of its own property, and continually manifests and declares itself . . . for each thing reveals its mother, which thus gives the *essence and the will* to the form."—*Jakob Böhm*, "*De Signatura Rerum*," ch. i., § 13-15.

"Throughout my books, the implication is that our lives, alike physical and mental, in common with all the activities, organic and inorganic, amid which we live, are but the workings of this Power."—*Herbert Spencer*, Article in the "*Nineteenth Century*," No. 89, p. 7.

"The final outcome of that speculation commenced by the primitive man, is that the Power manifested throughout the Universe distinguished as material, is the same power which in ourselves wells up under the form of consciousness."—*H. Spencer*, Article in "*Nineteenth Century*," No. 83, p. 9.

NOTE 38, p. 261.

"Perhaps you will admit that man is the culminating point in the system of nature here on earth; but will object that he is the inevitable result, not the contemplated end, of all its prior history. And if he were the contemplated end, would he not equally be the inevitable result, of the instrumentality instituted for attaining it? In insisting on this necessary sequence, you only declare that the purpose is not left without provision for its accomplishment. With or without design, this feature—of adequate physical efficiency—cannot be absent, and the specific mark of intention lies in the ascending scale by which the series of means *mounts* to a supreme result, and presents a hierarchy in which the lower serves the higher, and each succeeding step bears more the character of an end and less that of a mere means, till you rest on the summit which completes the scheme. To mere necessary causation no such ascent belongs : it is not physical, but intellectual, and speaks to *our* thought because spoken from nature's."—*Martineau*, "*Study of Religion*," vol. i., p. 318.

NOTE 39, p. 265.

"Religion, in its ultimate essence, is a sentiment of Reverence for a Higher than ourselves. Higher than ourselves, however, none can be, that have not what is most august among our endowments; none, therefore, by reason of size, of strength, of duration; none simply by beauty or by skill, none even by largeness of discerning thought, but only by free and realising preference of the most Just and Good. A Being of living Will can alone be nobler than myself, lift me above the level of my actual mind by looking at my latent nature, and emancipate me into the captivity of worship. In other words, reverence attaches itself exclusively to a *Person;* it cannot direct itself on what is *im*personal—on physical facts, on unconscious laws, on necessary forces, on inanimate objects and their relations, on space, though it be infinite, on duration, though it be eternal. These all, even when they rule us, are *lower* than ourselves; they may evade our knowledge, defy our power, overwhelm our imagination, but never rise to be our equals, or conspire to furnish even the symbol of our God."—*Martineau,* " *Studies of Christianity,*" *Anthropomorphism,* p. 368.

"With different writers, it is true, the offence begins at different points: in order to avoid it, Theodore Parker forbids us to say that God 'thinks,' but allows us to believe that He 'loves': Mr. Arnold will not allow that he either 'thinks or loves:' Caro insists that he both thinks and loves, yet declares that to conceive of him as resembling and transcending such faculties as ours involves us in the mischief of anthropomorphism." Professor Tyndall detects it in Darwin. "Of originating power he (man) has no personal experience; yet, in ascribing it to God, he is an anthropomorphist! From these examples it is obvious that the term so variously used has become a mere vehicle for the expression of dislike."—*Martineau,* " *Study of Religion,*" vol. i., pp. 334, 335.

NOTE 40, p. 268.

"Morality is the realisation of our destiny as reasonable creatures in the world of social relations, religion the realisation of the same destiny in reference to God. Social relations being based, along with the rest of the world-order, in God, the ultimate ground of all moral obligation consists in the religious feeling of dependence, which is reinforced by the feeling of trust, and by the striving after communion with and likeness to the Deity, which provide an encouraging and inspiring motive."— *Pfleiderer*, "*The Philosophy of Religion*," vol. iv., p. 272.

NOTE 41, p. 271.

On "the utter futility of the objections . . . brought against the theory of natural moral perceptions, upon the ground that some actions which were admitted as lawful in one age, have been regarded as immoral in another," see the quotation in Note 34 from *Mr. Lecky's* "*Hist. of Morals*," vol. i., p. 109.

NOTE 42, p. 275.

"When we consider that the worship of sacred human personalities is the one point common to the three world-religions of Islam, Christianity and Buddhism, which in other respects differ from each other so widely, we can scarcely help supposing that this pious reverence for human ideals, as the visible types and supports of the religious life and effort of the community, is the spring of the specific power of expansion these religions possess. At all events this point appears to me to deserve more consideration than it has yet found." —*Pfleiderer*, "*The Philosophy of Religion*," vol. iii., p. 180.

It is interesting to note that Mr. Lecky considers Islâm comparatively weak in this respect :—

"Barren Mohammedanism has been in all the higher and more tender virtues, because its noble morality and its pure theism have been united with no living example."—*Lecky*, "*Hist. of Morals*," vol. ii., p. 10.

Dr. Martineau well says: "Personality is not the largest, but it is the highest fact in the known cosmos." —"*Study of Religion*," vol. ii., p. 365.

On the personality of Mohammed, cf. *Bosworth Smith*, "*Mohammed and Mohammedanism*," p. 110, and the Article on "*Mohammed*," by *Wellhausen*, in the *Ency. Brit.* 9th *Ed.*

LECTURE VIII.

NOTE 43, p. 298.

"The rock on which they split was the character of Islam, which was then fixed or had been fixed from the beginning."—*Pfleiderer*, "*The Philosophy of Religion*," vol. iii., p. 181.

"From the stiff and rigid shroud in which it is thus swathed, the religion of Mahomet cannot emerge. It has no plastic power beyond that exercised in its earliest days. Hardened now and inelastic, it can neither adapt itself nor yet shape its votaries, nor even suffer them to shape themselves to the varying circumstances, the wants and developments of mankind."— *Sir W. Muir*, "*Rise and Decline of Islam*," p. 41.

"Tous ceux qui ont été en Orient ou en Afrique sont frappés de ce qu'a de fatalement borné l'esprit d'un vrai croyant, de cette espèce de cercle de fer qui entoure sa tête, la rend absolument fermée à la science, incapable de rien apprendre ni de s'ouvrir à aucune idée nouvelle."—*Renan*, "*L'Islamisme et la Science*," p. 2.

NOTE 44, p. 305.

"And, that you may learn that it was from our teachers—we mean the account given through the prophets—that Plato borrowed his statement that God, having altered matter which was shapeless, made the world,—hear the very words spoken through Moses." He then quotes the first chapter of Genesis.—*Justin Martyr, 1st Apology*, ch. lix., p. 57. (*Ante-Nicene Christian Library.*)

"Meanwhile, I think I may safely affirm that we must abstain from assigning to Buddhism the smallest direct influence on the *origin* of Christianity."—*Kuenen*, "*Hibbert Lect.*," p. 236.

"I can find no evidence whatever of any actual and direct communication of any of these ideas from the East to the West."—*Rhys Davids*, "*Hibbert Lect.*," p. 151.

"It would, of course, be going too far to deny that coincidences of belief are occasionally produced by actual contact of mind with mind; but it is no more necessary to assume that they always are so, than to suppose that chalk cliffs, if there be such, in China are produced by chalk cliffs in the downs of Sussex." —*Rhys Davids*, "*Hibbert Lect.*," p. 3.

NOTE 45, p. 306.

"Clement's Christology is often spoken of as meagre

and unsatisfactory. In one respect this is unjust. For Clement's idea of the Saviour is larger and nobler—may we say less conventional?—than that of any other doctor of the Church. Christ is the Light that broods over all history, and lighteth every man that cometh into the world. All that there is upon earth of beauty, truth, goodness, all that distinguishes the civilised man from the savage, the savage from the beasts, is His gift."—*Bigg*, "*Bampton Lectures*," p. 72.

"The barbaric (Jewish) and the Hellenic philosophy have in some sort rent the eternal truth into fragments, a dismemberment not like that mythic one of Dionysos : but a severance of the Divine wisdom (theology) from the Word of the eternally-existing One. Now, he who shall join together again the severed portions, and make the Word once more whole, and *at one*, such an one shall assuredly gaze on the truth without peril."—*Clement of Alex., quoted by Bunsen*, "*God in History*," vol. iii., p. 97.

. . . "Sic doctrinæ omnes gentilium non solùm simulata et superstitiosa figmenta gravesque sarcinas supervacanei laboris habent, quæ unusquisque nostrûm duce Christo de societate gentilium exiens, debet abominari atque devitare ; sed etiam liberales disciplinas usui veritatis aptiores, et quædam morum præcepta utilissima continent, deque ipso uno Deo colendo nonnulla vera inveniuntur apud eos."—*St. Augustine*, "*De Doctrinâ Christianâ*," Liber ii., § 60.

"A quocumque enim verum dicitur, illo donante dicitur, qui est ipsa veritas."—*St. Augustine*, "*Ep. ad Hieronymum*," Ep. clxvi., § 9. *Cf.* also *Justin M., 2nd Apol., ch.* x.

"The first of these claims put forth by Christianity is the claim to be regarded as an original law of the universe. Throughout the New Testament Epistles there is a constant reiteration of the statement that this religion, although a new manifestation to the world, is not a new principle in nature. Paul speaks of it as 'the mystery which hath been hid from ages and from generations, but now is made manifest.' What is this but to say that the Christian principle existed in the universe before it existed in the heart of man?"— *Matheson*, "*Can the Old Faith live with the New?*" p. 380.

NOTE 46, p. 315.

"Men wanted a Father in heaven, who should take count of their efforts and assure them a recompense. Men wanted a future of righteousness, in which the earth should belong to the feeble and the poor; they wanted the assurance that human suffering is not all loss, but that beyond this sad horizon, dimmed by tears, are happy plains where sorrow shall one day find its consolation."—*Renan*, "*Hibbert Lects.*," p. 42.

"The wants of humanity are diverse, its aspirations many, its aims contradictory. Politics are not everything here below. What the world wanted, after the frightful butcheries of antiquity, was gentleness, humanity . . . . . The establishment of Christianity answered to this cry of all tender and weary spirits."— *Ibid.*, pp. 26, 27.

"But there is no human virtue which the love, the truth, the righteousness of Christ will not inspire and draw out into a nobler form. Christianity is a religion for the weak, not because Christ is weak, but because He is so strong, because 'to them that are weak He increaseth strength.' "—*Campbell*, " *The Christian Ideal*," p. 220.

NOTE 47, p. 318.

"That virtue is knowledge, and conversely that knowledge is virtue, is, as Prof. Jowett remarks in his '*Plato*,' a truth which in the history of ethics is ever being lost and ever being re-discovered. Formulated long ago by Socrates and Plato, it was lost by the school that succeeded the death of Aristotle; rediscovered by Cudworth and Clarke, it was lost again in the philosophies of Shaftesbury and Hutcheson. Once more, it was set in its true light by the moral genius of Kant, however much its true significance has been obscured in the contemporary schemes of Scientific Ethics. For the truth is, that morality belongs to that creative and paramount Reason which science seeks to explain as the latest development of materialistic atoms and energies, but which vindicates its reality and its supremacy by the imaginative power with which it is able to form a theory of its own origin. Man is above nature, because it is due to man that we have a theory of nature."—*Courtney*, " *Constructive Ethics*," p. 130.

NOTE 48, p. 330.

"The noblest souls of whatever creed, the Pagan Empedocles as well as the Christian Paul, have insisted on the necessity of an inspiration, a joyful emotion, to make moral action perfect; an obscure indication of this necessity is the one drop of truth in the ocean of verbiage with which the controversy on justification by faith has flooded the world . . . .

"The paramount virtue of religion is, that it has *lighted up* morality; that it has supplied the emotion and inspiration needful for carrying the sage along the narrow way perfectly, for carrying the ordinary man along it at all. Even the religions with most dross in them have had something of this virtue; but the Christian religion manifests it with unexampled splendour."—*M. Arnold*, "*Essay on Criticism*," pp. 402, 403; 3rd Ed.

"The spirit who shall attain pre-eminence in moral obligation, and become support to others and fellow-worker in the realisation of their destiny, has solved the problem of the centre of gravitation for all souls—" he will be found to have grouped for ever around his person all who deserve the name of man. Of this problem Jesus first discovered the solution, and then actually realised it. He has been to humanity the genius of holiness."—*Godet*, "*Biblical Studies*," p. 84.

" The history of self-sacrifice during the last eighteen hundred years has been mainly the history of the action of Christianity upon the world. Ignorance and error have no doubt often directed the heroic spirit into wrong channels, and sometimes even made it a cause of great evil to mankind; but it is the moral type and beauty, the enlarged conceptions and persuasive power of the Christian faith, that have chiefly called it into being: and it is by their influence alone that it can be permanently maintained." — *Lecky*, "*History of Rationalism*."

" The radical difference between Jesus and Socrates

is that such a conception as Paul's [conception of *faith*] would, if applied to Socrates, be out of place and ineffective. Socrates inspired boundless friendship and esteem; but the inspiration of reason and conscience is the one inspiration which comes from him, and which impels us to live righteously as he did. A penetrating enthusiasm of love, sympathy, pity, adoration, reinforcing the inspiration of reason and duty, does not belong to Socrates. With Jesus it is different. On this point it is needless to argue; history has proved. In the midst of errors the most prosaic, the most immoral, the most unscriptural, concerning God, Christ, and righteousness, the immense emotion of love and sympathy inspired by the person and character of Jesus has had to work almost by itself alone for righteousness; and it has worked wonders."—*Mat. Arnold,* "*St. Paul and Protestantism*," p. 79, 3rd Ed.

NOTE 49, p. 332.

Richard Rothe has said, "Das Christenthum ist das allerveränderlichste; das ist sein besonderer Ruhm."— "*Stille Stunden*" (Wittenberg, 1872), s. 357.

"If, on the contrary, the Christian religion which proceeded from the prophets and apostles of the Bible, not only exhibited from the very first an unlimited impulse to spread, but also the capacity to enter into the life of the different peoples . . . . . if history shows all this to be the case, then it manifestly furnishes us with the most brilliant and irrefutable apology for the unique superiority of Christianity to all the other religions."— *Pfleiderer,* "*The Philosophy of Religion,*" vol. iv., p. 312.

"Christianity will survive because of its natural

truth . . . . . Neither will the old forms of Christian worship be extinguished by the growth of a truer conception of their essential contents. . . . . Christianity will find the ways for its own future. What is certain is that it will not disappear. Whatever progress may be made in science, art, and literary culture—however much higher, more general, and more effective than at present the value for them may become,—Christianity will be still there as what these rest against and imply; as the indispensable background, the *three-fourths of life.*"—*Mat. Arnold*, "*Last Essays,*" Preface, xxx, xxxi.

" Christianity has, it seems to me, been overlaid and obscured by the exclusive attention paid to miracle and dogma. Progress, as was said before, is conterminous with Christendom. Outside the pale of Christendom all is stationary; there have been notable outbursts of material wealth and splendour, transient flashes even of intellectual brilliancy, as in the Caliphates and the Mogul Empire, though the light in these cases was mainly borrowed; real and sustained progress there has been none. Japan, to whatever she may be destined to come, has kindled her new civilization with a coal taken from the Christian hearth."

* * *

"Philosophers speak of four universal religions, Christianity, Judaism, Mohametanism, and Buddhism. There is only one. No religion but Christianity has attempted to preach its Gospel to the world . . . . Mohametanism and Buddhism are more than tribal perhaps, but they are far less than universal. Mohametanism is military, as its Koran most plainly shows; in conquest it lives, with conquest decays; it also practically belongs to the despotic, polygamic, slave-owning

East; it has never been the religion of a Western race or of a free industrial community; by arms it has been propagated or by local influence and contagion, not by missions. Buddhism, if it is really a religion and not merely a quietist philosophy engendered of languor and helpless suffering, is the religion of a climate and a race: its boasted myriads are all enclosed within a ringfence, and it may have a prospect of becoming universal when an Englishman becomes a Hindoo, while in the heart of its domain Hindoos are becoming Christians. Judaism, after surrendering its universal and spiritual element to Christendom, fell back into a tribalism, which, as a relapse, is of all tribalisms the narrowest and the worst, being not primitive and natural but self-chosen and obstinately maintained in the face of humanity."
—*Prof. Goldwin Smith*, "*Evolutionary Ethics*," "*Contemp. Review*," vol. xliv., p. 801.

INDEX.

Abbasids, 138
Abstract idea, humanity an, 296
Abstract ideas silent to the soul, 266
Admiration, moral value of, 349, xli
African races and Mohammedanism, Note 24, p. 373
Agnosticism, xlix
    ,,   in Buddhism, 96,
    ,,   in Christianity, 325, 334
αἰδώς, 71, Note, 12, p. 362
Ajïta, 99
Albigenses, 116
Alfarabi, 138
Algonquins, Note 8, p. 358
Allen, Dr., " Continuity of Christian Thought," 111, 116, 118
Altruism is sacrifice, 235
    ,,   in Christianity, 230, 317, lix
    ,,   in nature, 351
    ,,   a substitute for religion, 219
Alva, 247
Ambiguity of the statement that religion is demoralising, Lect. V, and p. 206
Ambrose, St., 194
Amiel, influence of character on thought, 346
Analysis, God not discovered by, 326
" Angel Messiah," Bunsen, 94
Anthropocentric theory, 257
Anthropomorphism, 265
Apostolic brethren, 117

Arabian science, 136
,,   ,,   more strictly Greek, 140
Arianism, 110, 157
Aristotle, definition of happiness, 56
Arnold, Mr. Matthew, power in the world, 222
,,   ,,   definition of religion, 49
Art, influence of character on, 348
Aryan Religions, xxxi
Asceticism a witness for fellowship, 113, Note 9, p. 359
,,   not belonging to Christianity, 166, Note 27, p. 377
"As we are, we see," 28, 346
"As we think, we are," 21, 343
Athanasius, 110
,,   his ideas modern, 310
Atheistic tendency in Buddhism, 94
Augustine, fatalistic teaching of, 114
,,   yearning for holiness, 229
Automatic, action, Dr. W. B. Carpenter on, 355
Avalokitesvara, 99
Aztecs, ritual cannibals, Note 10, p. 361

Bailey, P. J., "Festus," 347
Baptism, wholesale, 190
Baring Gould, Mr., on powers of love, 353
Barrett Browning, Mrs., on Law II, 30
Beaconsfield, Lord, power of poets, 357
,,   ,,   temper is fate, 347
Beal, "Buddhism in China," 100
Belief, coincidences of, not necessarily caused by contact, Note 44, p. 397
Bernard, St., 117
Besant, Mr. W., on power of love, 353
Better poems, worse poets, 272
"Be yourself," 249
Bodhi-satwas, 99
Böhm, Jakob, on self-expression, 343
Bonaventura, St., 117
Book of nature, 118
Borlase, Mr. W. C., on Pagan customs, Note 29, p. 380; Note 31, p. 382
Bosworth Smith, "Mohammed and Mohammedanism," 136
,,   ,,   on Persian corruptions of Islâm, 138

Bosworth Smith on Wahhábites, 143
Boundary boys, Australia, 227
Brahmanism, 6
,,   demoralising, Note 30, p. 381
,,   deterioration of, 95
,,   pantheism in, 65
Buckle on religious persecution, 24
,, on progress due to knowledge, Note 34, p. 384
Büchner on present culture, 235
,,   on social egotism, 219, 220
,,   on the highest moral code, 236
,,   unconscious witness to Christ, 236
Buddha, his death, Note 16, p. 367
Buddhism, a complex term, 90
,,   agnosticism in, 96, xxviii
,,   a pessimistic quietism, 150
,,   atheistic tendency in, 94
,,   dependence demanded in history of, 99, 148
,,   ,, lacking in, 98
,,   developments of, 98, 148
,,   fellowship in, 94, 145
.,   Great Soul Theory, 148
,,   introduction into China, 100
,,   its reluctance to affirm or deny, 150, Note 25,
       p. 374
,,   no message for the poor in, 152
,,   number of its adherents, Note 13, p. 363
.,   no progress in, 102, 150, 299, 404
,,   salvation in, 93, Note 17, p. 368
,,   self-control in, 93, 96, Note 26, p. 377
,,   significance of life unrecognised in, 151
,,   undogmatic, 149, Note 25, p. 374
Bunsen, "Angel Messiah," 94
Burke, Edmund, 247
Byron, Lord, on Environment, 346

Caird, Prof., on poetical power, 357
Calvin, fatalistic teaching of, 112, 158
Cannibalism, religious, 67, Note 10, p. 361
Carlyle on sacrifice, 350
Carmichael, Mr. C. H. E., on man a religious being, 338
Carpenter, Dr. W. B., automatic action, 354
Character, education of, 259
       ., explains varying moral standards, 271

Character, is greatness, 259
,, Mr. H. Spencer on, 343
,, perfection of, through love, 330
China, introduction of Buddhism into, 100
Christ the Light of men, 306, Note 45, p. 397
Christian idea of incarnation, 283
Christianism not Christianity, 300
Christianity, 103, 159
,, alleged sources of, 305, Note 44, p. 397
,, and altruism, 317
,, and patriotism, 196
,, an original law of the universe, Note 45, p. 397
,, a religion for the weak, 328, Note 46, p. 399
,, Christ the foundation of, 301
,, conception of man, 310
,, exclusiveness of, 303
,, Fatherhood of God in, 308
,, fellowship in, 104, 159
,, fellowship demanded in, 109, 120
,, humanity preferred to patriotism by, 197
,, idea of redemption in, 314
,, inspires, 316, Note 48, p. 400
,, its relation to Druidism, Note 29, p. 380
,, ,, to Epicureanism and to Stoicism, 232
,, misunderstood, 106
,, Mr. Lecky on, 193
,, not ascetic, 166, Note 27, p. 377
,, not religionistic, 192
,, number of its adherents, Note 13, p. 363
,, origin uninfluenced by Buddhism, Note 44, p. 397
,, progress in, 104, 159, Note 49, p. 403
,, Réville on, 193
,, teaching of Apostles, 162, 303
,, ,, Christ, 159
,, the answer to men's needs, Note 46, p. 399
,, the increased importance of things seen in, 197
,, the survival of, Note 49, p. 402
,, unifying power of, 196, 232, 303
,, witnessed to by A. Comte, 236
Chrysostom, 194
Church of England, schools of thought in, 120
Clark, J. Freeman, 208
Classification, importance of, 342, xxix
Clement's Christology, Note 45, p. 397
Codrington, Dr., on man a religious being, 338

Index.

Comparative study of religions, 49, xxii
,, ,, ,, advantages of, 5
,, ,, ,, dread of, 50
Comte, Auguste, witness to Christianity, 236
,, ,, egoism of life, 220
Conscience, 208, 268, Note 35, p. 386
,, a social product, 221
,, Dr. Martineau on, 268
,, education of, 218
,, evolution of, 222
,, independent of public opinion, Note 35, p. 387
,, not a power apart from man, Note 35, p. 386
,, self-consciousness in regard to right and wrong, Note 35, p. 387
Consciousness of moral good anterior to experience, Note 35, p. 390
Constant, B., on man a religious being, 15
Contempt injurious, 52
" Continuity of Christian Thought," 111, 116
Copernican Theory, 257
Corday, Charlotte, 213
Cortez and Religionism, Note 31, p. 381
Courtney, Dr., on Morality, 385, 390, 391
Crawford, Marion, 9
Creed, no ideal in scientific, 281
,, witnesses to a person, 278
Creeds, a disease of intellect, 22
,, necessary to religion, 22
,, not the foundation of religion, 274
Croslegh, Dr., " Fruits of Christianity," 184
Crozier, J. B., " Religion of the Future," 288

Davids, Prof. Rhys, on salvation in Buddhism, 93, 96, 99
Definition of Religion by Prof. Caird, xxxvii
,, ,, Darwin, xlii
,, ,, Feuerbach, xlvi
,, ,, Fichte, 49, xxxix
,, ,, Fiske, 54
,, ,, Goethe, xli
,, ,, Gruppe, xlvii
,, ,, Hegel, 49, xxxvi
,, ,, Kant, 49, xxxix
,, ,, Matthew Arnold, 49
,, ,, Martineau, xlv
,, ,, Prof. Max Müller, xlii

Definition of Religion by Pfleiderer, xxxvii, xlv
,, ,, Plato, 54
,, ,, Réville, 55, xliv
,, ,, Schelling, 54, xxxviii
,, ,, Schleiermacher, 54, xxxv
,, ,, Spencer, Mr. H., xlviii
,, ,, Spinoza, xl
,, ,, Strauss, 55
,, ,, Teichmüller, xli
,, ,, Tiele, xxxvii
,, ,, Wundt, xlvii
Deism, a banishing of God, 307, lxi
,, reversion to, 157
Deistic idea, 310,
Dependence, 54, 209
,, becomes fatalism, Note 28, p. 378
,, depraved in history of Buddhism. 99
,, in Christianity, 103
,, in Egyptian religion, liii
,, lacking in Buddhism, 98
,, original in Islâm, 131, Note 19, p. 370
,, witnessed to in Brahmanism, 65
,, ,, ,, Islâm, 83, xxxii
,, ,, to by Khonds and Zulus, 64, Note 8, p. 358
,, ,, to in Vedas, 64
Dhammapada Sutta, quoted from, 97 ; Note 17, p. 368; Note 26, p. 377
,, ,, the moral teaching of, 153
Docetism, 157
Doctrinaire, the, 341
,, age precedes revolution, 26
Dogma inevitable, 22
Dogmatism absent in Buddhism, 149
,, denying God, 87
Dogmatist contrasted with prophet, 87
Döllinger on Fellowship, Note 9, p. 360
Drift, the theory of, 221
Druidism, Irish, Note 29, p. 380

Eckart, 117
Education of conscience, the, 218, 207, 252
Effort, the law of, 252
Elements of religion, Positivism alive to some of the. 296, 299
Eliot, George, on character-growth, 345

Eliot, George, on religious ideas, 185
,,   ,,   on sacrifice, 350
,,   ,,   on the law of indirectness, 355
Emerson on classification, 342
  ,,   creeds, 22
  ..   self-sacrifice, 351
  ..   the influence of environment, 27
  ,,   ,,   ,,   organism, 30, 347
  ,,   thought, 344
Energy withdrawn from the world by religion, 196
Environment, the law of, 21, 343
Epicureanism, 232
Ethics and religion, 188, 243
Euclid, 138
Evolution, moral, 222, Note 35, p. 386
  ..   physical, 259

Fa Hian, story of, 100
Fairbairn, Dr., on religions, 309
Fatalism, 112, Note 28, p. 378
  ,,   barrier to improvement, Note 28, p. 380
Fatherhood of God, the, in Christianity, 308, 112
  ,,   ,,   needed by man, 308
Feeling determines faith. 227
Fellowship, 54, 209, Note 9, p. 359
  ,,   and Athanasius, 110
  ,,   and Calvinism, 158
  ,,   craving for in Asceticism, 113
  ,,   demanded in history of Christianity, 113
  ,,   in Aryan religion, xxxii
  ,,   in Brahmanism, 65
  ,,   in Buddhism, 94, 145
  ,,   in Christianity, 104, 159
  ,,   in Egyptian religion, lv
  ,,   in Hellenism, 71
  ,,   in Judaism, 70
  ,,   in Mexican religion, 67
  ,,   lacking in Islam, but supplied, 84, 132
  ,,   Montanism, a cry for, 109
  ,,   Mysticism and, 158
  ,,   Patripassianism affirms, 156
  ,,   witnessed to in Saint worship, 114
  ,,   in the idea of sin, lix
Fénelon, 117

Fénelon, yearning for holiness, 229
Fetishism in religion, 189, 276, Note 30, p. 381
Fichte, definition of religion, xxxix
Fiske, Mr., definition of religion, 54
,, "Destiny of Man," 260
,, " Idea of God," 310, 340
Fouillée, 262
Foundation of religion of the future, 274
Fraser, Dr., on man a religious being, 339
Freedom in religion, xxxvi
" Friends of God," 117

Galen, 138, 183
Gareth, 254
Gautama, a person, 91
,, death of, 93, Note 16, p. 367
Geynes, Dr., excommunicated, 183
Gissing, Geo., on malice, 349
Gladstone, Mr. W. E., on Nemesis, 71, Note 12, p. 362
Gnosticism, 157
God, the Fatherhood of, 308
,, known by love, 324
,, misunderstood, 321
,, name of, in Hebrew, 70
,, not discovered by analysis, 326
,, trusting us, 268
,, consciousness, xlii, lvi
Goethe on kinship, 344
,, on power of vision, 346
,, on religion, xxix, xli
Golden age, belief in a, 230
Grace, doctrine of, misunderstood, 181
Great Renunciation, the, 92
,, Soul Theory, the, 149
Gruppe, his definition of Religion, xlvii
Guyon, Madame, 117

Hallam, on the benefits of Religion, 176
Hamlet, 214, 322
Hazlitt, 258
Hebrew religion, the, 70
Hegel, his definition of Religion, 49, xxxvi
Heine's dream, 234
Hellenism, 71

Herder on man a religious being, 14
Hinton on like seeing like, 347
Homer a sort of Bible, 25
Howells, " Undiscovered Country," 347
Human sacrifices, 66, Note 10, p. 361
Hubner, M., on the population of the world, 363
Humanity cannot be worshipped, 296
Hurakan, 68
Huxley, Prof., on rational order, 264

Idea of God in Christianity, 307
Ideas, combined with personality, 295
„ need character, 343
„ the power of, 344
Ideal of Christ unsurpassed, 236, 237
„ in religion of the future, 282
Imperialism in the Roman religion, 108, 112, Note 18, p. 369
„ in Christianity, 111
Incarnation, need of, 283
„ Christian idea of, 284
Intellectual judgment at the root of all morals, Note 35, p. 386
Islamism, 80
„ absolutism in, Note 19, p. 370
„ achievements of, 144
„ dependence in, 83, 131, xxxii
„ discourages painting, 142, Note 23, p. 372
„ fellowship demanded in history of, 85
„ „ lacking in, 84, 132
„ fixity of, 297, Note 43, p. 396; see Note 22, p. 372
„ foreign influences expelled from, Note 21, p. 371
„ mysticism in, 85, Note 20, p. 371
„ number of its adherents, Note 13, p. 363
„ persecuted science, 140
„ Persian influence on, 138, Note 21, p. 371
„ progress not original in, 136
„ Puritanism in, 143
„ sculpture forbidden by, Note 23, p. 372
„ submission in, Note 19, p. 370
„ not universal, 298, liii, Note 24, Note 29, Note 49

Jacob, God's education of, 59
Janet, Paul, on a perfect moral action, 208
Jehovah, the worship of, 231
Jesus Christ contrasted with Socrates, Note 48, p. 401

Jowett, Prof., on virtue is knowledge, 400
Judaism, 70, 404
Julius Cæsar, the play of, 30

Ka, lv
Ka'ba, the, 134
Kant, his definition of Religion, 49, xxxix
Karma, 102
Kellogg on the worship of Buddha, 99
Khárijites, the, Note 15, p. 366
Khonds, the, 64, Note 8, p. 358
King, Mrs. Hamilton, "The Disciples," 352
Knowledge, 216, Note 34, p. 384
,, and will, Note 34, p. 385
,, is virtue, Note 47, p. 400
,, sense of duty anterior to, 218
Koran, doctrine of uncreated, 141, Note 22, p. 372
,, hindrance to progress from the, 141
,, painting and sculpture forbidden by, Note 23, p. 372
Kuenen, on Buddhism, p. 376
,, on classification, 342
,, on Súfism, 135
,, on universal religion, 79
Kwan-yin, 100

Lamartine, 351
Latium, religion of, 188
Law of effort, 252
,, environment, 21, Note 3, p. 343
,, indirectness, 36, Note 6, p. 352
,, organism, 28, Note 4, p. 346
,, sacrifice, 34, Note 5, p. 350
Laws of man's spiritual nature, 19, 319, 343-357
Layard, Sir Henry, 142
Lecky, Mr., on Christian morals, 193, 401
,, on civic virtues, 196
,, on Mohammedanism, 396
,, on virtue, 386
Legalistic religions, xxix
Leighton, Sir F., on influence of character, 348
Leonardo da Vinci, 118
Letourneau, on man an animal, 227
Life, significance of, 311
,, all sacred, 314

Life, interpreted by love, 319
"Light of Asia," Kellogg, 99
Longfellow on the law of indirectness, 365
  ,,   on man as a religious being, 341
Lotus. "Self-creative force," 148
Love interprets life, 329
,, knows God, 324
,, purifies sacrifice, 41, 330
Lowell, Mr. R., on like seeing like, 347, 350
Lubbock, Sir John, on man a religious being, 337, lii

Maāt, lv
Macaulay, 272
Maitreya Buddha, 99
Malice, an intellectual defect, 349
Manjusri, 99
Mankind one in higher things, 291
Man, conceptions of, in Christianity, 310
,, naturally religious, 11, 16, Note 1, p. 337, li
,,   ,,   B. Constant on, 15
,,   ,,   Herder on, 14
,, his self-assertiveness, 248
,, his nature permanent, 7
,, the contemplated end of history, 261, Note 38, p. 393
Mantras, the, 64
Martineau, Dr., his definition of religion, xlv
  ,,   on Anthropomorphism, 393
  ,,   on conscience, 208, 389
  ,,   on perfection of man, 393
  ,,   on personality, 396
  ,,   on public opinion, 220
Matheson, Dr., 135, 313
  ,,   on man a religious being, 341
Melville, Whyte, on self-sacrifice, 351
Merit and virtue, 214
Mexico, the religion of, 66
  ,,   ,,   its tenderness, 67
,, the siege of, Note 10, p. 361
Michael Angelo, 119
Mill, J. S., on law of indirectness, 40
Mingwe Redskins, Note 8, p. 358
Mirza Kasem Bey on reformation of Islâm, 86
Missions, superficial at times, 190
Mohammed, his personal appearance, 80, Note 14, p. 363
  ,,   androgynous, 81

Mohammed, characteristics, Note 14, p. 363
 ,, an Arab, Note, 24, p. 374
Mohammedanism in Africa, Note 24, p. 378
Molinos, 117
Monier Williams, Sir, 376
Montanism, a cry for fellowship, 109
Montesquieu, 184
Moral elements correspond with the laws of man's spiritual nature, 208
 ,, aim in nature, 263
Moralism, 210
Morality of Pagan religions, Note 32, p. 383
 ,, and religion, 172, Note 48, p. 400
 ,, ,, increase of kinship between, 186
 ,, not a mere moral act, Note 34, p. 385
Morals, depraved, 183
 ,, high and virtue low, 214
 ,, low and merit high, 214
 ,, no fixed standard of, 270, Note 34, p. 386
 ,, orthodoxy preferred to, 194
 ,, the beauty of Christian, 193
Moral synthesis, 244
Morison, Mr. J. Cotter, misunderstands law of indirectness, 353
 ,, ,, on Christian saintship, 177
 ,, ,, on the unfortunate, 228
 ,, ,, on things seen and unseen, 197
Morris, Mr. Lewis, "The Epic of Hades," 356
Moslem scholars, 138
 ,, science, 137
Mo'tazilites, 89
Muir, Sir W., on the fixity of Islâm, 396
Müller, Prof. Max, his definition of religion, xlii
 ,, ,, on man a religious being, 339
 ,, ,, on religion inevitable, 287
 ,, ,, on Rita, 65
 ,, ,, on the Fatherhood of God, 308
Mysticism in Christianity, 115, 158
 ,, in Islamism, 85, Note 15, p. 365; Note 20, p. 371
 ,, in Positivism, 299

Name of God, three stages in Hebrew books, 70
Nations, unity of, 290
Natural moral perceptions, the theory of, Note 41, p. 395
Nature-consciousness, lvi
Nemesis, W. E. Gladstone on, 71, Note 12, p. 362

Neoptolemus, 245
Nicæa, Council of, 113
Nicolas of Basle, 117
Nutar, liv

Object of worship must be real, xlvi, 277. Note 36, p. 391
Oldenberg on highest offering in Buddhism, 146
Omayyads, 137
Orthodoxy preferred to morals, 194
Originality, true, 305
Othmar, 322

Pagan customs, survival of, 179, Note 29. p. 380 ; Note 31, p. 382
Paganism, Roman, 107, Note 18, p. 369
Pagan religions, Note 32, p. 383
Painting, Islâm discourages, 142, Note 23, p. 372
Pantheism, 307, 310, Note 9, lxi
  „ in Islamism, Note 15, p. 366
Parinirvāna, 102
Patriotism and Humanity, 196
Patripassianism, 156
Paul of Samosata, 157
Perfect morals, elements of, 207
Permanence of man's nature, 7, 9
  „ Longfellow on, 17
Permanent elements of religion, 54
  „   „ neglect of any, dangerous, 60
  ..   .. how far indigenous in universal religions, 131, *et seq.*
Perpetuity a test of religion, 300
Persian influence on Islâm, 138, Note 21. p. 371
Person, all great religions centre in a, 275, xxxiv
  „ witnessed to by creeds and sacraments, 278
Personality and religion, 246, Note 42, p. 395
  „ highest known fact, Note 42, p. 396
  .. in the future religion, 274
  ,. in the source of religion, 268, Note 39, p. 393
  .. in the subject of religion, 270, Note 39, p. 393, lvii
  ,. linked with ideas, 295
  „ of God, 265
Persons, the power of, in history, 275
Pessimism in Buddhism, 150
Petrobrusians, 116
Pfleiderer, his definition of religion, xxxvii, xlv
  „ on Islâm and culture, 371

Pfleiderer, on Islâm not universal, 374, 396
,, on objective reality, 391
,, on personality in religion, 394, 395
,, on superiority of Christianity, 402
,, on the Koran, 372
Philoctetes, 245
Plato, his definition of religion, 54
,, Justin Martyr on, Note 44, p. 397
,, on Virtue, Note 33, p. 384
Positivism a mysticism, 299
,, narrow foundation of, 300, xxvii
,, recognizes some of the elements of religion, 219, 296
Power behind all things, Mr. H. Spencer, 229
,, of history, a person, 275
Primitive revelation, a, 14, lvi
Progress in Christianity, 104, 117
,, in the theology of Celts and Tuetons, Note 11, p. 362
,, in Egyptian religion, lv
,, in Buddhism, 102, 150
,, not original in Islâm, 86, 136
,, sacrifice essential to, 209, 328, 350
,, the element of, 55
,, the Koran against, 141, Notes 22 & 23, p. 372
,, witnessed in Scholasticism, 117
Ptolemy, 138

Quatrefages, De, on fellowship, Note, 9, p. 359
,, on man a religious being, 337
,, on the population of the world, 363
,, religious races, 13, lii
Quetzalcoatl, 68, Note 11, p. 361
Quietists, 117
Quinet, Edgar, on art, 119, 359
,, the influence of dogma on civilization, 26, 344
,, the Romans and their religion, 370

Rab'i'a, Note 15, p. 366
Race-growth analagous to child-growth, 57
Rahula, 92
Rational order in the universe, 264
Raymond of Sabunde, 118
Reciprocity, 236

Index. 419

Redemption in Buddhism, 93, 146, xxxiii
„ in Christianity, 314, xxxiii
Redskins. Note 8, p. 358
Religion a dependence, 59, Note 7, p. 357, xxxvi, xlii, lvii
„ ambiguity of the word, xxi
„ and Ethics, 243
„ and Morality, 172, Note 40, p. 394
„ and personality, 246, 268, 396
„ change of arguments about, xxiii
„ contrasted with moralism, Lect. VI
„ definitions of, 49, xxxv
„ depraved morals not always due to, 178
„ energy withdrawn from the world by, 196
„ fetishism in, 189, 276, Note 30, p. 381
„ freedom in, xxxvi
„ inconsistency of followers not chargeable on a, 183
„ increase of kinship between morals and, 186
„ inevitable, 287
„ its principles not hostile to morality, 186
„ mechanical, 188
„ must inspire and instruct, 296, 316
„ of Aryan races, xxxi
„ of Egypt, liv
„ of Humanity futile, 229, 296, xxv
„ of Latium, 188
„ of Mexico, 66, 361
„ of native races, 12, l
„ of Semitic races, xxxi
„ permanent elements of, 54, lvi
„ recognition of the Infinite in, xxvii, xli
„ reverence in, xlviii
„ substitutes for, 207, 216, 219, 221, xxv
„ survives, 5, 7
„ tested by perpetuity, 300
„ the benefits of, 176
„ the Hebrew, 70
„ the organization of self devotion, 287
Religionism, a shadow of religion, 186, Note 31, p. 391
Religion of the Future, the, features of, 54, 273
„ „ Ideal in, 282
„ „ inspiring power in, 282
„ „ must be eternal, 293
„ „ „ unite man, 292
„ „ one or many, 288
„ „ on what founded, 274

Religions, book- and non-book, xvii, xxix
,,   centred in a Person, 275, xxxiv
,,   classification of, xxv
,,   comparative study of, 49
,,   die, 5
,,   Dr. Fairbairn on, 309
,,   Legalistic, xxi
,,   manufactured religions, xxv
,,   non-universal, 63, xxxi, lii, 403
,,   redemptive, xxxiii
,,   universal, 63, 79, lii, 403
Religious cannibalism, 67, Note 10, 361
,,   influences, a fact, 231, 401
Reluctance to affirm or deny in Buddhism, 150, Note 25, p. 374
Renan on Moslem Science, 137
,,   patriotism, 196
,,   self-devotion, 287
,,   the aim of Humanity, 263
,,   the benefits of religion, 176
Reversions to type, 227
Réville, his definition of religion, 55, xliv
,,   on abstract ideas, 266
,,   on Christian morality, 193
,,   on man as a religious being, 340
,,   on the death of religions, 5
,,   on the influence of disposition, 33
Richard III., 214
Roman paganism, 107, Note 18, p. 369
Rothe, R., 402
Rousseau, 183
Ruskin, Mr., on Holman Hunt and Rossetti, 31
,,   self-denial, 355
,,   Thackeray, 347
,,   the grammar of art, 343
,,   the influence of laws, 26, 344
,,   the love of nature, 119

Sabellianism, 157
Sacrifice, Carlyle on, 350
,,   essential to progress, 35, 328
,,   in Altruism, 235
,,   in Christianity, lix
,,   Geo. Eliot on, 350

Sacrifice, Geo. Sand on, 350
„ human, 66, Note 10, p. 361
„ none without love, 330
Sacraments witness to a Person, 278
Saint-Hilaire. M., on man a religious being, 337
Saintship in Christianity, 177
Saint-worship, witness for fellowship in, 85, 114
Sand. Geo., on Sacrifice, 350
Schelling, his definition of religion, 54, xxxviii
Schism, cause of, 279
Schismatic, the, the child of the Fanatic, 279
Schleiermacher, his definition of religion, 54, xxxvi
Scholasticism, its witness to Progress, 117
Schopenhauer on man a religious being, 341
„ on like knowing like, 348
„ on the influence of environment, 27, 345
Science persecuted by Islâm, 140
Sculpture, Indian, 345
„ forbidden in Islâm, Note 23, p. 372
Secretiveness of native races, 12, li
Secular and religious ideas, 314
Seeley, Prof., on love of history, 352
Self-accomplishing design in nature, 262
Self-consciousness and conscience, 268, Note 35, p. 386, lvii
„ danger of, 39
Self-control in Buddhism, 93, 96, Note 26, p. 377
Self-determination, need of in moral action, Note 33, p. 383
Self-expression, need of, 240
„ Jakob Böhm on, 302
Self-possession, need of, 250
Self-sacrifice, 250, Note 5, p. 350, lx
„ Whyte Melville on, 351
Semitic religions, xxxii
Sentiment and conduct, 195, 220, 343
Sense of duty anterior to knowledge, 218
Shakespeare, the influence of environment, 27
„ the power of thought, 30
Significance of life increased by Christianity, 197
„ unrecognized by Buddhism, 151
Simpson, Sir Jas., on law of Indirectness, 355
Sin, idea of witnesses to Fellowship, lix
Sly, Christopher, 256
Social influences on man's development, 261
Sophocles, 245
Spencer, Mr. H., on character, 343, 346

Spencer, Mr. H., on feeling and belief, 227
,,   ,,   religion essential in society, lii
,,   ,,   the personality of God, 266
,,   ,,   the Power behind all things, 229, 392
,,   ,,   the inevitableness of religion, 287
,,   ,,   the worship of Humanity, 296
,,   ,,   utility no substitute for religion, 226
Sprenger, 134
Smith, Prof. Goldwin, on Christianity, 403
Stael, Madame de, definition of happiness, 56
Standard of morals, no fixity in, 270, 387
Stoicism, 232
Strauss, his definition of religion, 55
Substitutes for religion, 207, 216, 219, 221, xxv
,,   ,,   defect of, 225
,,   ,,   knowledge, sentiment, drift, 216
,,   ,,   Mr. H. Spencer on, 226
Súfism a mysticism, 85
,, in Islamism, Note, 15, 365
Sutta-Nipâta, 147, 369, 375
Sympathy with goodness, necessity of, 210
Synthesis, need of moral, 244

Talfourd, "Ion," 351
Tauler, 117
Taylor, Prof., Altruism in Plants, 351
Telemachus, 71
Tenderness in Mexican religion, 67
Tennyson, Lord, on law of indirectness, 355
Tertullian, 166
Theory, Copernican, 257
,,   Darwinian, 257
Therapeutæ, 305
Thermopylæ, men of, 328
Thirst for Righteousness in Zoroastrianism, Note 28, p. 378
Timon of Athens, a type, 225, 322
Truth the only originality, 305
Tupper, Mr. Martin, on law of indirectness, 356
Tylor, Dr., on Khonds and Zulus, 64
,, on non-religious tribes, lii

Ulysses, 245
Unbelief, how far a sin, 327

Unconscious sacrifice, 38
Unfortunate, message of Christianity for the, 227, 328
,, Mr. Cotter Morison on the, 228
Unifying power of Christianity, 196, 232, 303, 402
,, none in Islâm, 297
Unity of Nations, 290
Universalism, two kinds of, 79
Utility no substitute for religion, 226

Vajradhara, 100
Vedas, the, 64
Virginius, 213
Virtue and merit, 214
,, and morals, Note 34, p. 384
,, low when morals high, 214
,, wherein consists real, 223
Virtues, masculine and feminine, 312
Voice of history on personality, 247, 275
,, nature witnesses to character, 248
,, science on character growth, 256

Wahhábites, the Puritans of Islâm, 143
Waldenses, 116
Walis, the worship of, 85
Wellhausen, pp. 366, 370, 371, 396
Westcott, " Christus Consummator," 351
,, on Judaism, 70
Will power in great men, 224
Winkelried, 254
Whateley, Archbishop, 6
Woden, 362
World-consciousness, lix
Worship of Jehovah, 231
Wundt, Prof., his definition of religion, xlvii

Yasodhara, 92
Yucatan, Hist. of, 381

Zeno, on friendship, 357
Zoroaster, 189, Note 28, p. 378
Zulus, 64

LONDON:
PRINTED BY PERRY, GARDNER AND CO.,
FARRINGDON ROAD, E.C.

www.ingramcontent.com/pod-product-compliance
Lightning Source LLC
Chambersburg PA
CBHW051856300426
44117CB00006B/418